BUSTED

ZUBIN DIO

Copyright © 2019 Zubin Dio
All rights reserved
First Edition

PAGE PUBLISHING, INC.
New York, NY

First originally published by Page Publishing, Inc. 2019

ISBN 978-1-64462-490-6 (Paperback)
ISBN 978-1-64462-491-3 (Digital)

Printed in the United States of America

PREFACE

These are the letters I sent home from a state prison that I was sent to after I was convicted for possession of cocaine, or what they call Devil Dust along with many other names. I was sentenced to a five-year term on a plea deal or take my chances, take it to trial, get fifteen to life for a jail sentence. All I wanted at that time was to get home as soon as possible to be with my family that meant so much to me. Now for those people who think that the amount of cocaine don't look like much when you buy it, just think about it, check out the laws before you get involved with that shit. I didn't. It didn't look like much, and it was no larger than a pound of sugar. I had so much at that time because I didn't want to keep on calling up the guy that I bought it off that often. He told me that he was going to stop selling the product. He said that he made his money; it was time for him to stop it. Or maybe it was a setup and he was working with the police to bust people because he had probably got caught selling. This was a deal he made with the cops, like a lot of people do these days.

The first time I called, I ordered eight ounces; after I got it, my wife said, "Maybe you should order more because you might run out." At this time, my wife had a thousand-dollar-a-week habit. She was sucking it up as fast as I could get it. So even though I didn't want to get more, I called him, ordered another eight ounces but to be split up for two of my so-called friends also. I was looking at my wife. She was starting to scare me real bad. I didn't know what to do but tell her to take it easy. I was running an auto body, mechanic business out of my home along with teaching at a vocational high school, but a lot of my money was being used for bad to feed a habit. She was working. I never thought of asking her for money to support her habit. I just paid for it like a man who loves his wife would do anything for her.

A couple of guys that I knew for years came by like they did a lot of times on a Friday to just smoke some weed, drink some beers. They started to ask me when I was going to get any more coke for my wife and if I could get it for them, also for their wives or whatever they wanted to do with it. By me doing this, it was like helping me with the expense of the product to support my wife's habit. But after a while, I noticed that my wife started to come home at lunchtime to do coke.

I would yell out, "You better not be doing any coke!"

She would say, "No, just to eat." She would say, "I'm not touching any of it, I'm just eating a sandwich," and then say, "I'm so damn hungry."

It got to the point that as soon as she would walk into the door, she was downstairs in the cellar, sucking it up, and then whenever she decided to come upstairs, she would have a ring around her nose. I would say to her, "Wipe the coke off your nose."

It wasn't long before she stopped taking showers, just wasn't taking care of herself; everything was a sponge bath. I did say, "Can't you take a damn shower because you worked all day. It's hot out."

She would say, "I already took a sponge bath. I didn't work that hard."

This bothered me a lot because I had to sleep with her every night. She had a bad odor to her, like a dry sweat smell, and her breathing was erratic. The inside of her car looked like a Kleenex box. They were all over the inside of the car, in her pockets; she always had a Kleenex in her hands along with a ring around the nose. She wasn't listening to me. That was when I knew our marriage was falling apart because of this shit. At this time, I had noticed that my cash to pay the mortgage was disappearing along with the product. I did confront her and ask her if she was taking it. She said no, said

BUSTED

what a rotten thing to say to her. So the next best thing to do was to set her up, so I put some coke in a place where I knew she would go to. Of course, she took it. I was hoping that I was going to be wrong, but I wasn't, so I sat down in a chair next to her, not telling her that I set her up. I started to talk to her, said we had to stop doing this shit, told her that I thought that she had a real problem. Then the day came when she asked me, "Come on, just do a little with me. I won't ask you ever again. We will go upstairs, have great sex afterwards." That was all I needed to hear.

Again, of course, I did because misery loves company, so I did it with her. I guess it was something we did together that one time. But we got around talking that day; again I said to her, "We have to stop doing this stuff." Her reply to me was, "I'm not ready to do that just yet." The phone rang at that time, so the conversation came to an end. It was a good friend. He asked if I was going to be home. I said yeah, and he asked if he could come over. She asked who it was, and I told her that it was John. She looked up and said, "He will do more with me if he's going to get it for his wife." I said, "Do more, after all you have done tonight?" I just couldn't believe what I was hearing. This guy, I considered him to be a good friend, but I always wondered about him lots of times. He would ask me if I was going to be home, and I would say no, but when I would come home, he would be here. To this day, I still wonder if my wife was selling to him all the cocaine that I found missing, and was putting the money in her pocket, and if at the same time he was helping himself to my wife. I guess I will never know because he doesn't talk to me anymore after I went to jail. I tried to call, but he never returned my calls. Maybe the guilt was killing him.

This stuff will make you do stuff that you would never do if you were straight. If you're involved with this stuff, just take a moment, just look at your family. Say, is it really worth it to lose them over this stuff? What is one day of your life worth if you're sent to jail. If

I had at the time of my bust a large amount of money, I would have given it all up just to be free, to be with my family. The only ones that can sell drugs and get away with it is the government. They can do what they want, have no one to judge them for their actions. Just remember they are the ones that make up the laws. They can break them when it's in their favor, so that leaves you as the one who gets fucked. Do you really think you can get away with selling drugs and not give the government their share, or should I say their tax money? Everything you do in this country, the government wants their share. Always remember this: you work; the government spends.

They said that the Mafia was bad, but just look around, open your eyes, ask yourself, where does all the drug money go that they get from busts that's enough to rebuild the country? I have nothing bad to say about the Mafia. They just love what makes the world go round—that's money. Now look at most politicians in office now (that's most of them), they wouldn't know how to do a real job if it bit them in the ass. If you still feel that you still want to get into selling drugs, first find yourself a real good crooked lawyer, retain him, keep him happy. If not, when you get caught, you're going to do a lot of time. Once you're in jail, doing time, you're there for a real long time, waiting for an appeal or a revise and revoke. There is a good chance you can get more time than you already have if you look at the words revise and revoke. Your lawyer better be good before you go in for one.

I ended up hiring a lawyer from Boston. From the time I hired him, I must have talked to him about three times. I just saw him once through jail cell bars. The only reason he took time to see me was because he had a case in that court that day. This lying mother told me through the cell bars that he was in the room talking to the narcs about my conviction. Another lying piece of shit lawyer. I guess this made him look like he was doing something for me in regards to my case after taking money from my wife.

In the five years that he so-called represented me, I got used to being hung up on because this is what they do when they are not going to do anything for you. They take your money, put it in their banks. It's like you never existed to them and thinking that you will forget about it. Well, at least this is what happened to me. My so-called bigshot Boston lawyer held on to all my money. This kept me from retaining another lawyer, and that was all the money I had at that time. Then if you don't fight to get your money back for doing nothing for you, they keep it. If you do get it back, they still collect interest on the sum that you gave them until they return it. This so-called great Boston attorney held on to my money for four years, and I never got a penny in any of the interest he made on my money. I could keep on going, but it would take a whole chapter to discuss what lawyers do to guys who are incarcerated, what they take people for. So all I can say is if you're in the business, you have done well, get out before you get busted, get convicted for the possession of drugs, and whatever else they can add on to that. Or even worse, get a murder charge because some dumb bastard who may overdose on the product dies, then it's a murder rap. But now I'm thinking about it, you would probably get out sooner on murder charge than on a drug charge because it's not a mandatory sentence.

In this story you will find how some decent family member start to drift further away from me every day that passes by. As time passes, they all forget about you. Before you know it, you're all by yourself, doing the time. All you have are your memories, thinking about the life you had before you got busted, day in, day out. What really hurts is your love that you have for your family, for your wife, and hope you stay married. But most often as time goes on, your marriage ends or goes sour, then it just falls apart. That's another thing you carry around with you the whole time that you're incarcerated along with watching your back.

After about three years, I started to really know what kind of a woman I married; that was when I started realizing all the bad things she was doing in letters I was getting from unknown people on the outside. The things she did will be included in this story. The worst thing about it is that your hands are tied and you can't do a damn thing about anything for anyone or for yourself. But no matter what, I will always love her, but just in my heart that she broke, now knowing how many guys she has fucked in the past, how she turned her back on me after I was incarcerated. Well, being on the inside, I tried to talk to a lot of my friends I had before I got in trouble. Not one wanted anything to do with me because a lot of them owed me money for working on their cars when I had my garage. There was something I needed while I was in jail, and that was money.

When I called some of my so-called friends, if they answered the phones to talk to me, it was like they didn't even know me, and cut short the phone call. The biggest hurt was my cousin whom I trusted with everything I did. He always said he could be trusted no matter what; he would always be there if I needed him. But now I look at him as a piece of shit because he spilled his guts to the police, told them a lot of what I was doing in life. Knowing him, when the police pulled him over, he probably shit his pants then spilled his guts out, and that's probably why it was a fast search of his car. I haven't talked to him ever since I got sent to jail. I don't ever want anything to do with him for the rest of my life. In my eyes he's dead, just like his mother said to me when I came home one day and found my chair turned backward, my plate upside down. She looked me in the eyes and said, "You're dead to me." I could see the hate in her eyes. This was all because she found a little weed in my pants pocket when she decided to snoop though my stuff in the room that I was renting from my uncle. That day my aunt took it upon herself to do my laundry without me knowing and found the weed in my jeans pocket. I just couldn't believe she would do something like that, go through my stuff. Just before that, I even found money missing that I had in the closet, but I think it was her daughter who took it. What I would like to know is what she was doing going through my pockets anyways. I'll never know, never wanted her to do my laundry. This is something that will be with me for the rest of my life also, but who needs family like that anyways.

This story that you're about to read is about the time I spent in a state prison after getting busted with a large amount of cocaine, how it messed up my life to this day with jobs, friends, family members, other things that come with being incarcerated. Everything you'll be reading are some of the things that happened while I was incarcerated. I wrote it down in letters I sent home from day to day, from year to year, to my wife and daughter along with other family members.

BUSTED

What was really hurting me was watching everyone in my family start to disappear from my life after I was sent to jail. At the time of my incarceration I was married. My wife and I were very close until we were busted for drugs, and I was sent to jail for the possession of cocaine. That week that we got busted, I told her that she had to stop doing cocaine. She said to me that she wasn't ready to quit, but she would slow down. At this time I had so much work to do repairing cars in my shop. I didn't know what to do first because I was watching her all the time. I was worried that something was going to happen to her because of the amount she was doing. I just didn't have enough time to keep my eyes on her and work in my shop. I didn't know what else to do. Her appearance, her looks were looking real bad. I was noticing it was affecting our marriage, and she was always hiding out in the cellar. The woman that I married, that I thought I knew, hid her secret real well. Her knowing that I could get the drugs she needed, being married to me, was her way of not paying for it. She was a longtime user of cocaine; she was able to hide it really well, so I was told by some people that knew her throughout the years.

Well, the first of day of spring was finally here, and my cousin came by to see if I had got the cocaine that I was telling him about. As he pulled up in front of my house, we went walking around my backyard. I told him that I had been trying to get in touch with my supplier for weeks. I told my cousin that my coke dealer friend had called me, asked what I needed, and I put in my order. I just received it that day. I told him that I was going to get what I could, because he told me that he was going out of business, so I should get what I could. Because he made the money he needed, he wanted out, as he had told me so many times before. So at first I bought eight ounces. I told my wife what I had got, and she said, "Maybe I should get more in case we run out."

I said, "This is more than enough."

She said, "Just a little more, we don't want to run out."

What she meant was *she* didn't want to run out. So I started to call him until I got hold of him again. I got eight more ounces, then told her that I got enough to last her a while. All she had to say was, "Good."

I did start to notice that as long as her face was full, she didn't give a damn about anything or anyone else. She was driving me crazy, wanting to do the cocaine that I just bought. She was on my case all the time until I got ahold of him for the last eight ounces. She bugged me to call him over and over again until I got ahold of him. When my cousin was over, I told him about the additional eight ounces of coke that I just got. I told him how bad my wife was driving me crazy wanting to try the new stuff that I just got. Then while we were talking, I told him how much she was doing, then he said that he noticed that she was looking real bad. It sounded just as bad. He asked me how much I got. I just said I got enough of shit that it could choke a horse. It should keep my wife supplied for a long while, but I kept it where she couldn't get to it. I got so much because I didn't know anyone else to get it from. Plus he had been a friend of mine since we were ten years old. He then told me that I should tell him where it was just in case something should happen to me; he would be able to gain access to it and not to tell my wife where it was. I said that she didn't know. I then told him that my wife was doing more or sometimes less than an ounce a week.

I told my cousin just about everything because we had at that time the same problems in lives with our wives. At this time we were almost like brothers, so my aunt always said, but he always thought his shit didn't stink, thought he knew it all, thought he was better than everyone else. This guy ripped me off so many times that I couldn't count it if I tried, and he thought that I would never figure it out, but I did right from the start. But I never wanted him to know that I knew because he was family and thought he was so much smarter than everyone else.

After I told him where it was, we went back to the house and went down in my cellar to smoke a joint. He was such an asshole. If he was to take a joint out, he would smoke it with you and charge you for it. Put it in this little book he carried with him at all times. Then the conversation led to him asking me if I could get him some cocaine so he could start to distribute it again. I looked at him and told him that this was the last time I was going to get it. I was going to stop getting this shit and try to get my wife into a program. I then said it was not worth it and not to get back into it. I said I was just going to tell my wife that she will have to stop because I no longer knew where to get it anymore. The stupid mistake that I made was telling my wife how much that I just got. I just told my cousin that I was just sick of looking at the shit. I was just scared and didn't want my daughter to find out because she would hate me because it was for my wife, at least most of it was going to be.

My cousin Charley the Rat said, "Your wife isn't going to like what I'm going to do." So he asked me for a joint and a little coke even after he just did some. Of course he got it for free, and that was his middle name. But when this cocksucker was selling it, he wouldn't give you the time of day, and everything that came out of his mouth was, "You're in my book." Whatever you got off him and you didn't have the money, he would write it in his book that he carried with him all the time and would want something of yours to hold for collateral. Then when he left, I told my wife that he was acting real funny. He made me feel uncomfortable by just asking me stupid questions as he never did before. Then I told her how he insisted that I tell him where I had buried the coke I just purchased, and she said that sounded real funny.

It must have been at least fifteen minutes since he had left, then I got a call from him. He said, "They are on their way over your house."

I said, "Who?"

He said, "The Narcs."

I exclaimed, "What!"

He then said that he got pulled over. They just got their heads inside his car then searched to see if he had any drugs in his car. Then they questioned him, asked where he was coming from. He said that he was coming from my house, and then he said he didn't tell them any more than that. As we were talking on the phone, he said, "I didn't tell them anything about what you were involved in, you know, the coke." This fuckin' dickhead said this over the phone, and I just couldn't believe it! But when this dickhead was selling it, he had codes for everything, and if he had to wait for you on a delivery, he would charge you a late fee for not being on time. While I was talking to him on the phone, I said to him, "I got to go, the police just pulled up in front of my house."

But it was a local police car at first. The doorbell rang. As I opened the door, a cop rushed in. He asked me if the dogs bit, to chain them up because he said that he didn't want to get bit. I started to look for their leashes. Before I was just about to open the closet door, I heard a shot, then another. My dog named Coda just ran by me rubbing her paws over her head, and I just figured that she had been shot by a piece of shit Narc that busted into my home at first. The bullet that he shot her with hit her in the head, and the dog was running around the house and then ran down into the cellar, falling down the stairs, where my wife was. My wife was able to catch the dog as she ran under the stairs to, I guess, get away, and I yelled at the head honcho Narc, saying that he didn't have to shoot her. They called the dog officer so she could restrain both dogs and rush the one that got shot to vet to see if she could be helped. The bullet went though the top of her head out the corner of her eye, through the roof of her mouth, and came out the bottom of her jaw. This dog was a great dog, never bit anyone ever. There was no need to shoot her. She just wanted to know who was coming in the house. I think they just shot her because she was a Doberman Pincher, because my cousin always called them vicious attack dogs. That was the same words they said to me as they entered the house. As the cops ran down into the cellar, they saw that my wife was doing cocaine. The table was covered with it, and she told them that she had a problem with the drug.

Well, they started to tear the house, the cellar apart, found one of my wife's stashes right away, one that I didn't even know about. Then they found a place where only three people knew about. They went right to it like maybe someone told them where it was, like my rat cousin or this guy Bob who'd seen me take it from a couple night's prior to me getting busted. Of course, my cousin just left the house, who knew where everything was at all times. Very funny thing how the Narcs went right to the spot I buried it. What a fuckin' cocksucker my cousin was, and that's why I call him Charley Rat. They had me handcuffed upstairs and kept asking me where the rest of the cocaine was. I kept telling them that I didn't know what they were talking about and kept repeating it time after time. My wife was sitting right beside me. I got her attention and said to not say a word, to keep her mouth shut, that she didn't know a thing because she was married to me, and she didn't have to talk to them about me or anything they found.

They just kept throwing things all around the house and made me open a safe I had in my room, where my wife's jewelry and paperwork for the house was. While one of the cops was looking in the safe, the head honcho grabbed me by the handcuffs, picked me up by them, called me a choice of names, and said, "I don't care how long it takes, we will find the rest of the drugs if it takes all night." How did they know that there was more to be found unless someone told them that there was more, and the only one that knew was my cousin Charley Rat. He kept telling me that he knew that there was more to be found. Of course the cops said that they gave me my rights, but that was bullshit. No rights were given to me that night at all. He was too busy shooting my dog in the head and belittling my wife along with mentally abusing me in the other room. Now my wife was probably as bad as my cousin was and was spilling her guts out as my cousin did just to save her ass and telling whatever the Narc wanted to hear. On the court papers that were handed to me that I never got a chance to read fully, along with the search warrant papers, all I got to read was the first paragraph. I never got a chance to read the whole thing. When they say they gave me my so called rights that were just bullshit they never gave me my rights. Of course they will say that I read the search warrant. No matter what I was to say, they will say I did read it. All cops stick together unless they are out to fuck one of their own. Just remember, their job is to put you in jail no matter what it takes. They don't listen unless it helps them convict someone else in another case.

They placed me in a chair, handcuffed, and a couple of different cops came into the house. One said, "Look at what I found in the back of the garage." It was the cocaine that I had just bought, and they found it buried in the back of my garage under an exhaust fan and was buried about a foot down, and there was a board on top of it, and it was hailing out at the time, and they found it. (Right.) When I buried it there, I put it down in a hole I dug, covered up real good, and there was no sign that anything was buried there. Along where they found the cocaine, there was stuff thrown all over where I buried it. They found it where I told my rat cousin where I put it, that same day, a couple of hours prior to them coming over. They went right to the spot, like you see in the cartoons on TV—X marks the spot. They said there was a shovel already. There was no shovel there. You know someone had to have told them where they could find it. All the houses the cops raid come from rats, motherfuckers like my cousin, so they get their deals that the cops offer them. These rats, they make deals with the prosecutors to cover up bad deals that they made in the bust. If they give information on someone, it's a stay-out-of-jail deal. In jail, they just say throw a chunk of cheese in the corner and see who goes for it, or drugs in this case.

In this case, one was a guy named Bob and a girl named Joyce that was with him when he came over my home. My rat cousin Charley told them where I buried it. I know one thing for sure: there will be one person that will go out of his way to read this, and that will be rat cousin because he will want to know what I wrote about him in it. But knowing him, he will love to see his name in print, but it won't be here, just the name of Charley Rat and to me, we will be a piece of shit!

When they took my wife into another room to question her, they showed her a bag of wallpaper paste. The cop said to my wife, "What's this?" I could hear her crying. Of course, she fell apart, thinking that they were showing her cocaine. What a stupid bitch. She was just in that room wallpapering with me, and she was mixing the wallpaper paste with water. That's what they were showing to her, and she kept saying, "It's my husband's." She then said that she didn't know anything about it now. How can stupid can stupid be. Now who was down in the cellar with cocaine all over the table, had cocaine in places I didn't even know about? My wife said she didn't know anything about the drugs that they just found buried in the yard. The cops must have said, "We really believe this one no matter what she tells us." The cops started taking everything that was white, from wallpaper paste to all my baking soda I had in my storage closet. As long as it was white, it went with the cocaine they found. DUH I wondered why. They took everything that a person could weigh stuff with. I mean everything, right down to the ornamental scales a friend gave me before he died.

I was then brought out in handcuffs to the police cars that were outside my home. As I walked out of my home, the whole street was lit up in blue from all the lights from the cop cars. I was so ashamed of myself. My father would have killed me if he were alive. I was brought to the police station in the town that I lived in, booked for possession of drugs, and put into a jail cell. They tried to ask me questions; however, I refused to answer anything they asked me because they were saying things that I never said but trying hard to convince me that I did. But really I had nothing to say to them because the way they just shot my dog and the way they treated my wife, to me, I had no words for them. So back to the awaiting cell I went. I was later shipped to the west end of New Bedford to a prison they called Ash Street Correctional. All I could think about was my wife; I didn't want her to go to jail and into a jail cell. I was hoping they would let her go if I said the drugs were just mine and she didn't know anything about it, but fat chance of that.

When they sent me to the Ash Street jail, the cell they put me in had a glass bulb that was broken. I took a piece of the glass and was going to try to cut my wrist with it, but the guy that was in the cell with me ratted me out and called the CO. The piece of glass wasn't sharp enough to cut anyways. There were marks from the handcuffs that cut into my wrists and wasn't put there from me. They took me out and put me in a separate cell after I had seen the shrink. This guy was an idiot. The first thing he asked me was if I would be able to go into population. I looked at him and asked what the fuck was population. I had never been in jail before, and he was asking this. I just didn't understand what he was trying to tell me about population, and I said, "What the fuck is that again?" to no answer. When the shrink was done with me, they took me out, put me into a paper Johnnie, and put me into a dark single cell. The paper Johnnie that they put on me was ripping off little by little, and I was cold. I tried to talk to the COs in charge, and they just ignored me the whole time I was there. The COs could give a flying fuck what was happening to you or what could happen to you. They would wait till it was over. I mean whatever was happening before they moved in. To me, this night was the longest night of my life. It seemed like the day would never come, and I was scared when it did come.

I did try to go to sleep but couldn't. It was because a woman CO was talking outside the cell I was in, talking about her piercing that she had all over her body. She was telling a couple of COs that she had one going through her cunt, belly button, her eyebrow, also her tits, etc. The guys that she was telling this to were guys she was just cock teasing; they were too stupid to realize it, as a lot of them are. They must have gone home and jerked off their dicks till they were raw. This woman CO did this to them all night long, and she wasn't giving it up to these two jerks. She was just too good-looking for these two fools. For me, it was not a turn-on, but if you want to do this thing to your body, it's a so-called free country. You can do almost anything you want to yourself except fill it with drugs.

My wife was right down the hall. I was thinking about her every second of the night. I was very worried about her safety because she was very fragile. She would be a pushover if someone wanted to fuck her up, and it would be easy to fuck her up. All night long, I was freezing because the Johnnie they gave me to wear was falling apart. By morning I just had enough to cover my lower half because it just kept ripping into small pieces throughout the night. I knew when morning was here because the birds made so much noise I couldn't sleep if I tried. This is the loudest that I've ever heard birds ever.

Along with that the breakfast came. I got some cornflakes and milk. When I poured the milk on the cornflakes, it came out in chunks. It was sour. I told the so-called CO about it, but he just said, "Deal with it." I asked the CO if I could use the phone, and he said no. Then I asked if my wife was okay. He said the last time that he'd seen her she was okay. As I was talking to the CO, I noticed someone coming around the corner of the cell that I was in. It was my father-in-law. I thought maybe I would be getting out of there along with my wife. But he was just there to pick up his daughter, my wife.

When she came by where I was, she just gave me such a dirty look. If looks could kill, I would have been dead. That would have been fine by me.

I told her what would have happened if they raided the house; she said that she wasn't ready to quit doing the coke. She did look at me and said, "This is me. This is my way of relaxing, and I'm not hurting anyone." She just blew off what I just said to her. Well, they just left me there, didn't even try to get me out. I just couldn't believe the way she looked at me. I remember it clearly to this day. I will never forget it. This is the woman I married for better or worse, whom I loved so much. That was a short-lived event. Now that I think about it, I can't believe that she told the police that she didn't know a thing about the drugs. There she was downstairs in the cellar when the narcs came powdering her nose.

On that following Monday, I went to court. Of course, the news station was there. Boy, did they blast me all over the news, in the newspaper as a big dealer. They made it look as if the police made the biggest drug bust in their careers. How much of a big-timer I was. Fuckin' dicks they were. I couldn't get to use a phone. No one was there to help me retain a lawyer, so I ended up with a public defender to represent me at the hearing again. What a fuckin' asshole, and even to this day, I don't know his name. Well, I said yes to him representing me thinking I could get out so I could clear things up, try to talk to my wife, check out what they did to my home. What a damn asshole this lawyer was. He just made things worse than they were in the eyes of the court along with myself. He was the stupidest lawyer I'd ever seen.

When he was speaking to the judge, I realized he had a lot more stupid, didn't get a chance to use it at that time. What a dumb motherfucker. I would like to put down his name but don't know it, but I think he was put there by the police to keep me in jail. It worked. I don't know where he got the part of me having guns in my possession. That must have come from the police because there were no guns at all in my home, and why would I need one. Again why would I need a gun when it was mostly for my wife. A couple of friends I knew said it was a setup. I tried to tell the lawyer that there were no guns. He said for me to be quiet. Then he said that my case was just thrown at him; he didn't get a chance to really look at the case. I just said to him, "What the fuck is wrong with you?"

He then said, "I got your bail down. You can get out with a bails bondman."

I said, "Who the fuck is going to get me a bondsman? I have no one helping me on the outside."

They set bail at a hundred thousand dollars; I could get out on eleven thousand dollars. I looked at him and said, "Boy, did you fuck things up for me," and he just walked away and said, "Deal with it." The police closed out all my bank accounts. I had no money at all to get out on bail. I know that's what the courts wanted for bail. Toward the end of the day, at least I think it was, I was moved to Dartmouth Correctional. As I was in the cell, I watched guys that were in the same cell as I was in fighting over boiled hot dogs that they brought to the holding cell for lunch. It was like the COs were there to feed the animals, and they acted just as I said, because they all lunged for the hotdogs on the tray. I was able to get a couple on the second round when all the guys thought there was no more food coming. After that we were brought out of the cell to join another bunch of guys in a room where there was a good-size line. We stripped and, we were powered with this white stuff, given a plastic bed to sleep on. It was an experience that I will never forget, at least I know I won't. I was getting really fucked in the head. I didn't know which way was up, just kept thinking about all the things at my house that I worked on for so many years of my life. I was thinking that they were going to take it. I bought it with money my mother gave me before she died. All the stuff I worked so hard for and wanted to leave to my daughter will be confiscated, put up for auction.

Here I'm in jail; there isn't anyone at my home to make the payment on my house. As I'm thinking about it, I'm rubbing my leg against the cell wall, and I had rubbed a hole right through the side of my pants and didn't notice it until I started to feel sick and real weird. I was going through Valium withdrawal. I had just helped a guy a few minutes before and said that could never happen to me. They came to get me and brought me into a room. I don't remember much of what the room looked like, but they tried to give me liquid Valium, and I spit it out. They busted me for drugs, and they tried to give me drugs, but I did have a problem with Valium at the time but just couldn't understand why they were giving it to me.

As I was thinking, I just couldn't believe my wife just took off. She left holding the bag, probably going nuts to find some coke. That was just about all she probably had on her mind. After a few days, I did got bailed out by my cousin. He put up the bail money for me so I could get out, get my shit together. At the time of my bail, I wasn't thinking my cousin set me up; I was just happy to see him, but the whole time I talked to him, he was negative toward me, saying fucked-up things to me. I didn't lead on that I thought he had something to do with me getting busted. I played the game with him. I thought his bailing me out was from the kindness of his heart, but just prior to me getting in trouble, he said that he would like to find a way to make the dirty money he had legal. This was money he had made from selling drugs prior to me getting busted. Then things started to click in my head. Well, I guess he found a way to come out smelling like roses. He used the money he got from dealing drugs to bail me out, then it became clean with a court check—no taxes.

At that time, I started to realize that my cousin was part of me getting busted. I just didn't want to believe it, but cleaning my act up, I was able to put two and two together. I figured out that he was a piece of shit. He was asking questions like he wanted to get into the business again. He was telling me this before I had gotten busted. Then out of nowhere he asked me if I had any more cocaine buried anywhere else that I didn't tell him about that the cops didn't find. He took me to a restaurant to eat, but all that was on his mind was if I had more cocaine buried somewhere else in my yard. He said that he could sell it, make me some money for lawyers, plus make some of my money back that I owed him for the bail that he used to get me out. I looked at him and said to myself, This fuckin' asshole really wanted to sink the hook in. Then I knew not to trust him after that. That's the last thing to ask a person when they get out of jail, like I just got out of. He told a friend of mine whom I talked to all the time that he had nothing to do with me getting busted. I said yeah, that is why he asked me if I had more cocaine buried that the cops didn't find. I took in account everything he asked me, and to me, he had guilt written all over his face. This prick is guilty as sin. He has never approached me to try to make me understand that he had nothing to do with it.

The other thing I noticed about my rat cousin when he was talking to me was he was always looking toward the sky, never into my eyes. Shifty-eyes motherfucker. I could never trust a person that ever did this. The only reason he put up the bail was to launder his dirty money that he had from selling cocaine. That was the only reason he bailed me out. He got it all back in a check from the courts all cleaned up. That same week, my brother saw him at the dog track betting on the dogs. He told my brother that he had nothing to do with me getting busted. This was what he kept telling friends that we both knew whenever they asked him if he had anything to do with me getting busted. This is another reason I know he set me up. He feels that he needs to convince the people that he didn't have anything to do with me getting busted. So I just kept my mouth shut just to see if I was right in what I was thinking. I just wanted to be sure before I accused him of something like that. I just had to get this out of my head because I had too many other things that needed my attention, like making mortgage payments, getting an attorney to represent me in court.

My daughter was in Florida living with her mother. Her knowing what I was involved in was upsetting me, and this is something I didn't want her to know. I was ashamed of myself. I was trying to get in touch with my wife so I could see her to see where she stood, what she told the police. I wanted this to end as soon as possible. I was so glad to get out of jail. It happened to be a real nice hot day, I really needed it after being in that hellhole. The first thing that came out of my cousin's mouth was that I stank real bad. All I said to him was "You would too if you were in that fuckin' place, going through what I went through. You would stink also. I was in a closed area for seven days and didn't take a shower. I think this could make anyone stink, and even now the odor was still stuck in my head to this day. After being in that place, I couldn't wait to get home to take a shower, get the stink off me. But to this day, I don't know if it was me who stink or if it was the power they threw on me. I'll never know. I really don't want to know."

I remember when he turned to my street. I saw my house, and I was so happy but was looking around to see if they sealed the doors with tape, saying not to enter. I walked up the stairs to my house, and I realized that the police had the keys to my house. I couldn't get in, so I broke a window to get in. I couldn't get in touch with my wife to get the other set. The next thing that came out of my cousin's mouth was "You better enjoy it because the police are going to take it because it was involved in drugs. They are going to get it for one of their cop buddies."

Now this really bothered me real bad. I just started to think of what to do. All I said was, "You think so?" He said that he knew so. He looked at me and said he thought that maybe I should sell it. I said, "How I can sell if you think the cops are going to take it?"

He said, "All you can do is try before they take it."

Then I said, "No damn way. They will realize that I was no big-time dealer. I will just get charged with possession, I'll still have my home." Then I said, "I'll take my chances with the courts. I can tell them where all my money came from. I had all the proof that it didn't come from the sale of drugs."

Then something started. He started to talk my wife down. I felt heat throughout my body because I love my wife a lot, and I told him so. He better stop because I was ready to bust him in the face. He then said, "Look, she left you in jail, didn't do a thing to help you or come to take care of the house or even go to pick you up, so what do you think she's going to do?" Then he said that she would forget about me and would be fucking someone else before the end of the week for drugs.

I guess they say love is blind. I must be really blind. Even after she did what she did to me, I still had a lot of feelings for her. He said, "Let's get all her stuff together, dump it off at her father's house." Then he started to throw her stuff on the floor. I just stopped and said, "Don't throw another thing of hers on the floor again." Then I said, "What if she comes home? She has nothing to wear, then what will I do. It's like I'm kicking her out. I would never do that even after what she has done to me."

He then said, "Wake up, she is not coming home. She was going to let you rot in jail." And then my cousin that I named Charley Rat said, "Think about that." I somewhat listened, and in time, my wife did fuck me over as he said she would do.

But still I took all her clothes to the cleaners to be cleaned even though at this time I didn't have much money. I finally got a chance to get a decent meal. I didn't have to watch a bunch of guys fighting over a tray of hotdogs after they had their hands down their pants. I noticed when you're in a place like I was in, you got to watch every move these guys make in case things come your way. After I had something to eat, I started to look around my house and realized what a mess the cops made. A lot of it wasn't necessary. I just started to pick up all the broken stuff up, family pictures, dishes, papers scattered all over the place. It smelled real bad. It needed to be cleaned up. But as I started to clean up, I noticed that the house was a mess to begin with. I just couldn't believe I let it go so far.

My wife was no housewife. She couldn't clean house if her life depended on it. She had trouble even taking care of her own even when it came to taking a damn shower. My mind was all messed up; the only thing that was going through my head was me losing my home, my wife, what my daughter would think of me. I worked so hard for this home, buying and selling cars and putting up with so much shit from people, but what a good business I had before all this happened. There was no big-time sale of drugs going on, as the cops told the newspaper. They also said that I was selling drugs up the whole East Coast, but all I was doing was just taking care of a coke-whore wife along with a couple of friends who also had the same problems. It took a month for me to really realize how bad she really was, until I started to look at her real closely. I started to get scared because of what she was turning into. I didn't know it until I started to see her starting to steal and hide the drugs. When she said she needed more, this is when she started to show her true colors.

The police took all my cars, closed out all my banks accounts; they even canceled all my car insurance, along with my home policy without me knowing until the bank called me. I would go by the police department and park across the street from the police station just to look at my cars that were in there lot. It was killing me inside. There was nothing I could do at that time. My Corvette stood out like a sore thumb because it had a cream color paint job, and it could turn heads. During the night, I could hear my alarm going off at the police station and knew it was my Corvette because I knew the sound of its alarm. When you get caught for just about anything related to drugs, they want to take everything you own away just because they found drugs at or in your home.

My mother left me a good amount of money, but I didn't know about it until the later years after her death. It was in a safe-deposit box. I didn't know about it until the bank called me. This is one thing I didn't tell my cousin about because this is one thing I wanted to keep to myself. This was because of the falling out we had when the business we had together fell apart. Another thing, if he knew about the money I had, he would somehow try to hustle it away from me. The reason that it fell apart is I was the only one working. He was too busy going out during the day to Fall River, picking up, fucking whores, and paying them with cocaine. Then I came in one night and caught him breaking up coke on the office desk. After that, I found out that he was hiding drugs in the shop, and that was it. I broke up the partnership.

I started to clean the inside of my home again. It stink real bad after the cops tore it apart. This was because they left the refrigerator door open, and all the food was rotting. That was where the smell was coming from. My wife did come by when I was still in jail and took a lot of stuff she wanted but didn't pick up a finger to clean, not even to close the refrigerator door. My cousin is the one who bailed me out. I thought I could trust him, but I noticed that he had a big smile on his face when he picked me up from jail. I noticed it right away but paid no attention to it. I never questioned him about it.

When I got home, I kept calling my wife to see if I could talk to her, to let her know that I was home. Of course, she wasn't home, so I said "fuck it" and was just hoping that she was all right. I just wanted to hug her so bad. My cousin came by to take me out to eat again, so I just paid close attention to him. He said that he would pay, and I said "Yeah!" and that was a shock, and it wasn't put in his book he always carried. He was coming by a lot to see if he could hustle me out because he thought I was going to lose it all. I knew this because of what I've seen him do in the past. He came by one night, and we went out to eat. For the second time, he again asked me about the drugs, if I had any more hidden anywhere. Then he looked at me and said, "At least you smell better." I gave him a dirty look that said, "What a fucked-up thing to say after all the shit I've gone through," including all the shit that I had on my mind at that time.

As the conversation went on, he looked at me again and said, "Do you have any more cocaine buried?" This was the third time he asked me that. He kept telling me that he could make me some money to live on; this was the only thing that was on his mind. I just couldn't believe what I was hearing, what he was asking me over and over again. I looked at him and said, "What, I said no." Well, I looked at him and said afterward, "Yeah, there is a good amount that they didn't find in the house." When I came back home, I crushed the rock of cocaine into chunks with the back of a plunger in order to flush it down the toilet. There was at least four more ounces that I buried next to a big rock outside my home but not on my property. I was scared to get it because they were still watching me. I was being followed on a regular basis by that piece-of-shit narc that shot my dog. I ended up telling my so-called best friend John about it, and he dug it up with my daughter's boyfriend and fucking me over while I was in jail. My cousin at the time of the bust was the last person to call me. When I went downstairs to clean, I just happened to look at the caller ID, and it said Mobil One on it. That means that the call was from a cop car. This just goes to show you that when I got busted, my cousin was the last person I talked to. The night when the cops raided my home, he was the only person I talked to. I know it was his call because I just erased all calls prior to his call. The cops have their own phones, and they are not going to use my phone to make their personal calls. The time matched when he called me and when the Narcs busted me.

BUSTED

Now think about this, how could he be pulled over, have his car searched, go home to call me and start to talk to me, and do this all in twenty minutes (bullshit). Then he also said on the phone, "They are on the way to your house." As he was talking to me, they pulled in front of my house and were at the door. I would love to know how my cousin knew that they were on their way to my house, were ready to knock on my door, unless he was in the car. This slimy rat bastard also knew when they were at the door right to the second. Now I told my cousin I had to go and went to the door. Just as I opened it, they busted in. This is when my dog was shot in the head because they were told that they were vicious attack dogs.

Seeing that I worked at a school, of course, the police said that I was selling drugs to the students at the school that I was at. I would never do that ever, no matter what. I have never sold any drugs ever to any kids. They said this so they could get a feather in their hats. But drugs did go around the school a lot. On one occasion, one student brought in his car after I had fixed a lock on his car trunk. As I opened the hatch, I smelled weed, found it in the wheel well of his car. I just looked at him and said, "Get this car out of here." He just looked at me and said okay. Toward the end of the day, he came up to me and asked me if I was going to report him. I said, "For what?" He just said, "You know," and I just said, "I don't know what you're talking about. I just said never bring that into the school ever again if you have drugs in it, do you hear me?" He just said yes. I then said to him that I didn't see anything. If they were going to ask me, I would say I didn't know what they were talking about.

What was I going to do, get him kicked out of school, get him a court case? He would never be able to attend school again, never be able to go into the service if he wanted or attend another trade school. I couldn't do that to a kid that was in his last year, was about to graduate, was a real good kid the whole time I had him as a student. I made it look like it never happened. All his buddies knew what I did, I wasn't going to ruin a kid's life like the cops did to me. I loved my job at the school. It was the best job that I had in my whole life. It's because I was teaching something that I knew to kids who didn't know it. It felt real good to be teaching it. I was respected.

I see the head instructor of the school that I am teaching at, and he is my so-called boss now. When he sees me, I get nothing but dirty looks from him. He stares at me now like he's better than me. When I see him doing this, I want to go over and punch him in the throat. He's the type that if you say the sky is falling, he will believe you, as he believed the story the cops told him. If he was so smart, he would be able to figure out that I was making chump change. If I was a big-time dealer, what was I there teaching for peanuts. Some people appear to be so smart, going to big-time colleges, yet are so stupid and gullible.

When the police went through my home, they found my bankbooks and withdrew all my money that I had at the banks. I guess they put it in the police accounts, so it was tied up, so I had to find another job to make money. The job that I had at the school was gone; they made sure of that. Everything at my shop was gone. All the customers that I had were scared to come to my shop for repairs on their cars. So I got a job working at a Toyota dealership. I worked till it was almost time for me to go to jail. I think the police contacted them. My job was terminated after a couple of months. I was able to collect unemployment. This was enough to pay the mortgage on the house, to be able to put some money away so I would have money in jail to live on, which I gave to my wife to send me while was in prison. That was a real stupid thing to do, giving it to a drug addict.

At this time my daughter found out that I got in trouble, and she was living in Florida with her mother. She told her mother that I would need help. She wanted to come back home to help me out. Her mother said, "Forget him, stay here, go on with your life. He got himself in, let him find his way out. You're settled in here now. This is your life now." My daughter said, "He raised me, I have to go back home to my father, help him, because he will need me." As I always said, family always takes care of family when they are in trouble. My daughter just left everything behind to come home to help me get through it. She was the only one that stood by my side, the only one that I could really trust. Her mother sold most of the things my daughter left behind, as she did to me when she kicked me out. It was just her way.

BUSTED

It took a while to get my shit together. I went to see a lawyer I knew for years. He was the best of the best. His name was Joe, and he was very straight with me, said that he didn't handle this type of case. He sent me to a drug lawyer who just handled these cases. The court date was coming up; I had to get a lawyer to represent me in court. Let's just call him Mr. David. So I did go to see him, and he took the case on. A good friend of mine, I thought at the time, covered the bill because the cops tied up all my money. After the lawyer got his money, he looked at me, and he said that he had to talk to the prosecutor to see where I stood. Well, he got back to me, and he said that they told him that they wanted fifteen to life and would not budge. He called in someone else that he knew. He was talking to me about my case to see between both of them if they could get a halfway mark. Well, when the other attorney came in to talk to me, asked me what kind of money I had, I told him, and he said that the money was tied up by the cops. He then asked if I had money somewhere else other than what the cops had of mine. I said no. He then said do the time, start over again.

"Where is all the money you made dealing drugs?"

I said, "There was no money made." I explained that my wife was a drug addict, and I split the cost of the cocaine between my friends. Whatever they did with it, I didn't know. It was mostly for their personal use, so I was told; I just went with whatever they told me. I just needed help for my wife's drug habit.

It took about a week, then I got a call from my attorney, and he said that he had to see me as soon as possible, so I made an appointment for the next day at a time that he could see me. I walked into his office, and as I opened the door, there was a loud noise coming from behind it. When I looked, it was a bag of empty booze bottles hitting the back of the door as I opened it. They were spread all over the floor. I just couldn't believe he had all those empty bottles behind the door, where clients could see them. He said, "Sit down there." He put a deal on the table from the prosecutor. They said three years. I looked at him and just fell apart. Just the idea of leaving my wife and daughter for three years hurt me so much that I could never put it into words. He said that they were still talking; maybe something else would come up. He then said, "Make another appointment with my secretary and call me back in a week."

Well, another week went by, and again I was in his office. While he was talking to me, he said they gave him a deal to talk over with me. He said that it was a good and fair deal. So I said, "Are they going to tell you three years again?"

He just gave me a look that could kill and said, "No, five fuckin' years."

I looked at him and said, "You said last week three years."

He looked at me and picked up a glass ball that was on his desk and threw the glass ball through the door. I heard it roll down the hallway. Then he said, "Five fuckin' years, did you get that? You got caught with a lot of fuckin' cocaine. Who the fuck do you think you are, one of the fuckin' Rollin Stones? Get all your shit together because you're going to jail real soon." Then he said that my cousin was trying to pull all his money from the courts; the courts were going to revoke my bail.

I then started thinking, no wonder he wasn't coming around. He made sure his car was fixed first. He used me like he always did. He knew that I knew the money that he used to bail me out was dirty money. He was trying to find different ways to clean it up. He found a way, which was to use it for bail money. He wasn't doing this from the kindness of his heart because he didn't have a heart. He treated his family like shit. Also, his wife hated him to no end, and she told me this more than once. She told me that I really knew him like I thought. I didn't know him as she did. Boy, did I find out and realize it was just a way to hide his dirty money. Then my cousin got his money back as clean as it can be, right through the court system. Paid no taxes either. What better way to clean dirty money than through the court system. The courts have no idea where it came from because the courts are the only ones who can do this and get away with it plus get it back in a check, and knowing him, he probably said it came from his mother.

Well, this was January of 1998. My daughter just had a baby boy, and I considered myself very lucky because I got a chance to hold him before I went to jail. I shortly got a call from my so-called lawyer, as I expected. He said, "You're going to jail tomorrow." He said it just like that. Then I remembered what the bail bondman said to me when he put up the bond for me. He said, "Don't make me come looking for you. Don't fuck me over on my money. If I have to come looking for you, it will be real bad for you." He didn't scare me. If it wasn't for my wife and daughter, I would have been gone. Such a long sentence for possession of drugs. It was a nonviolent crime, on a first offense. In my whole life, I never ran away from anything, and I wasn't going to start now. That just wasn't in me. If I did, I wouldn't ever be able to see my daughter again. I couldn't do that to her.

I called my wife, asking maybe we could see each other before I was sent to jail because we had to be at court the same time in the morning that week. Well, she said that she had things to do, like take a bath. I was very surprised about that. Then she said that she was scared because of what was going on during the week and that she was going to stay at home. I kind of knew that it was bullshit. She already knew what she was going to get, and she was probably going out to fuck someone, because she took a bath. She was real scared and was hoping that she wasn't going to get jail time because the one day she stood in jail, a black girl took her jacket. She left without it. She was really scared of black people because she was beat up outside her house by a black guy for her pocketbook, so she said.

Well, my daughter came, and I went for a ride. I just figured that we would go by my wife's hangout where she had been hanging out since she was young with her friend. This was where I was told she was selling coke to people she knew. This girl was so stupid she would sell it to a cop and then tell them where she got it from. Something just told me to take a ride by her hangout. I wanted to see if she was going to stay home or go to her famous pit stop. When my daughter and I drove by the place, we saw her father's caravan in front of the place because her car that I gave her was still at the police station. Of course, she was there. We parked a little ways from the place. Of course, she came out, and we watched her come out with a guy, and she pushed this guy right up against the building and started making out with him. I pulled up right across the street from her. She saw me but just got into her father's caravan and drove off.

I watched the guy she was making out with start to walk off and real fast in the other direction. She just left him standing there. At this time I had nothing to lose. I was going to go after the guy and beat the fuck out of him, but my daughter stopped me from doing it. She just said, "No, leave him alone, it's not his fault." I chased my wife down in my car, and at a red light, I ran up to her window and said, "What the fuck are you doing?"

She just said, "Leave me alone. You don't tell me what to do!" And she sped off. I was going to call this girl to have her beat up bad, but my daughter again said, "It's not worth it. Just let it go. Let her do what she wants to do. It will all come back to her."

Just watching her hang all over this guy was getting me sick because she was my wife. All kinds of hate was going through my body. I realized she would do just about anything for cocaine. Just then I realized she was a coke whore. I never figured that out the whole time I was with her. I was so mad at what I'd seen that I still wanted to beat the hell out of her, and that would have been the first time I hit a woman. My wife ended up being just like most of the girls that I knew and could have got with coke.

She said, "You're going to jail. I'm not! So what am I supposed to do? Should I just stay at home? Just wait for you? I have a fucking life!" I just couldn't believe what I just heard at that moment. Looking at her, I knew she was high after all I did for her. Now to this day I wish I never told the cops that she knew nothing about the drugs. I should have let her do time alongside me. Maybe she would have been a better person as she said to me in the few letters she sent me. They would have sent her to Framingham woman's prison, where she would have been on her knees for a CO for cheeseburger or a stick of pepperoni that she could use for sex purposes. Yes, I have clipping of the shit that went on in prisons like that, how they covered up things right down to getting women pregnant. I would read it once in the newspapers, but I've never read any more about it. They brushed it under the carpet. Even though the COs treat you like shit, they sometimes show their true colors, show that they are somewhat human. They also do messed up things in life, as most humans do from time to time. No one is perfect, but judges and prosecutors, they are above the law and never make mistakes.

I did call my lawyer the day before I was expected to go to court. This was in January 10, 1998, I think, or around that date, and asked if he could get me a continuance for a couple of days because I really wanted to talk things over with my so-called wife. He then said to me, "You have been out for ten months, waiting for this day. You want another continuance? No. You're going to jail tomorrow, and this is the end of this conversation. I also want to let you know that your cousin pulled his money from the courts." I just wanted a couple of days more so I could treat my coke-whore wife like the whore that she really was. After I saw her press that guy against the wall, I wasn't going to get a piece of ass for the next five fucking years. I was going to treat her like the guy she threw up against the wall.

I looked up one of my old girlfriends that I really loved and took her out for dinner, and we ended up making out, and at that time, she was also in a bad marriage. My so-called wife called me up that day because she had plans to go somewhere with her father, but I know it was an excuse. I kind of knew it was another one of her bullshit stories, but what could I do. When I went to see this girl that I knew, she told me what she saw my wife doing, but I didn't want to believe her because she wanted to get back with me. I just wanted my wife back even after what she was doing to me. But what this girl was telling me probably was all true because she worked in a restaurant my wife and I would go to when we were together. This girl had seen her there with other guys more than a couple of times and never told me.

Well, I had so much hate in me, of course, because of my wife and what I was hearing about her, that I ended up seeing her, and I had sex with her because I knew I wouldn't be for the next five years. I fucked her instead of making love to her. I treated her like the whore she was and was probably what all the other guys were doing to her. This was the first time I can say I just fucked her instead of making love to her, and she probably knew it too because it was noticeable. It was in my sister's bathroom, standing up against the wall, as she did to the guy I had seen her with in front of her hangout.

When I walked into the courtroom knowing that I was going to jail, I was hoping that she would be around when I got out of jail, her knowing how bad she fucked up. The night before, I didn't sleep; I just walked around my house all night, looking at all the stuff I owned, wondering if it was going to be there when I got out. There were so many different things going through my head at the same time that it was almost unbearable. Wondering, thinking about the place that they were going to send me to. Was it going to be like all the other places that I was at? (I mean a fuckin' hellhole.) In the morning I must have hugged my daughter at least ten times and said, "You stay at home because I'm going to jail today. I don't want you there. You won't be seeing me for a long time." I told her not to worry about me, then gave my grandson a good look and told him that I loved him. Off I went to court, ready to go to jail. Just another obstacle placed in front of me that has to be tackled.

My daughter told me not to worry about the house, that she would take care of it because if she had to rent another house, it would come out to the same as what I was paying. It was more than my wife offered to do even though she hoarded all her money and lived with me for free for so many years. I never took into account that she was putting her money in her own bank account. She never told me until the cops told me. I couldn't believe how fast the night passed. Before I knew it, the next day was here. My friend John came by to give me a ride to the Superior Courthouse. That was when I saw my wife. All she said to me was hi. She sat right beside my friend John. She looked real friendly toward him, as she always did when he came over without me being home lots of times. That bitch had a smile on her face like she didn't have a care in the world because she knew she wasn't going to do any jail time. I was all fucked up in the head from the day of the bust to the court day just knowing that I was going away for five fuckin' years. All I did for my family, not even one of them showed up in court for me, not even my cousin because he had his face full. Greedy bastard. I guess because he got what he wanted, his money cleaned by the courts. He also didn't have to pay taxes on it, so of course, his face was full.

BUSTED

When they called my name, I looked at my so-called lawyer. They said, "Come up to the post." As I was there, I was glancing back at my so-called attorney, and he was fiddling with papers, paying no attention to what the judge was saying to me. There was no response from my lawyer at all. The judge started to ask me questions, asked me if anyone put me up to this plea or if I did it on my own. I turned to look at my so-called attorney for an answer, to see if he was even there. He looked at me and started to go through his paper again in his briefcase and again paid no attention to me or to what the judge was saying to me. To this day I know in my heart my lawyer traded me for some other case, made a deal with the prosecutor, but who could prove it. He's dead. He took it to his grave with him. So I answered the judge's questions because the prosecutor wanted to give me fifteen to life if I didn't plea out for the five years. I just was thinking, For what! Fuckin' asshole. It's like I killed a bunch of people.

When I started to purchase cocaine (to me now I call it shit), I had no idea what kind of trouble you could get into if you got caught with cocaine. To me it didn't look like much, but I guess it was all of that. It was real funny. I tried to get in touch with the guy I always got it from; he never made me wait so long before. I should have known that something was wrong, but I trusted my school buddy Larry. When I was bailed out of Dartmouth Correctional, I went back to the bar where I got the coke from. It looked like it was being torn apart. Things were being taken out the back door, then I realized that my school buddy Larry must have been made by the narcs also. He helped to set me up. Those pieces of shit narcs cops set me up for a fall. It must have been a slow week for them, or somebody was bucking for a promotion or a star on their forehead because they did it twice to me. I think about it now, and this was something like a setup or a good case of entrapment.

I was told by my friend named Larry, when I bought it from, that he was going out of business. Then he said that I should buy as much as I could, and that's what I did because I didn't know anybody else to buy it from. This was from a guy I got high with. I was brought up around guys who smoked pot, drank, so on. It was just part of my life that I fell into, and I paid no attention to it. I just did what everyone was doing at that time. Now I'm here waiting for the judge to pass sentence on me. I don't have enough money to get a real good attorney now, so I'm going to plea out to a five-year term. The fucked-up thing about it is if I were a big drug dealer, you would think I would be able to afford a good lawyer, not some dick wipe who was also acquitted for having a large amount of coke and still be able to keep his license to practice law, doing no time for possession of coke.

    The judge looked at me passed sentenced of five years like he was swatting a fly. It was to be a mandatory sentence. This means day for day, no good time. That's when it hit me. He said I was to be shipped to Cedar Junction, before I knew it, I was cuffed, put in a van, was being shipped out to jail. The CO that brought me out to the van was a real dickhead, as I found out that they were all the same as time went on. I was just shoved into the van, told to have a good trip, and never got a chance to say goodbye to my wife. Now that I think about it, she probably didn't give a flying fuck because the last time I looked at her, she was smiling at my so-called friend John. After I was in jail, I received a letter telling me that they saw my wife at a restaurant with my friend John eating a meal. This is because he just got some coke from me before I got busted. I told him where I had another four ounces buried. Knowing him, he most likely told my wife this, and she was most likely sucking, fucking him for it. I've always said, a stiff dick has no conscience, and a lot of guys don't think who they can be hurting when they are fucking a friend's wife. I know he was a dog because of all the things he told me that he was doing behind his wife's back. But to this day I always will be wondering if my so-called good friend John fucked my wife. This will haunt me for the rest of my life. It wouldn't bother my wife to do something like that because in one phone conversation, she told me that she had fucked more guys than I had fingers and toes. I guess if he had coke, he was going to let my wife know that he had coke so that he was sure to get something off her if she knew this.

    Soon after I was able to get mail, I got a letter from someone just to let me know that they saw her at a restaurant with my so-called friend John again. They both would have gotten a little something from the coke he got from me a couple of days earlier. When it came to John, he always said nothing was for free for him. All he probably wanted was to get his cock sucked or fucked. All he would have to do was turn her on to some coke. That would be a treat for her in more ways than one. If he did fuck her, it really wasn't going to be good because she was always a bad fuck. I guess guys that she fucked just fucked her to bust a nut but didn't take time to make love to her as I tried to. They just treated her like a whore. But stupid me couldn't see it all those years. I never saw it in her. In my heart, I still loved her; you just can't change what's in your heart no matter how much you try. Just want to let everyone know I never married a virgin. I married a woman who just grew on me. I never did a background check on her. She just knew how to blend right into my life.

I was sentenced on Martin Luther King's birthday I thought the courts were closed, but I was so wrong. I thought I would get another day to be with my wife before I was sentenced. Weird thing about being sentenced on Martin Luther King's birthday is that the whole time I was incarcerated, the blacks were the ones who gave me the hardest time the whole time I was incarcerated. My wife received two years' probation, that's all, but I was going away for five damn years. The way I stood up for her, she fucked me over real good. Before we were sentenced, I noticed that she started to treat me like shit, or should I say the way all her ex-boyfriends treated her, so that's why it was no problem for her to do it to me because she knew how to do it so well. Now that I think about it, I wasn't in my right mind because everything was so cloudy to me. I should have let her do the time that they wanted to give her and shut my damn mouth. At the time that I was sentenced, I wasn't thinking how bad jail could be until I got to Concord Correctional. I then wished I had done drugs and drank, but after they stripped me, I felt like I was high because I couldn't believe what they put me though.

I arrived at Cedar Junction on January 15, 1998, in leg chains, handcuffed like I just murdered a person or robbed a federal bank and shot up a bunch of people. I was put in a large cage and was wondering what was next. In the cage they put me in was a bunch of good-looking guys (yeah, right) who looked like they never did anything wrong in their lives. They took out so many guys at a time, then it finally came to my turn. I was put into another cage with another CO. He looked at me and said, "Strip down. Everything off."

I looked at him and said, "What!"

He looked at me and said, "What part of strip don't you understand." He then said, "This can be easy or it can be your way. Whatever you want. I can put you back in the cage with your buddies, we can try this at a later time."

Well, I did what he told me to. I felt really weird stripping in front of a guy, but I did what was expected of me. I went through my second strip search, and it got even weirder than the first strip search because he was looking up my ass, under my balls. At that time I didn't know why. I then said, *I* better get used to it. *I* think this is going to happen a lot as time went on. Of course I was right; it did. When I got strip-searched, I would just look up at the ceiling and say, This will be over soon. Do what they tell me to do. Get it over with. The CO looked like a professional at what he was doing. I did try to talk to him, but he didn't want to hear it, like all the others I tried to talk to. I told him that I was not like the other guys. This was my first time in jail.

He said, "You're no different than all the others." He just laughed at me then said that I wasn't going to be treated any different from them. He said, "Stop trying to be my friend. Do what I tell you to do, we will get along real fine."

I then said, "I'm not trying to become your friend. I just wanted to tell you that it's my first time in jail. I'm not going to pull anything on you."

He then said, "Whatever you say." Then he said, "What are your sizes in clothes? You take waist first, then I'll see if I have it."

I thought I was going to get a jumpsuit like you see on TV, with stripes, but to my surprise, it was a pair of jeans. It looked like a blue work shirt like I wore at most of the shops I worked for. He took my street clothes and asked me what I wanted to do with them, if I wanted them destroyed or sent home. I said, "I want to send them home to my wife." He took my wife's address and shipped them to her father's house, where she was living at. This was the first place that came to mind.

At this time, I asked if I could use the restroom. He said, in a real cocky way, "In a little while. I have to log you in first. Also the nurse has to see you, and then you can use the restroom."

The first thing I said to myself was I'll be talking to someone with somewhat more intelligence, a professional person at that. she will let me use the restroom, but I was again mistaken. She was as dumb as all the rest. The CO brought me into a large room with COs locked in another room covered in plexus glass, like a control room. They were in their own world and watched everything that walked by them. I was told to stay sitting on a bench until the nurse was ready to see me. I was sitting, and it felt that I was there for hours. Then I saw a CO that looked like she was a nurse coming out of a room holding a cup of Dunkin Donuts coffee, staring at me as she was walking by and just kept staring at me. Again as she was walking, I asked her if I could use the restroom. This CO that looked somewhat like a nurse said, "In a little while."

I said to myself, Dunkin Donuts must make a lot of money in these prisons because everyone I see is holding a cup of fuckin' Dunkin Donut coffee.

I sat there for even longer after I had asked to use the restroom and she made me wait longer. After a while, another CO that looked again like a nurse came out of her office, still holding a cup of coffee, and said, "Are you here for a medical checkup?" It felt she was asking me the reason why I was there. I thought that she would already know why I was there. I thought she was going to take me right in, but to my surprise, she disappeared again. I thought I was going to piss myself, but of course, I didn't. This time she was gone for even longer, and I still needed to use the restroom. I could just about taste it I had to go so bad.

I must have been there for at least two hours. She came out of her room-office again, looked around, walked back in, came out with a clipboard and a pad, and said, "Step into my room." I asked her if I could use the restroom, and she said, "In a little while." I said to myself, Great, another one. She asked me if I had taken any medication. I said yes, it came in with me. I told her that the CO who checked me in took it from me and said that he was going to give it to her so she could check out what I brought in with me. She said that she would check into it. Then I asked if I could use the restroom, but yet again her reply was, "Yes, in a little while," when she was done with her exam.

She looked at me, said that she had to ask me some questions about my health first before she would let me go and use the restroom. I then said, "Whatever you need to know, I'll answer it if I can." Then she began. She asked what my doctor's name was, where he was located. Then she asked if she could contact him to ask him about my medical record. I said no. I just didn't want them calling my doctor, telling him where I was at, especially saying where they were calling from then asking him about me. I was ashamed enough; I didn't want my doctor knowing where I was.

I really didn't think I was going to make it in jail because of my bad attitude, not being in my right mind. I would say anything that was on my mind. I just kind of knew that I didn't fit in to a place like this. I was still in a real bad fog, couldn't think straight, didn't know which way was up. I was just thinking of home all the time and my wife and wondering if she was trying to get me out of this place.

The nurse took my weight along with my height along with a few more questions then told the CO that she was done with me then turned me over to him. The CO brought me to another room so that they could take my picture for an ID, for their records. They asked me to strip down again so they could see if I had any tattoos. I said that I didn't have any, but they still wanted to check anyways. If they did find any tattoos, they would have to take pictures of them to see if they were gang related. If they found any, they would have to send me to that special unit just for gang members. I think it was called Section 8. I was talking to a guy that was in the same room, and he said, "What a great bunch of guys to hang with. It looks like they want to kill each other, and they all kept to one another."

I asked the CO again if I could use the restroom. He also said, "In a little while." This went on for hours. I told this guy, "Everyone that I've seen has told me 'in a little while.'" He looked at me and said,

"Get used to it. You piss, shit when we say you can." It was getting so bad I was saying to myself, "I'm going to piss my fuckin' pants." It was hurting so bad at this time that I didn't know if I wanted to piss or crap. Maybe both. If I did, they wouldn't give a damn. This short time in this place I already had a built-in hate for these guys because they were treating me like one of their kids that they probably treated like crap also. These COs think that they're better than me. I didn't think that much of them at this point, especially the ones that I was dealing with at this time. I mean, dumb motherfuckers like the ones that put me in the cage. I knew I'd find someone that I'd be able to carry on a conversation with. I said, "Please, God! Don't let them be as dumb as the ones that were in the cage with me. Those guys were at least four quarts low. If they are all like this, I'm in real trouble."

They were talking to each other, but I couldn't understand what they were saying to each other. I could never speak or understand stupid. But I had to understand I was just walking into this place. I'm white and look nothing like them. They were speaking a language that I never heard before, and most of it wasn't understandable to me. Their language was much different from what I was used to hearing. What makes me say this is that it felt like I was in another foreign country, not America. They looked like a lot of them didn't give a flying fuck and didn't care that they were incarcerated. Just looking at these guys I just wanted to keep to myself. Listening to them talk, I would just shake my head in confusion. Most of the time I was thinking that it was a language that they made up so that the COs would not be able to understand what they were saying to each other. To me, nothing that they were saying to each other was understandable, but right now I was not working with a full deck, so I just watched them very carefully.

I heard some of the COs making fun of these guys. I heard them say it seemed like being in jail didn't even bother them. I was regretting every minute of it, wishing I never got involved with drugs. I overheard some of the COs. They were talking about who they were going to mix together to start trouble tonight. These were the new guys coming in after me. They were finally done with me. I was brought up to the third floor, to where my cell was, and it was really late at night or early morning. That's all I can say because all the lights were turned down. Everyone was still in their cages, and I was heading for mine. At this time, I was just hoping that there was a toilet in the room so I could take a piss or whatever. I was holding for such long time I didn't really know what I had to do.

The CO led me to a cell and said that this was going to be my cell, and the door was opened, and he said, "The top bunk is yours to sleep in." Then the CO said, "Now you can piss and whatever you have to do," and laughed. I heard someone snoring in the room, and it was loud, and the room smelled like shit from whoever was in the room. Now I know what the CO meant by saying "Now you can use the restroom" because it smelled like a restroom, and he laughed, then the door was closed. There was a toilet in the room, and it was all stainless, but it had no toilet seat, just a bowl. It still looked great to me. I had to use it real bad. I looked for toilet paper, and there was none to be found, but I had some tissues in my pocket, and to me that was enough. I had to take a dump real bad, and it was an all-day dump from early morning. When I was downstairs, I really thought I was going to piss and shit myself but didn't. I hit the toilet, and I blew it up bad, and I heard a voice yell out, "Flush the fuckin' toilet!"

I yelled back and said, "The room smells like shit anyways, so what's the difference?"

Then he said, "Just do it out of respect."

Then I said, "Okay, I'm sorry."

It must have been at least four o'clock in the morning, and I was just getting checked into a room, so it took all day and most of the night to get this far. As I got into the top bunk, a voice came from below, and it said, "Don't get too comfortable. They will be calling breakfast and count very soon, and you must stand for it." I said to myself, What the hell is count time? Then I found out very shortly. I was on the top bunk, and I heard CO over the intercom yelling out "Count time!" and the voice from below said, "Get down so they can count you. Then after they clear count, you then can go for breakfast if you want. They must see you standing in case you're dead in the room and to make sure that you haven't escaped, and that was just about impossible to do where they had you."

The guy in the bottom bunk I called him the Voice because I never saw him, just heard him, and when I did see him, he was standing below me before I even stood for count, and he was always wrapped in a blanket. He said that they were going to be calling count all day, and you got to stand for it. Then he asked me if this was my first time inside. I said, "Yeah."

He laughed and went back to bed. He then said one more thing. He said, "I have the bottom bunk, you have the top."

I said, "No problem."

I started to think I had to spend five years in this room with this fuckin' asshole. I could see all the interesting conversations we are going to have. I had just started to close my eyes, when they called out, "Count cleared." He said, "Go to chow now if you want to eat." Then all at once the door opened. I was just waiting for them to bring breakfast to us. I saw everyone going in all different directions, so I followed them, and they led me right to the chow hall. Before I left the block, the CO said, "You're in the kitchen tomorrow to work." I was trying to figure out what he meant by "You're in the kitchen tomorrow to work," and then he said, "Pots and pans" and laughed.

As I walked out of the block, I had no idea where I was going but knew that I was very hungry, so I just followed everyone else. When I was walking, I was looking around at all the cells and was very confused but again was so damn hungry; all I wanted to do was eat. What a long walk, so many guys as far as the eye can see. I just kept following everyone else. I finally could see the so-called chow hall. Still, I noticed that there was a long line even before I could get to the chow hall doors. What a long line of guys there was. As I approached the chow hall, the doors going into the chow hall were slamming against the outside of the building from the wind. It was a cold winter day in January. The air smelled weird, the doors were wide open, letting what little heat there was in the chow to escape. All the guys were just pushing to get in to eat. When I got a chance to look in to see what it looked like, there were still long lines of guys inside just as it was on the outside. As I passed, I looked at what the guys were eating. It was pancakes. I said, I could do that, but what a lot of guys.

There was so much noise that I couldn't hear myself think. When I say it was loud, it was loud. There was wall-to-wall scum with COs at both ends. I finally got my pancakes, started to eat them, and was watching everyone that was around me, staring at all the guys, also watching who sat beside me. I didn't trust anyone, didn't know what to expect when I finished eating. When I started back to the unit, I was saying to myself I hoped I could find my way back to my room because they all looked alike to me. I didn't know how much time they gave to eat and get back. I found the third floor and my room number, but when I walked in, there was someone else in the room. I then said, "Oh shit." I got everything right but the wrong block. I didn't know what to do.

It didn't take long; the COs were on me like flies on shit or white on rice whatever. When they found me, a lot of them were yelling at me. I said that I didn't know where I was at and asked for them to stop yelling at me. He said, "I'll stop when I feel like it."

I said, "I just got in last night. I haven't figured out the place as of yet."

He said, "Okay, but don't let it happen again."

I got to my room, and the guy in the blanket on the bottom bunk was laughing, just couldn't stop, and he said, "I knew it was you when count wasn't cleared." Then I told him that my wife was trying to get me a real lawyer to get me out of this fucking nut house. He asked what I was in for. I told him, "Drugs."

He said, "Good luck, it's not going to happen to a druggy. You will never leave, and you're going to do all of the time they gave you."

I said that my wife was looking real hard. "She will not give up until she finds one. I know her."

He said, "You have a better chance of seeing God. She will give up on you. She is free, will forget about you."

I said, "She will never forget me. She will get me out of here. She won't let me rot in here."

Then he just said, "Remember what I said and what she is going to do to you."

I just said, "She will never do that to me."

Then he said, "You're just wasting your money."

I was hoping he was wrong. I was hoping that she was in the process of trying to get me out of this hellhole. After that, my wife took up so much space in my head that I almost couldn't think of much more because I really thought she was going to try to help me. As I was lying in my bunk, I was saying, "Please, God, get me out of this place. I'll never touch that stuff again," and just rambled on under my breath. I was here no more than one night, and I knew it was a fucked-up place. I was thinking, *Five years in here. Oh shit! What did I get myself into?*

Well, next count came, and off to lunch I went. As I was walking into the chow hall, I felt the wind hit me. It was cold as heck. It was the coldest month of the year, January, 16, 1998. They did give me a jacket, but it was so thin that the wind just blew right through it. I was hoping to get into the chow hall as soon as possible, was hoping that there wasn't a long line as before. As I entered the chow hall, it was as cold inside as it was outside, but being in a place like this, you learned to adjust to this stuff. As I soon found out, you have no choice but to do so. I started to figure it out after one day living in this hellhole. I just couldn't believe my eyes in what I was up against.

When I was waiting in line to get my breakfast, I looked to the left, and I asked the guy that was ahead of me if this was where they had visits. He said no. I said to him that it looked like there was a woman sitting over there. He then said, "No, it's a man dressed like a woman. It's a he-she." I just couldn't understand how they could dress like that in a place like this. Then he said, "Don't mess around with it."

I said, "No fuckin' way, that would never happen." I said that I just couldn't believe my eyes. He or she really looked like a woman.

He then said, "The dude next to him is doing life, that his bitch, you just don't fuck around with someone else's property." Then he looked at me and started to laugh.

I then said, "It looks real."

He said, "Yeah."

There were plenty more in here as I started to see in days to come. As I was standing in line, I heard some guys saying to each other, "Let's see who's meal we can take today." It was chicken being served, and I told the guy that I was talking to, "They are not going to get my food. They better think twice if they think so."

He said, "Don't worry, they just go for guys who won't give them a hard time, like old guys, young guys." I told him that it looked real good, and he said, "It's one of their better meals. Looks can be real deceiving, wait till you taste it." I got my piece of chicken; it had no taste to it at all. I mean no taste, nothing. The guy that I was talking to in line was sitting beside me, and he said, "Try this." I looked at it. It was salt and pepper. He said, "Give it right back to me or it will disappear real fast if you put it on the table." Then he said, "Look at that guy across the table, he already made a mistake. He put his salt, pepper on the table. Watch it disappear." As he said that, it went right down the table. "He won't see it again. He just supplied to all the guys sitting at this table. I never let it leave my sight, keep it in my pocket. It's something that you need in here for their food because their food never has any taste to it."

When it was time to leave the chow hall, you tried to take food with you, so in case you got hungry during the night, you always had something to fall back on. When you're in lockdown for twenty-three hours, you get hungry. Guys would cut holes in the sleeves of their jackets and stuff things in them, so when you walked, you would have it in your sleeves. You let it slip down after they checked the bottom of your jacket. But you just got to time yourself before you get to the door and slip around the COs when they were searching someone else at the door and hope you get out with what you have. The guy that I was at the chow hall with told me to make it look like I had something in my hands. He would be carrying a lot of stuff out, and he said that he would share it with me if he got out with it. I said no problem. They stopped me, and he just went around me. We split it up when we left the chow hall. I guess they would search you in case you carried out something from the chow hall that could be used as a weapon, like a knife or a spoon, that you could hurt someone real bad with. Just can't believe the weapons that I've seen in the places that I was at and how they made them. I never looked at it that way. I learned so much in such a short time what these guys were capable of doing, stuff I would never imagine that could be used as a weapon.

When it was time to leave, I was able to find my way back to the right block, the right room, with no problem even though I was in another world. Plus the COs had their eyes on me all the time. I just counted all the cell blocks, made a map in my head of where I came from, and just retraced it back to where I came from. What a long walk. As I was walking back from the chow hall, one of the guys came up to me and said, "You're a newcomer, right?"

I said, "Yes!"

He said, "I noticed you yesterday looking lost, confused."

I said, "It was my first day. I'm hoping that my wife gets me a good lawyer or I'll have many more lost, confused days." Then he asked me if I was ever in before. I said no, and he said, "You're in for a real lesson in life, one that you will never forget. It will be with you for the rest of your life. Trust me when I tell you this."

I said, "What you mean by that?" I was just feeling him out to see what he was going to say next.

Then he said, "You will see jail, feel jail now for the rest of your life, right down to your first day."

Then I thought, I have another eighteen hundred more days to go. Shit. I looked at him dumbfounded.

He said, "Just look around good, what do you see? You will have to spend time with these guys for a long while."

I listened to him because he was the most intelligent person I met so far, but of course, all I have to do is look around and then said, "Never again. Fuck no."

Then he said, "Good luck."

"I'm out of here very soon. It was my first, my last time I'll spend in a place like this. What an experience, one that I will never forget either!"

He said, "Look around, look at the guys, what a great bunch of guys to carry on a conversation with." Then said, "You got past the point of DUH, that's why I'm talking to you. I mean, a lot of these guys are stupid motherfuckers, and you can't reason with most of them. Maybe you can find someone that you can hang around with in here as you will. When you get out of here, you can talk war stories with him."

I said, "No fuckin' way. I'm going to keep to myself, do what I have to do to get out of here sooner if I can."

Then he said, "You're not getting out any sooner than the five years they gave you because you're doing a mandatory sentence, and that's day for day, as I told you during lunch. Keep your shit together. Being in a place like this, you're your best friend. Don't let them get to you. Remember, don't lose your mind." He said that he knew because it almost happened to him. He said, "This place can eat you up inside if you let it."

I said, "Being in the lunch hall with these guys is fuckin' up my head."

He said, "It will pass. It did it to me also. Just watch what you say to these guys. They are a bunch of motherfuckin' rat assholes, and that's the good part of them. I'm not saying all of them, just most of them. Just be careful. Just as I was with you when I first met you, remember." Then he turned to me and said, "Does that make you feel much better, me telling you what I'm telling you before I leave this place?"

I asked, "Where do you live when you leave to go home?"

He said, "I'm not going home. I'm going to be transferred to another prison, as you will be. This is just a holding place till they send you to another prison."

I said, "You're shitting me."

He replied, "No, you will see when you're here for a couple of months. You go to all the units they have here, then they move you out to another prison. Why, did you think you were going to spend your whole time here?"

I said, "Jail is jail, this is what I thought."

Then he said, "Fat chance of that. Look around, don't they look real happy being incarcerated? Doesn't bother them at all."

I said, "I noticed that."

He said, "That's because they have been in and out their whole life, are used to it. Most of them are repeat offenders. This is their life, they just go with the flow. To most of them, it's a bed, food.

They need someone to tell them what to do, they like it. But the worst thing about it in this place is that they mix everyone together if they don't have all your offenses together. I mean, they mix Skinner, Diller's with everyone else."

That was when I asked him, "What are you talking about?"

"These are guys who rape kids and women along with beating the hell out of them. Real low-lifes. Everyone who is in here who's not accused for that crime hate them as I do, or at least most of the guys in here do."

What a change of life. I was a real green bean in here. I didn't know which way was up. I was totally lost.

Then he said, "Why we don't just stick together till we are moved to another prison."

I was all for that, someone to talk to. I said, "That sounds good to me."

"Or until I get my move, which will be sooner than you."

I said to him, "Okay then."

He said, "Good luck in the kitchen tomorrow, you will need it. Plus you will get a kick out of it." He said that he was just moved from pots and pans to being a cook, and to him it was an upgrade to a better position a couple weeks ago.

To this day, I don't remember what time the CO got me up to get me to the kitchen, because there were no clocks at all anywhere. I just know it was very early. I think it was at 4:00 a.m. Well, I was led to the kitchen. I never in my whole life seen so many pots and pans in my life as I did that day. When I say pots and pans, I mean pots and pans. They were large. I had to wash them all. There was water all over the place. I neither had nor did I get any waterproof footwear. All I had to wear was what I came in with from the street. They got soaked real fast right through the second I walked in. The CO didn't give a damn when I asked him for footwear and just looked at me with a dirty look. He really didn't give a flying fuck if my feet were wet as long as the pots and pans were washed.

Right after that. I went to lunch to eat. I was told that I'd get paid for working in the kitchen and wondered how much. I was told that I was to earn a whole five dollars a week. Yes, five dollars a week.

I was talking to my buddy; he was more or less telling me what to expect, what was going to happen to me while I was in Concord. As the days went by, it got more and more messed up. He asked me if I liked the food in Concord. I said it sucked and my dog's food I fed my dogs smelled better. Then he told me that he was working with a CO that made the food, and he was showing him how to prepare the food for the whole place. He said the whole time that the CO was cooking, he was smoking a small tiparillo cigars, and it just hung out of his mouth as he puffed on it. Lots of times the ashes would fall into the large colanders as the CO was cooking the food for the inmates. The CO told my so-called buddy that it wouldn't hurt anyone and said it hasn't hurt him any in all the years he's been smoking. But my buddy who was working by his side, it was killing him because he was a smoker. He would try to inhale as he was exhaling. Then when the CO was done smoking, he would break it up and throw it into what he was cooking, said this way no one could get his butts. It killed my buddy to see this.

What I can't understand is, what makes it so right for the COs to smoke but not okay for the inmates? He said he knew better than to speak to the CO that was cooking about anything because he was a real asshole, and he needed the money that he was making for his canteen. But if you looked at it all, the COs were all assholes. I think it was all in their training that they went through. What really sucked in my head was what my buddy told me about my sentencing. I had to do day for day with no good time. No matter what I did in here and was able to get good time, I couldn't use the time I earned to get out earlier. It's just not right. I had just entered this Godforsaken place, and I already wanted out, and I had five fuckin' years to do and kept thinking this.

The guy that I was hanging around with already wanted out. He just wanted his move to come so he could get out of Concord. He was in for attempt of murder. What sense did this make? I didn't try to kill anyone, but I got a mando sentence for a nonviolent crime, and he was going to get good time to get out sooner than I would. At this time, everything was so confusing to me. My mind was so messed up I just couldn't put things together. This is because my mind was

BUSTED

all over the place. Just being confined to a cell for twenty-somewhat hours was really fuckin' with me, being on the top bunk with the lights on most of the time blaring down on me. At this time, I was hoping that my wife didn't forget about me and was trying to get me a good lawyer to see if I could get out sooner. My wife was holding all my money that I got back from the courts. My hands were tied, and I couldn't do anything from where I was, so I was hoping that my wife was doing something for me.

They finally cleared my telephone numbers, so I tried to call my wife quite a few times, and all the times that I tried to get in touch with her, she wasn't home. She was always out. This was the girl I married, and she told me that she would always wait for me, stand by my side the whole time I was in here. At this time I was thinking to myself what she did to me when I was put in jail the first time. What I remember very clearly was her walking by me with a dirty look on her face, staring at me with hate in her eyes as she walked by me. The worst part was my wife leaving me there, but in that case, her father was the one putting up the bail money up to get her out. But the whole time that she was out, she never even tried to bail me out of jail, and she had plenty of money to do so. I did get in touch with my daughter, and I asked her if she could call my wife, see if she was working on trying to get me another lawyer to see if she could get me out of here. Well, it took her a week to get in touch with her, and she was on the outside. All my wife told my daughter was that she was working on it and was trying to come up to see me.

As I was approaching the chow hall early, just the door to the chow hall alone was sickening and was getting to me. My shoes were starting to fall apart. I mean, the soles were coming apart because of the water. I was standing when I was washing the pots and pans. I was looking at the back of the CO's neck as he was walking me in to the kitchen; I hated every part of him. I didn't even know him. I think it was the way he treated me when he walked me to the kitchen in the morning for work. (Cocky mouth motherfucker.) On the outside, I knew some of COs that worked here. I thought they were decent guys. They always treated me good, until I was on the inside, then I saw the other side of them. I grew to hate every CO that I came in contact with, and the weird thing about it was looking at them, but it was more like I was looking through them. The hate I had for them I could never put it into words. It's because of what they put me through and the way they degraded me in front of women.

The guy that I was hanging around with really isn't my friend, so I'll just call him buddy and so forth. He's just someone that I met in this place. He keeps calling me his brother, and it bothers me somewhat. I have only two brothers, and none of them were in here, and they are my blood, not this guy. Well, I was walking with him to the chow hall when I saw a guy lying on the ground. I started to walk over to him, and the guy I was with asked what I was doing. I said, "The guy is hurt."

He then said, "Do you know him?" I said no, then he said, "Fuck him. It was probably a payback for something he did. Mind your own." He said, "The COs will take care of that problem."

Then I said to him how much I hated the COs. He looked at me and said, "Do you think you're the only one that hates them?" Then he said to remember what he said to me about keeping my eyes open, said, "You're not on the street. These are totally different types of guys, can't trust them."

From that day on, I started looking around as I walked from place to place, always checking my back. I really thought I was going crazy, and I just stopped talking to everyone, just staying on the safe side. Guys were starting to stick bedsprings in their waist where their belts go and up their sleeves, but I was way ahead of them. I had already done that along with pens I always carried. I was always carrying a pen and paper with me everywhere I went. It made it look like I was writing. I was most of the time, but the pen would be my first weapon if I needed it. You have to protect yourself at all times. Carrying a pad with your pens also makes it look better. But because of that, I was searched a lot, but they always gave most of my stuff back. The rest they threw on the ground and said that I didn't need it. They did ask me why I carried it with me all the time, and I said that I was writing letters home, telling them what I was going through in this place, and they just laughed and started to leave me alone after a while.

BUSTED

When these COs did search you, they really searched you. They felt you up and made you drop your drawers. I really think they love looking up your ass a lot of times. When you're behind the wall, I want to know what kind of contraband you can have, especially be able to have it tucked up your ass. Give me a break. Unless the COs were bringing it in. But in time, I really found out what guys could tuck up their asses and just couldn't believe it. A lot of the women COs were weird also. When they were searching a guy or seeing a guy getting searched, they would all come walking over to look to see what was going on. I really think it's because these women don't get it at home. But some of these women COs are as bad as they act, look it also; this is the closest they will ever get to someone's ass. I'm not talking about the real good-looking women COs. I'm talking about the ones that could stop time, look like ten miles of bad road. Those are the ones you want to stay away from. You don't want time to stop by what they look like. You want time to go on. Boy, some of these women COs sure are ugly. The real good-looking ones would just do their job like normal people do and when there shift was over, they wanted to get out of there, go home as soon as possible. People don't know how lucky they are to be able to leave when they wanted to. I do now.

I guess if you were to look through a CO's eyes, as I did sometimes, you can see why they feel that way, but they did this because so many of the inmates were fuckin' scum. That's the way I also see them as. That's through my eyes also. But after you're there for a while, they should know the ones that just want to do their time, get the fuck out of there. They just treat everyone like shit. They should have shrinks give them evaluation on the guys that are not in for violent crimes to see what kind of people they are, what you are capable of doing before they judge you.

I got back to my room and realized that my roommate was gone. I never got a chance to find out if he was black or white or even Spanish because he always had a blanket wrapped around his whole body all the time. At that time, I didn't know if he went home or was shipped to another prison but really didn't care as long as I was going to get the bottom bunk. I really got to enjoy the bottom bunk because it was easier for me to write my letters while standing for count, but I had to use my mattress because all mattresses had to be returned to the property room when you moved out. Today I was called downstairs; they wanted to know what I did with the drugs that I brought in with me because they just found the empty bottle. The pills were gone. I kept telling the CO that was part of things I was going to have sent home to my wife. They asked me where the valiums were, and I told them again that the CO took them from me when I came in. Then the CO asked me if I sold them to the guys in jail. I looked at the CO that was called IPPS (this means Inner Perimeter Police) and said, "How would I get them upstairs when you checked me out before I was sent upstairs?"

He looked at me and said, "By shoving them up your ass."

I looked at him and said, "No damn way would I shove anything up my ass." I said, "Your CO downstairs took everything I came in with, including my medication, said that he was going to give it to your so-called nurse before he sent it to my home. What he did with it is on him."

The IPPS CO looked at me while shifting the other medication I came in with from hand to hand and asked me what it was for. I told him it was for my ulcers. I had stomach problems. He just said, "Oh really." He said that he was going to give them to the nurse, make sure I got them as I needed them.

I told him, "Forget it. After you were playing with them, moving them from hand to hand, do you really think I want them after you played with them from hand to hand. I don't know where your hands have been."

If looks could kill, I would have been dead right then and there. He just threw them in the barrel. They ended up catching an inmate with the Valium I brought in because he was all fucked up, falling all over the place. I just couldn't believe that they thought I'd stuff them up my ass, and still they thought I sold them to the inmate that was all fucked up. I was there for a while; the regular CO was also asking me a while later where my medication was. Stupid assholes. I just told them I talked to the IPPS already about it. Then I told the CO that they just sent me back up to my room, and they said they better not find out different. I just said, "Ask your CO downstairs about it." I never heard any more about it. I guess they found out that the CO that took them away from me put them down where an inmate got hold of them. I hope he lost his job. He was a cocky fucker anyways and a smart-ass.

It had been a while, I was still trying to find paper and a pen so I could send more letters home to my daughter and wife to find out if my wife was going to come up to see me. I missed them so much. I know my daughter couldn't visit because she had a newborn baby, my grandson, but I was hoping to see my wife real soon. I found some property sheets; I used them to write my letters on to send home and to make envelopes out of. All I needed were stamps. They just started to let the new guys out of their cells for what they called recreation time. This was including breakfast and lunch. This meant you were out of your cell for about three hours. It was great to be out of your cell for that amount of time. To lock a person in a closed room for twenty-plus hours a day is not healthy. All you can do is stay in your bed or sit at a table that's shared with another guy. I was already getting bed sores on my back, and one of the guys gave me some Jergen's lotion for them. I thought it was something worse.

When I was out of my cell, I would look real hard for anything to write with, to write on, also something to read. I mean anything at all to read. You can't believe the things that I was reading while being locked in my cell like this. If I couldn't find something to read, I was reading all the labels on all my cosmetics. I really can't remember if I ever read any labels on any product ever until I was locked up. I was still waiting to get my money put into my canteen so I could get stuff I needed from the canteen, like razor blades, some candy, of course, tuna because a lot of their food was so bad I just wouldn't, couldn't eat it. I would just go without eating or wait till I went into work, would eat raisins, drink milk when I could get it instead of the food they made in the kitchen. One of the times that I was out of my cell, I got into a conversation with a guy, and he said that he would let me have a couple of stamps and pen, some envelopes till I got my canteen, but in trade he wanted some candy because he didn't have a canteen. He got his writing stuff though the mail. This was one thing that was real good in Concord: they would let you get stamps though the mail. This is something you could trade with if the COs didn't steal them from the mail.

As I was talking to this guy, I noticed this guy running across the tear, because I was looking over the guy's shoulder that I was talking to with my back to the wall. I saw this guy running across the tear with a sock in his hand. He ran past me and bashed this guy right in the face with it. I just saw it happen and couldn't believe what I just saw. All I could see was blood, teeth that came flying out of this guy's mouth, all over the floor. The sock that he used ripped a hole in the bottom. The lock flew out and hit the wall, lockers. I was just lost for words, just shocked and couldn't believe what this guy just did to another guy. Well, the guy just fell to the floor and started to shake. It was like someone just tried to escape from the prison, so the alarm went off, and everyone had to return to their cells. While the guy was down, the guy was calling the guy down all kinds of names. I don't recall the names, but it was a lot. I don't know if this guy knew him from the outside or from jail. I really didn't care as long as I wasn't involved in it. The COs were on him like flies on shit. I didn't care what they did to the guy. I was able to get what I wanted, and that was my writing stuff and a book to read.

At this time I was told that the so-called canteen was like a store. You could get all kinds of stuff, but I know I couldn't get much because I was making peanuts working in the kitchen. The courts took what I brought in for court fees. I was not able to get in touch with my wife because every time I called, she was never home. That was no surprise to me after all the times I called prior to this. I left all my money I made at the dealership with my wife along with all my unemployment checks. They were being cashed by her, but they were sent to me first. I would sign them, send them back to my wife so she could cash them. She was supposed to send some of the money to me, never did I wasn't getting any of it. I needed money really bad but as long as her face was full she didn't give a flying fuck as I started to realize this. But still in my heart I never thought she would do what she did to me while I was in jail, keep and all the money I gave her to send me. She was just about never home when I called so

I could not talk to her, nor did I even get a fuckin' letter from her. At this time I had so many chosen names for her it always ended it with me saying to myself that I love her.

Another week went by, and I finally got a letter from my wife, and she sent me eighty dollars from one of my checks and told me to be strong and that she loved me. Boy, did I suck that in. I was real glad to get something from her, but she could have sent me at least one of my checks that she had cashed. I was able to buy a damn candy bar; these are things that you never think about when you're on the outside. I really rarely thought about candy and different types of junk foods, but being locked up in jail, you think about what you can't get. Of course, I was already thinking the worst about my wife. I was just thinking, I probably was right that she used the rest of my checks for drugs because it was months before I got another check from her. Then I received another letter from her and waited to read it after chow. All it was was a letter stating that stopped my checks, nothing else. The COs probably had something to do with that and called it into the security office to stop them, and I never thought it was wrong because it was money I earned. I was able to get in touch with my wife, and she was really at home this time when I called, and all she wanted to talk about was to tell me that they stopped my unemployment checks because I was incarcerated. Of course, the letter that I got before hers said that I was a ward of the State. I could no longer get any more of my check from unemployment. This was what she was telling me the whole time on the phone. It sounded like she was upset about it. It killed me when she was living with me, she was a tight bitch with her money. I paid for just about everything. Now it was killing her to give me some money so I could get canteen. It was my money that she had and acted like she earned it. She was probably upset about it because she probably already went through all the money I left her before I left for jail. Yeah.

I wrote the rest of my family and asked them for some money. I never got so much as five dollars from any of them. They all turned their backs on me, so I had to do it on my own. Even five dollars would have been great. My older brother disconnected his phone. My younger brother said all the time that I called, was talking to him on the phone, he always said, "You're not missing anything. It's all the same. You're better where you are. You don't have to worry about bills." I just couldn't believe what I was hearing. What he just said, at that time they all were making good money, never sent me a dime the whole time that I was incarcerated. Not one family member helped my daughter with any bills that were coming into the house. All I did for them when I was on the street, and they wouldn't even call her. When my family had bad time, they always came to me to help them with their bills, to fix their cars. I never got paid for any work that I had to do on any of my family's cars. To this day when it comes to my family, I really think they have no clue on how bad it was in this place. Even now to this day they ask me to tell them stories of what it was like. When I was in all these different jails, they never thought once about me. They just went on with their lives like nothing ever happened. Well, it didn't to them. It was just like my aunt said to me one day. She said in her eyes I was dead to her, and I will never forget it to this day.

I was able to get in touch with my wife again during the week. I talked to her on the phone and asked her if she had gotten in touch with any lawyer to see if she could get me out of this fuckin' place. I couldn't believe she just had an excuse. She said that she was working real hard, but she hasn't had a chance to talk to one as of yet. It was like I never existed. No one gave a damn about me, and all she had on her mind was to go out and party with her so-called girlfriends. What a self-centered bitch. I knew she was doing this because I was getting these crazy letters from the outside telling me what she was doing. I never knew who wrote them (bullshit girlfriends). I just felt like saying to her sometimes, "Do you know where I'm at you, stupid bitch?" But I didn't because you need outside help the whole time you're in a place like this, even though I wasn't getting any help from her but was always hoping.

What a waste of life this place is. You don't know which way is up most of the time. They could have given me community service for five years and gotten me to work for free for the State. I was no big-time dealer. What good did it do by putting me in jail. I could have paid my debt by working for free. I was very serious the whole time that I was in jail. Many times I would just look around lots of times and would see all these guys just having such a good time. It was so hard for me to grasp. I just couldn't understand it. I asked one guy, "Why do you sleep all day?" He said, "What else is there to do in a place like this?"

There are no programs, there is nothing to do, all the programs that they do have I can't earn any good time on doing them, so why even do them. They lock you away in a place like this, give you a number, they just forget about you, and don't care if you live or die. There is no training courses to get you prepared for the outside. They just let you rot in here and belittle you every chance they get. All that's on my mind all the time is how I am going to get my business going again, get my customers back after what I got in trouble for, how much of my family would be left when I get out. What worried me the most was getting back to my old self, getting out of the fog that I was in all the time. I just couldn't understand what was happening to me. The psychiatrist never helped me in any way. She wasn't helping now. All she really did was just ask me questions that she had on a pad in her lap. All the questions that she was asking me was just something that the prison probably put on paper to ask me, but she was most likely doodling in the notebook she held. But she played it real good and looked like she was trying to help me, but I know after a while it was just an act. What I was really thinking was it was just time out of the other nuthouse. I mean the unit. What she so-called did for me wasn't for me. It was just to make her look good in the eyes of the intstitution, to make it look like she was doing her job.

After a while, I found my own way to waste my time. I just started to write about all I had seen going on in this fuckin' place in letters and mailed it all out to my wife and daughter. I was still trying to sleep during the day when I can, write at night when I'm awake so I could see what was going on during the night because I didn't trust any of these fuckin' guys. There was too much happening at night besides sleeping. This is another way I could watch these fuckin' guys. I don't like to sleep at night because of the things I'd seen going on. Right now it's about 2:00 a.m. The CO just left the unit, and as soon as he does, the animal noises start. It gets real loud, monkeys, wolves, hyenas, just about any animals you can think of. It sounds like you're in a jungle. Now these are all grown men doing this. I can just say I'm in a nuthouse. I know I will never be happy ever again because I don't know what it's like to be happy anymore. I know I'm going to lose my wife, and she made me happy, but I realize you can't change a person. She just went back to her old ways doing what she knew best. I was just saying that I have to put up with what she was doing, hoping she could find some time to get me a real good lawyer. All I could think about was Get me out of this fuckin' place. I tried not to give up on her. At this time I asked the CO if he had any kits to give me so I could shave my beard off. He said, "No, just deal with it." The reason was that my wife was still holding all my money. I was hoping she didn't spend it all on partying, because she hasn't sent me much any of it as of yet. I just couldn't believe how bad she was treating me. I didn't get any of my money from the kitchen yet. If I did, I wouldn't have enough money to buy even razor blades if I wanted. In my whole life I have never had a beard; I didn't like it. It just made me feel dirty.

Today I was told to pack up my stuff. The CO said to me it was moving time. They don't give much time to get your stuff together. They want you packed, gone, your mattress taken off the bed, brought down to the property office like the day before. This means fast. You don't understand. At this time I was just wondering where I was going, hoping I was going to a place where I could get more freedom outside of the cell along with wreck time. The COs don't tell you anything. They just say, "You're out of here, get moving or I will have you moved out. You're going to lose a lot of stuff." I was just getting used to this place, and they just move you. I guess they notice that you're getting too comfortable and say, "Got to move this guy." I thought I was getting moved to another prison, but I wasn't. They were just moving out of the main building, moving me into the old mechanic shop building across the way from where I was. As I was walking in, I saw the guy I met when I came into Concord. I thought they moved him out to another prison and said I have one person I can talk to. I thought when they moved you out of where you were, it would be to another institution, but they just move you to other places in Concord. I noticed that he walked into where they were so-called transferring me to. That was into a machine shop where they moved in all kinds of beds to house inmates.

When I talked to him, he said to me that they did that to make room for new guys that were coming in. That's because they need the room. It was a good business for them. It was a big money-making scam for the rich investors. When I walked in through the door, I looked down to the end of the building, and I saw a guy taking a shower. The door was open. It was real cold. This was in February. There was no privacy at all. His ass was just hanging out; it didn't bother him a bit. As I walked in where the door was, it was removed. I mean gone. There were strips of plastic hanging down from the top, like what you see in warehouses where fork trucks would just drive through to get to a freezer. I can't even tell you how cold it was, but it was so cold that there was ice in the doorway as you entered the room; you had to be careful not to slip on it. A lot of the floor was wet from guys coming in and out of the unit over and over again. The overhead heaters were blasting nonstop all day and all night long just to keep it somewhat warm. Even as I was in the room for a while, I could still see steam coming from my mouth as I exhaled. This told me it was going to be real cold in here.

I looked over to the right, there was a CO locked in an old tool crib where they must have kept the tools at one time or another. At least he was protected if a real fight broke out because the COs would take their time to get there because they wouldn't want to get hurt. He really didn't look too happy. He looked like he was doing time right along with us. He was surrounded by radios I guess in case there was trouble. There were bunks lined up against every wall in this place. They fit them in so tight that you could touch the other guy with just reaching across. The CO that brought me into the unit showed me the bunk that they issued me. I had a heater just above me, and it was blowing heat on to me all the time, so at least I wasn't freezing like some of the guys that were in here. I needed all that because it was real cold in this unit as I was unloading my stuff into a locker they issued me.

As I was doing that, a guy came over to me and said, "You're lucky with a heater right over you." He said that he asked the CO if he could move to where I was, and the CO said maybe. Later he was told no, that he was busy and someone else was coming in. Then he said, "I know it's not going to happen now because you're here now." He had to deal with the cold the best that he could, as we all did. He was down at the other end of the unit. He was making some chicken that he took from the kitchen, and he asked me if I had some rice to mix in. I gave him some to mix in with the chicken. I walked to where was he was cooking, and he showed me a glass of water that was next to where he slept. It had ice in it, that's how cold it was where he was. To my guess, there must have been at least a hundred beds or more in this unit. That was just a guess. It smelled real bad. It smelled like shit or like a sewer backed up. It smelled just like the first room they moved me into when I arrived. The footlocker that they gave me had no lock, and I was told that I had to buy one, said that I should get one before I got any canteen because they didn't have any time to watch my stuff that I have in my locker. "These guys will steal your stuff every chance they get."

The guy that I was talking to said to keep my eyes open at night because a lot of shit happened at night in here.

"These guys steal, beat guys up, so forth. You will see."

I looked at him and said, "I know." I said to myself, "I have to figure this place out." I got one of the CO's tryed to talk to me on the way out to chow. I asked him, "Is this place hell?"

He looked at me and said, "Welcome to population." Then he gave me a roll of toilet paper said, "Don't lose it or you will have to use your fingers to wipe your ass." Then he said, "Move on."

I looked around. I wanted to know where the bathrooms were. As I was looking around, I saw a bunch of guys standing in a line with rolls of toilet paper under their arms, so I thought that was the toilets. I said, "Why are there so many guys standing in the line to use the toilets?" Then I realized that there were only two toilets; one of them was overflowing on the floor, and it was right in the open. There were so many guys standing in line to use the toilets. I wondered why they didn't fix the other toilet, and then I remembered that the guys loved to stuff toilet paper rolls down them. Why? I will never know. Just to see them overflow. I had to use the toilet, so I just got in line and was waiting my turn. There must have been at least forty to fifty guys in line waiting to use the toilet. What a long damn wait. Then it was finally my turn. I got in, wrapped toilet paper around the seat to sit down, and as I looked up to the door, there was a picture of a naked girl plastered on the door. As I looked at it, it seemed very hazy. Then I noticed that the haziness was jizz or come shot, whatever you want to call it. It was so bad that it was dripping all down the door, where there was a large puddle of cum on the floor. I just couldn't believe that these guys were going to use the toilets just to jerk off in it. You couldn't see the girl clearly because there was so much cum on it. They were doing it with other guys waiting outside the door. I just pulled the cuffs of my pants up so they weren't hitting the floor, to keep it from getting cum on them. This got me sick to my stomach. I watched myself when I left the toilet, being careful not to step in the small puddle of cum on the floor as I left the stall. The next guy just about ran into the toilet. I guess he had to go real bad or had a load he had to drop.

    I then heard a bunch of guys laughing, yelling a short time later. One of the COs walked over to see what all the yelling was about. I saw a guy standing in front of the door to the toilet. The guy that ran into the toilet left the stall, and when he did, he slipped on the cum as he was leaving and fell right into the cum that was all over the floor. He had it all over himself, I mean from head to toe. All the guys were laughing at him. He just turned and started to yell, "It's not funny!" When I looked at him, it was soaked right through his clothes, on the side of his face. It was even in his hair. Whatever was on the floor was on his clothes now; there was a lot of cum on the floor now. Most of what was on the floor was on what he was wearing. The clothes that he had on was what he just came in with. I don't know if they gave him more clothes because what he had on was what he owned until he got his things from the last place he came from. The CO just walked back to where he was before this happened, of course laughing also. This must have been a disgusting moment for this guy. He was a big motherfucker too. I guess this was something that must have happened before because the CO didn't bat an eye at it, but they all treated all the guys the same no matter what happened, unless there were trouble in the unit.

As I walked around the unit, I noticed another guy I met when I came in. I said to him, "I thought you got your move." He said that he did. It was where we were now, that we would be moving again very soon. The noise in this place was real loud, as all the other places were. We had to just about yell at each other because everyone was just talking over one another, and it was that bad. It took me a while to find the phones, and when I say you've got to look around, I mean it. Well, of course, I found them when I noticed a bunch of guys standing around in a circle. By the time I noticed them, they were all being used. I kind of knew it would be a long wait before I got to use one. I must have waited at least a half hour. I finally got a chance to use the phone, so I called my wife first. She was home, to my surprise, and the first thing she told me was that my niece had just died from a Prozac Lithium mix the doctors had given her, that she had gained a hundred pounds and just died. I just slid down to the floor and started to cry. She was just one in the family that helped me before my daughter came back from Florida. I loved her. This girl did so much for me when I got in trouble that I can't even put it all into words. Now she was gone. I never got a chance to say goodbye to her because I was in jail.

It was so damn loud in the unit that I had to put my finger in my other ear just to hear what my wife was saying to me; even then it was hard to hear her. As I was talking on the phone, there was a guy talking to his wife on the phone. He had just gotten busted with five pounds of pot, and he got less than three years. He didn't get a mando sentence either, and it was for drugs. I was able to talk to him, and he did tell me that he had given his father forty thousand dollars before he got busted, said that it was some of the money that he made selling weed, and he just gave it to his father to hold for him in case he got busted as he did. Then he said that the forty thousand didn't hurt him a bit, and to him it was pocket change. He then said he still had a good amount of cash left in other places that the cops would never find. We just kept talking for a while. He said that he was selling weed for a long time before he got caught, told me that he had it hidden away real good. He didn't tell anyone where it was but his father.

After talking to this guy for while, he told me that his father had a farm, and it had a trapped door in the barn, and his father had a bunch of hay on top of the hidden door. They raided the house, checked the barn, but the narcs never looked under the hay, where the trapdoor was. That was where his next shipment was. He said going to jail was a break for him because he was getting tired of selling drugs and needed a break. I was so pissed off at him thinking jail was a break. He did give me his lawyer's name. He was from Boston, said that he was real good on getting guys out of jail. When I called my wife again, I told her to give this lawyer a call, see what he thought about my case, and to give him a retainer if he said that he could reduce my sentence. I told her to show him the warrant, the court papers, see if it was worth taking on my case, if I shouldtook a chance at an appeal. I gave her all my money to do this for me before I came in because all I wanted at this time was to get out of this hellhole, away from all this scum, and get back to my family.

When I walked away, I asked myself how someone can say that being in a place like this is a break from selling drugs, not thinking about his family, being on the outside. All I can say is stop selling drugs, because being away from my family is what was killing me the most. Being away from my wife, daughter, it was with me every hour of the day. The really fucked-up thing about it was he was telling me that he was going back to selling weed as soon as he got out. The weed he got caught with was heat sealed, put in fifty-five-gallon drums. He said that the sentence that he got was real good; he just got three to five years, and he'd probably be out in two years. At this time I wish I had sold weed and didn't have a junkie wife. I probably would have had a good amount of money on the outside, as this guy did, then I could have bought my way out of this place if I got caught. If they caught me, it wouldn't be for much.

Well, I was just starting to get somewhat used to this place. As I got up, I went to the mechanics sink to wash up because there is no place to wash up, so I wash up in a sink that looks like a trough, like the one they used to feed animals out of, drink out of. I waited in line to take a dump and watch out not to step into cum puddles that guys deposited on the floor. I stay up at night, sleep somewhat during the day, and just stay awake to go to chow when they call it because I don't trust anyone during the night. I was up at 4:00 a.m. just to beat the rush to use the toilet. I've been here for a while now and still haven't seen or got any visits from my wife. I thought I would have had one by now.

The bunk that they assigned me, where the heater was, had a pipe right above my head, and the pipe was torn up. I saw insulation coming from it. I thought it was just regular insulation, but now I found out that the insulation was asbestos. The reason I know this is that on the outside of the building, they have yellow tape stripes all over the place stating "Asbestos removal." They never thought of moving any of us. They know this; they don't give a flying fuck what happens to any of us. Now every time I go to the chow hall, I bring back fruit. I stick all the stickers that come on the fruit over the holes to keep it from falling on me when I sleep because I ran out of my scotch tape. Now they are starting to let us go to the yard during the day, then at night we go to a hall where everyone can use sports equipment, or go to the gym. I'm in the gym every chance I get; it keeps me from going totally nuts, to try to keep myself in shape, which I let go to hell. I'm still having trouble dealing with things in here. I'm still in some sort of a fog. It just won't clear up. I really think it's permanent. It's hard thinking straight. The shrink tells me it will clear up after a while. It's because of where I'm at. I really think she's the one who's nuts. It will be with me for the rest of my life. I know this in my heart. Just my con number, which I was told never to forget, so of course it's burned into my head, and that's running through my head continuously.

I have so much hate in me still that I just wish the head honcho narc that busted me, the one who shot my dog in the head, gets the same someday, that fuckin' piece of shit. He just went too far when he shot my dog in the head. I hope I live long enough to hear one way or another he got fucked up on the snitch job he holds. Well, today I finally got a letter from my so-called wife. She said that she wanted me to be strong and pray to God. He will see me through it all. She would be up to see me real soon. I just wish that she was in here right now. Even after all the shit I had been through, I miss her so much even knowing what she is and what she has done to me. As we were talking, she told tell me that she would be up every week to see me. I really needed to hear that. Really, this was something I really wanted to hear from her because I really loved her so damn much that it hurts me inside even though she kept fucking me over ever since we got busted. I know she is going to let me rot in this place. As I read on in the letter she sent me, I noticed she put down that me being in jail would make me a better person. I would learn a lesson for messing with cocaine. That made me laugh. This brought out the hate in me and made my body heat up. She was the cokehead, not me. I did find out that she was going out with a dealer at the time of the letter she just sent me. She was keeping it from me. I was still getting letters from some guys I knew on the outside except one unknown writer telling me what she was doing. The weird thing about it is some of the letters were from friends of hers from the place she hung around. I've always believed in God. I didn't need her to try to teach me religion. This from someone who was fuckin' sucking Tom, Dick, and Harry off and telling me to believe in God. One thing she's got to realize is if she doesn't right what she did wrong to everyone, she would pay for it. If there is an afterlife so they say. I was already paying for everything I had done wrong in life, I think, by spending five years of my life in hell.

Everywhere I looked there were guys on their knees, praying to get them out of jail, but to me, I think God doesn't come into a place where people have done so many bad things in life. The other thing about being incarcerated is, in my whole life, I had never seen so many reborn Christians and seen them do things that they tell you not to do. That same day, I got a call for a visit. I thought it was a visit from my wife, so I left the unit and started to run. I was yelled at and was told not to run, but I had a pass for a visit. I just couldn't wait to get there. I guess they have to do this in case it's an escape, so I started to walk real fast, thinking my wife came up to see me. I got to the visiting room, but it wasn't my wife. It was my cousin that I started to call Charley Rat in writing this. He said that he was up to see me, to see how I was doing.

The first words out of his mouth were "How are you doing?" I walked over to him, and while standing up in front of him, I was told by the CO in charge to sit down, but I paid no attention to what he was telling me. I looked my cousin right in his shifty eyes and said, "What the fuck are you doing here?" He said that he wanted to know how I was doing. I said to him, "You're part of the reason for me being in this fucking place, you motherfucker, you fucking rat. I'm in here with these fuckin' garbage people because of you, fuckin' rat." I kept calling him that.

Then he said, "How can you say that to me after all I did for you?"

I said, "What you did to me?" I just got up and started to walk away from him.

He started to yell at me, started to say "I had nothing to do with it" over and over again. The CO started to lead him out of the visiting room. As I walked away, I heard him through the walls as I left the visiting room, yelling out real loud, "I had nothing to do with it!" He was told to leave. As the CO led me out of the visiting room, I was told to go back to the unit. He turned to me and said, "That guy is as guilty as sin. He is lying through his teeth." I just said, "I know."

Later that week I got a letter from him saying again that he had nothing to do with it, how could I even think that way about him? He then said the reason he didn't talk to me for the last couple of weeks before I went into jail was because I didn't go to his birthday party that his family put together at his house. He was going to be fifty. I was looking at jail time, and I was expected to go to a birthday party? What the fuck was wrong with him. I was expected to forget that I was going to jail? Another dickhead, another scumbag I needed to cross off my list. It was so very easy for him to give the cops the information that they needed to pull a raid on me that night because he probably got caught with something in his car, so he told them what they needed to know. He had done this before. I overheard someone who was there when I was getting busted that it was thanks to him that they got the information they got to carry on the bust.

BUSTED

Of course I couldn't believe that he would do that when he was at one time a cocaine dealer himself. In all the time that I was incarcerated, I never got any more letters from my rat cousin just trying to convince me that he had nothing to do with what happened to me. If someone accused me of something like that, I would try to make it right, but not him (Rat). Even years later when I got out, I saw him quite a few times, but he never tried to talk to me at all, just tried to keep away from me, make believe that he didn't see me. That's because he is guilty as sin, piece of shit.

The way that I look at it is that it all comes back to you three times over; I can't wait to see that day when it happens to him. He talked to another friend of mine, and he said that he didn't want to try to talk to me because of what I called him, because I didn't attend his birthday party. Fuckin' jerk. This was what he kept telling people. He never went to any of my birthdays, never did a thing for me when I made him my best man when I got married. What I would love to know is, who does he think he is? He thinks he is the Godfather. I think he seen too many reruns of The Godfather. At that time, I was hoping that it was my wife. It would have been real nice to see her face. I could have told her in person about this lawyer. I found out that he took on hard drug cases. He was out of Boston who helped out a lot of guys in here.

When I go to sleep, I still see the things I went through when we got busted. I still can't block it out no matter how much I try. It runs through my head over and over again day after day. This place is one big nightmare. I waste most of my time just thinking of what I was going through before I got busted in this place. The COs sometimes ask you questions about things that go on during the night because they see me up during the night because they walk around night after night, shining the flashlight in your eyes until you open your eyes. I just say I don't see a thing. I really do see a lot that goes on, but I keep it to myself and just do my own time, as I learned.

Today a new guy came into the unit, and he said that he spent time in Vietnam. He was a bomb expert, so of course he had a lot of stories to tell everybody, and he got the interest of a lot of the guys in the unit. He was the new guy, and the entire unit just wanted to hear the entire stories he wanted to talk about. It was like a nighttime story before most of the guys went to bed. Nothing like a good war story. The other thing they liked was all the money that he had. He made large canteens every week. This guy would give a lot of it away. He had a lot of the guys cook for him. He would just give up the canteen so he wouldn't have to cook it. Plus he didn't know how to cook. This guy never left the unit, but he would have guys all over the unit cook for him but my friend. I watched him very closely, and I found it very strange that he never went anywhere. He always stood inside. My bed was really close to him, so I just could hear everything he had to say. I would say to myself, Can't you just shut up? I knew it was just bullshit; he was just blowing smoke up the guys' asses, but they wanted to hear it. He had his little group of followers, so-called slaves that he bought, but I just kept to myself, just watched how they kissed his ass for free canteen. As for me, I'd rather just go without.

A friend of mind named Kenny Gomes, who was in the war, no matter how drunk he got, he would never say what went on in the war, said that's best that it stood there. Even to this day, I remember what he said to me very clearly like he told me at the time I'm writing this. He said he was not proud of what he had to do over there. It's best that no one knows what he had to do. He also said guys who have served don't tell all, just enough. That's why he'd get totally fucked up all the time. This stuck in my head. This guy had so many stories that I knew it was all bullshit and paid no attention to him. I think it was too many movies on TV that he watched, just like all the guys who knew people in the Marines. There were stories starting to go around saying that he was a skinner. It went throughout the unit like wildfire. When that starts, you stay away from whoever or you will be on a shit list also. This went on for about two months. I came back for lunch, and he was gone. I asked the guys who rolled up his stuff; it got around that he was a woman beater and a rapist, and this went right through the unit. This is the only way they could stay in a place for a while, that would be by buying their way into a place that they were sent to. It's real weird the way they make themselves out to be this great person, until they get found out of what they got convicted of, then they were gone as fast as they came in. All it takes is one guy spreading a rumor, then it takes off, and everyone stays away, or they pay the price. Stuff like this never settles too good with most of the guys that are in jail, and things like that travels through a unit in about two days. That is it, then he's trashed. The mail finally came in, and I got a check from my wife. Again it was just eighty dollars. It was like she was giving me an allowance. It was my fuckin' money. I just held my anger back and thought at least I could get some food from the canteen. It was mostly rice, fish pepperoni, and what we could take from the kitchen. My so-called buddy would still bring stuff back from the kitchen, and we would mix it all together, make what they call a rice meal. That was eating good in this place. The food in the chow hall was real bad. Most of the times I just couldn't eat it unless they mixed it all together then made some sort of soup out of it. The Muslim don't eat any meat or pork, so everything was turkey meat, with no spices added. This made life real bad for guys who did eat meat, so we all were eating like Muslim, but most of them were just putting on an act again. Turkey is meat.

Most of the time I had toilet paper stuffed in my ears because it was so damn loud, but there is nothing you can do about this. You just put up with it because it was an everyday event. All this week I've tried every day to get to the phone. It was just about impossible to get one, then when you did, you were lucky. The noise was real bad. Still to hear the person you were trying to talk to, it was like you see on TV, a large flock of birds squawking. It was like one guy trying to talk over another. This went on all day long. When you get a phone, you have to press the phone really tight against the side of your head and hope you can hear who you're talking to. You're just allowed to make one call on the phone, then when it hangs up, you do have to move to the end of the line when you're done out of respect for the next guy. There are so many fights over the phones because of the assholes that try to make more than one call. You have so many minutes on the phone, then it hangs up automatically because there are so many guys waiting for the phone. The worst part of waiting for the phone is the guy who wraps socks over the phone receiver and has the other hand down their pants playing with their dicks. It's a bitch when you're next in line.

I just can't believe the things I see in this damn place. All the stupid fights over guys using the phones with their hands down their pants also. When you finally get your numbers cleared by the superintendent, you're so glad that you don't care who you talk to as long it's from someone from the outside, this means even people you didn't like on the outside. Sometimes just to hear someone from the outside makes you feel good inside because you're surrounded day after day by a lot of scum all the time. You don't know who you can trust, so many backstabbers in this place. In my case, my first call was to my wife. I always wanted to talk to her because I thought she was trying to get me out of this damn place and back home again. The first question was, "Did you talk to an attorney yet?" Her answer was that she has been working real hard, as she would usually say. She hasn't had a chance to do it as of yet. If she was on the inside and I was on the outside, I would be right on it and not let her spend one more day in this place that she had to. Then I would get so damn pissed off that I can't even put it into words. Under my breath I would say, "You're not in this fuckin' place. You just don't give a good shit as long as you are free to do what you wanted." Then out of nowhere while I was on the phone with her, she would say that she had to change the subject because it was getting her upset. She should try staying one fuckin' day where I'm at. At this time I would have to just go along with what she was telling me because you need people on the outside to help you, so I thought this was what she was doing for me. What a joke that ended being.

I wanted so bad to call my daughter to ask her if she could help me with getting a new lawyer, but at this time, she was taking care of my house, paying all the bills and everything that came along with it. This girl did it all by herself and was in the process of getting beat up all the time by her so-called boyfriend. This piece of shit wouldn't be beating her up if I was on the street. I would have had his legs broken, but I never would have told my daughter that I had it done. The people I knew on the outside, damn, but they all went in different directions when I got in trouble. It was like they never knew me. My daughter had her boyfriend kicked out because she couldn't take getting beat up anymore. The money stopped, then he started to say that his son wasn't his. He wasn't going to pay any support. She had to start stripping at a strip club so she could pay for the mortgage until the courts found out that her boyfriend was the father of her son. My daughter was a very beautiful girl. It was killing me when she told me that she was working at a topless strip club to pay the mortgage. I felt like shit. She told me that she asked my wife along with other family members for help with money, but they all said that was up to her to pay for it and not to call again.

My daughter ended up calling my wife's father, and he gave her some money to help her out at that time that she needed it. I told her to put the house on the market to sell it, but she refused to do so. I know she is as stubborn as her father is. I always told her that the house was like an investment to her, and when I die, it all goes to her. I didn't think I was going to make it in jail because of my poor attitude toward these guys, then I said if I kicked off in here, my daughter could cash in my death policy, until I found out my wife cashed it in earlier. Money-hungry bitch. I raised my daughter from a little girl, and she took on all my habits as well because her mother couldn't deal with her and really didn't want her because she was a pain in the ass, but I wanted her still. Her mother would tell her that she was from a failed past relationship and had no place in her new one. She would spend most of her younger life living in her mother's home, but I had her most of the time until I got custody when she turned sixteen. To this day I couldn't ask for a better daughter, but she still is a pain in the ass. Even now she drives me crazy, but this is what daughters do to fathers. You always put up with it because in your heart, they do no wrong. To this day I always wondered if my daughter knew that my wife was into doing coke. I know she hated her. She told me to kick her out a lot of times. I should have listened to her because she was right. But as they say, love is blind. I was so blind to the fact that she probably was able to see things that I couldn't. I did keep my daughter from the drugs. I never told her about it and always told her that drugs were bad and to stay away from them. To my knowledge, she always did.

One day my daughter took me aside and asked me about drugs and told me that she had seen my wife with white powder around her nose, to watch for it, and she was always blowing her nose then acting weird then said that I made a mistake in marrying her. This came to mind lots of times through the years. When you're in a place like this, you tend to start using the brains you had on the outside. Put your dick aside because you don't need it in here. Well, at least to me. It's real hard when coming into a place like this. It just gets hard being yelled at, especially being told what to do day in and day out, along with being told if you don't like it, you can go back behind the wall again. What gets me real mad is that you're treated like you're a slave, or even worst, like an animal You are also called a choice of names, and you tend to take it like it was never said to you. The COs know this. They use it in the best way they can, so they do the lowest amount of work as possible. They just have inmates do it for them. If you don't do what they tell you, they have you lugged to higher security. It also benefits them as well unless you're already in high security. If you get lugged to prison, transportation gets work to transport you to another institution. You have to start all over again plus lose your entire canteen, then wait for your clothes to arrive at the new place, which can take up to two weeks, sometimes longer.

At this time, I was at the gym as much as possible. I always would come back to a shakedown and find all my stuff all over the place on the bed or on the floor. A lot of it was stolen by other inmates. The COs don't give a damn. In this unit, you had to wait for just about everything, from the toilet to the shower. It was a nonstop thing because there was just too many guys housed in this unit. But the COs controlled everything from inside a cage. It was an old tool crib used for tools at one time. That's what he sat in. He had some radios in with him, which probably made it his control center. What a joke. If things were to go off in this place, no one would have to touch this CO that was in his control room because he would have shit himself to death. If you fucked with them, they find ways to fuck with you every chance they get, let you know what they are doing to you but always remind you that it was their house. You would have to do as they say. This is what they say to you every chance they get. They keep saying it over and over again: "You're in my house, you got to do what I tell you to do." They used these exact words on you all the time.

During the day, I would try to sleep because the dreams that I was having were really bad, thinking family members that were dead were coming back to life. It haunted me all the time. I guess this was my mother and father telling me how bad I fucked up. It is really hard to explain. It was like I was still visiting the dead all the time. It was really hard to think. It was like my memory was being erased. I didn't want to do anything at all but just what I was told to do. I started to realize I was really fucked up in the head. The stuff that I was always thinking about was my daughter, my wife, getting out of this place, but if I really think about it, my mind always drifted by to when I was busted by the narcs. It was like a VHS tape playing over and over again, everything the narcs did to me. It just made me hate them to the point that I wished that the head narc got a bullet right between the fuckin' eyes as he did to my dog. Fuckin' cocksucker, you know who you are. To this day I still hope for it. I would have such a big party that I would make a loan to have such a party even if I had to pay for it in the next five years, fuckin' scumbag.

The guys that I went to the gym with started to come around, saying to me, "It's time that you started to go back to the gym to exercise. Stop thinking about stuff that can't be changed. What happened is what happened. You should just move forward." I put in a request to see the shrink to see if they could help me again, just to be able to talk to someone about what I was going through, even though I know they did me no good, but it was someone to talk my problems over with. But just like I was told, they are not there to cure you; they are there to somewhat help you. But if you look at it, they are just there to make a paycheck. As I said before, they really don't give a damn if they help you or not. They were not that good at what they did. I was just there to pay off their student loans probably, part of that was going to prisons to try to treat inmates with their problems.

The worst thing about waiting to see a doctor was the time I had to wait in the cage to see them. While in the cage, I watched guys looking to beat each other up or stuffing toilet paper down the toilet, then watching it overflow onto the floors. The big thing was them calling the CO, telling him that the toilet was overflowing onto the floor, then him seeing what they did then walking away like he was going to do something. Most of the time, they would say, "Oh, looks like you did it again, so you will have to wait to get someone down here to fix it, so for now you will have to live with it." It didn't bother the inmates at all. They would use it just the same, then it would overflow all over the place, shit, piss, it didn't matter to them. But out of it all, there were some good guys; they were not all scum, but you just have to look for them. In this place you need someone to talk to from time to time, or you will really will go nuts.

Then from time to time they would send me to the stomach doctor, and she would ask me how I was doing. I would tell her that I was doing okay even though I wasn't taking my stomach medication for the ulcers I had. She would ignore what I was saying to her. Every time that they sent me to see her, all she wanted to do was stick her fingers up my ass. This was every time I saw her. She would never examine me but would cut to the chase and always asked to stick her fingers up my ass. I wondered if this was a fetish thing of hers or if she just wanted to check my prostate. I said that I'd just have a real doctor on the outside do that to me. What a face she gave me. Even though it was a real good-looking woman, she always had a lot more guys in jail. She could stick her fingers up their asses. She said that I should be checked out every year for cancer. I told her that I didn't care if I lived or died while being in this place, then I told her that the COs checked out my ass a lot during their inspections. She said that I could go back to the unit. I wrote a note to the superintendent properly, saying that I didn't want to see that doctor again. She couldn't help me in this place; I never did see her again.

I started to walk the track again as I was doing prior to issues that I was going through. This was a long track, and I feel it helped me a lot but thought about the outside as usual, thinking about working in my garage on cars again, just hoping that clears up the mental problem I'm having. When I always got back to the unit, I would always look around and say, "I can't let these crazy motherfuckers rub off on me," as I was watching grown men running around acting like kids then doing real stupid things to each other. I caught myself one time doing stupid stuff and stopped it right away, thinking, What am I doing? The bad part was I started walking around talking to myself out loud. I was starting to do this every day from the time I woke up to the time I went to sleep. Maybe this was why no one fucked with me, because they kind of knew I was losing it. I caught myself doing this because some of the guys I walked the track with noticed it and brought it to my attention. They told me about what I was doing and told me to get ahold of myself. After that, I had to convince myself to stop doing it. I knew it was because I was in this hellhole and just had to deal with it. The other thing I had to convince myself when I was talking to myself was this is not going to be forever. I will be going home again someday if I don't die first. You have the attendance to think this way because of the things you see going on in this place. I just can't believe the things I've seen. I have to deal with this shit every day then say this is what happens to people in places like this if they are in for a long period of time, as it did to me as well as time went on.

What I did forget is this is a correctional institution. They teach you the correct ways to do things. Of course, it's the right ways so you don't make the same mistakes again when you're released from this place (ya right). If you believe this, you're as stupid as they are trying to make you into, a puppet and pump bullshit into your head that they said that it will help you on the outside so that they can say they taught you a thing while your incarcerated right up to your release. I mean, the only thing they do very hard to do is brainwash you so you don't know how to live on the outside anymore and you end up coming back. This way you have to go back to crime and you end up going back to jail. I guess this was what they called job security. In one session I had with myself, I started to realize all the fucked up stuff that I was doing, then realizing that no one in this place could help me but me.

In the time that I was in this unit, I'd seen so many guys come in like they ruled the world; then within six months, a lot of them were on their knees, praying to God like all the rest I saw in the past to get them out of jail or see them preaching the Bible to others so they can get early release before the parole board. I would just shake my head and say, "Now you're into God." I wonder if they did that on the street. As for myself, I've always believed in God, so there were no put-on, as they would say. No matter how much I prayed, I was not going to get any time off my sentence unless my case was somehow overturned, if or when my wife retained me a lawyer. My sentence was a mandatory sentence, as I said. This means day for day, as I was told by one of the guys on the way to breakfast one day. This meant no good time could be added to it. I mean, no good time at all. You do every day they gave to you in the sentence.

But I was told by some of the guys that the COs told them that Governor Romney was trying to change the mandatory sentences. When they had it on TV, they were going to vote on it, but it was always carried on to another session, so it was all bullshit. It just got my hopes high after I was told that. I watched TV for a good month thinking that they were going to change the mandatory sentences law. What an asshole. I was lying around watching all the stupid laws they put out there and nothing about changing the mandatory law at all. I guess they intended to make it for a later time or just put it out there to make them look like they were working for their big buck jobs. All they do is put on a good show for people, but it amounted to nothing at all. Mitt Romney put on the best show of all. Nothing was said about the mandatory sentencing. Now I wouldn't vote for him no matter what he ran for. Even if it was for dog catcher. All the COs were laughing at most of the guys, saying, "They are not going to change the fuckin' laws because they would lose too much money you guys bring into the jail. It's money in the bank." I just will never trust anything he will ever say again. Everything that comes out of his mouth is just bullshit. He just got everyone's hopes up in jail. All this sentence does is destroy families, put families on the street. I lost my wife because of this and put a heavy burden on my daughter to maintain my home so I wouldn't lose it. All I was doing was just taking care of a drug addict's needs. Just remember, a lot of guys don't know what the law carries when dealing with drugs. In some cases, people are just doing it because they have a drug problem, as my wife did. I get it for a couple of friends, so they can afford to buy it for themselves, and it helps me with the expense for my wife. But the fuckin' narcs, the courts don't see it in this respect. They just say you're a drug dealer, throw a mandatory sentence at you, unless your family member is in politics or you have a cop in your family, they are exempt from prison time as a lot of politicians are.

I was calling my wife all the time, maybe getting through one every three weeks, writing her every day, wondering if she had a chance to talk to any lawyer from the guy in jail who helped him with the weed crime he was accused of. Of course, she would say she was working too many hours and didn't have a chance to do so. Of course, I would ask her to send me some money that I left her before I came in, and she would say it will be in the mail the next day. I wouldn't get it several weeks later. After that I started to make cards, sew guy's clothes, even opening combination locks to make some canteen for the week. I waited to get some money from her and little at that. I left this bitch with a good chunk of change; it came to me very slowly, as if it were her money. It wasn't. Everything that I had on the outside that she could suck me dry of or to get money from it was gone. I think it went for drugs. Some so-called friends were still sending me letters, saying that they see her. She was getting high. Her lifestyle never changed except fucking around with different guys. As I was waiting for my wife to get off her ass to see if she could get me another lawyer, I tried to call the one who helped to get me the five years term that I was serving, but of course he would hang up on me. While I was waiting, the court took what little money I had in my canteen then said it was for court fees. If I disagree with the decision, I could prove that I was indigent, and the courts would stop taking money out of my canteen. Come on, I was just making five dollars a week, and they wanted it.

No one family or so-called friends would or could help me on the outside. I was able to write a letter from in jail, and they got all the information from I guess the superintendent. They found me to be indigent, then they stopped taking money out. I said one thing done, and I even did it being in in jail. My mind was getting worst; I guess it was like people who get Alzheimer's. It was like my mind was being erased. I put in again to see the shrink, and again the CO was a cocky bastard and said, "I hope you go out of your mind, then you be one less guy to take care of." Well, I got my appointment, so of course, I went to see the shrink. Of course, I was put in the cage with all the other assholes. I see the same old stuff: clogging of the toilet, watching the guys still shit and piss in it and it flowing on to the floor, then just saying to myself, what fuckin' assholes.

My time came to see the doctor, as I was hoping for. As I entered her so-called office, right from the start she asked me what the problem was, asked what she could do for me. I said, "What a professional," then thought she must have taken the same jail course as the COs did. Course number one: how to turn inmates off. I began by saying, "I'm still thinking about things on the outside, just can't stop. It feels like a dream to me, but it's like I'm in a fog. I think I'm going crazy."

Her reply to me was that it's all normal to think this way because of where I'm at, then she said, "It will all clear up in time when you get used to where you are."

After that, I started to think, Now I know she's nuts. I thought this was something that she had written on the notepad that she held in her hands all the time because she never looked like she was writing to much down on it. I'll bet for sure she was doodling on it as she was talking to me because it didn't look like she gave a fuck.

Then she said, "You're not used to having everything done for you. What you're going though is a normal reaction for guys who have never been incarcerated before."

I told her that I think that my sentence was too harsh, that I was going in for a revise and revoke, then she said that it won't do any good. "They will not lower your sentence because to them it looks like they made a mistake in sentencing from the beginning." Then she said, "Did you do the crime?" I said yes. Then she said, "If you did the crime, do the time." I gave her the dirtiest look ever and said, "I am through with you." Again, I thought going to see a shrink would help me, but it was no help at all, just time out of the cell, and that was what it amounted to every time I went to see the shrink. I realized that she didn't have nearly enough time under her belt. She was just another pretty face. That's all she had going for her. Well, at least it was some time out of the unit.

BUSTED

I learned that most of the guys that I had seen doing fucked-up things were things that they did all or most of the time. I started to talk to the guys that I came in with, and they made more sense to me then the shrink did. The guys just said, "Just do your time. Wait to see if the next lawyer helps you in any way. Maybe he can help you get out or have your sentence reduced. That's all you can hope for." One of the guys said, "Don't listen to any of these fuckin' doctors. They are as fucked up as the CO are. Just hope for the best, do what you have to do to keep working out in the gym." I then realized that they were right. They talked me into going back to the gym to work out again. That helped out a lot. He looked at me then said, "I thought we were going to lose you. They were going to send you to the nuthouse."

I looked at him and said, "There is plenty of time for that, isn't there." I then started to think back at all the stuff that I was doing then realized that I was doing some fucked-up things; I just couldn't stop doing them. It started to be habit. I was basically thinking about my life on the outside all the time, what my wife could be doing. I just stopped thinking of where I was, was letting myself get fucked up being in the place that I was at. I started to think about the kids that I used to teach at the high school, how much of a good teacher I was, teaching them the stuff that took me so long to learn right up to the schools I went to. The fuckin narcs really dirtied my name the best that they could by telling the newspapers that I was being checked out very closely to see if I was selling drugs to the students. This was really working on me to no end. In my life I never did anything like that, and I would never do such a low thing like that ever, to sell drugs to kids, no damn way. I was basically supplying my junkie wife. I just couldn't afford the amount of drugs she was putting up her nose. Then I started to get it for a couple of my so-called friends to help me with the expense for their wives or girlfriends whatever.

From the time I entered Concord, the fog that I said I was in was getting even worse. Most of what I was teaching the students in school was disappearing from my memory like it was being erased. The math and all the major subjects were disappearing; I just didn't want to remember any of it anymore and said to myself, "I'll never have a job like that ever again, so why do I need it." When I started to think about it, it was too much for me to want to remember it. I would start to get headaches. I had nothing to take for them. Forget about these asshole doctors. They would say, "Get your medication through the canteen." Being in here trying to talk to lawyers was just too much for me to do in this fuckin' place. I really needed someone on the outside to help me with the lawyers, things that needed my attention at home. Things that I did at school I wouldn't need any of it in this this damn place because who would want to learn stuff like this in here. Plus I had to watch my damn ass in here at all times; that was a full-time job. Lots of times I would look around the unit from the top bunk, look around at all the guys, then say, "What a bunch of fuckin' assholes that I had to do time with." I'm not saying all of them, but a hell of a lot of them.

They were too busy thinking of how they were going to do what they got busted for over again. Most of them thought that they all found a different way to get away with what they got busted for. The next time they do it, they would tell me, they will get away with it. Some of them in conversation would tell me, "I know what I did wrong, I know how to do it over again without getting caught again. I will make loads of money on just doing one big job again." Most of them didn't have a clue what was going on in the world. Them being in a place like this, they adjusted very well in here. For a lot of them to come back, it was like a walk in the park. None of them even thought of getting a job in all the conversation I had with any of them. When I would talk to myself, I would have to keep telling myself to try to keep my shit together; don't get burned out like these fucking guys.

There were so many black guys and Puerto Ricans in here they outnumbered the white guys by far. I tried to keep away from them because they just stuck to their own kind. In my whole life, I never heard the word Nigger so much as I heard it in this place. This is how most of the black guys talked to each other, by addressing each other by calling each other Niggers. In one occasion I was talking to one of the guys that I worked at the gym with, when a guy came over, cut in on our conversation, then started to talk to him regarding another so-called story. I replied to it. The guy turned and said to me, "Hey, this is a—AB Conversation. See your way out of it." I just gave him a dirty look then walked away. This happened again. I think he was just trying to piss me off. I turned to him and said, "Do you know what you said to me one time about a AB conversation?" He said yes. Well, that's when I asked him if he knew what "Fuck off" means. He said yes. That's when I said, "It means the same as you telling me about a AB conversation," so I told him just to walk away. After that when he sees me talking to someone, he never cut into any of my conversations ever again.

    I did start to have another conversation with the guy that I was talking to prior to that discussion about our next move. I then asked him about our next move. He said, "Yes, we are not going to stay here. We are going to a different place at any time. This is also a holding place." At this point a I knew I made an enemy by saying what I said to the last guy that cut into my conversation. I had to keep my eyes open, see where this was going to take me. After this slight disagreement, I really couldn't sleep at night at all, just in case this guy was really pissed off at me. I was in fear I would get hit with soap in a sock in the middle of the night, then I would have to pay him back like I'd seen so many times before at night. It was okay. I was already staying up at night, somewhat sleeping during the day. I would doze off now but never at night unless I was in a locked cell. It was also an advantage to me. I also would use the toilet at around 4:00 a.m. so I could beat the morning rush. I would not have to step around the cum that would be all over the floor in the morning and smell the odor that came off some of the guys who didn't wash up. After that, I would shave in their mechanic sink that looked like a turf that animals drank out of and jump back into my bunk because it was real cold in the unit, and I mean freezing. I'm glad I had a heater right over my head. I would look at the pipe that I put sticker to keep the asbestos from falling on me. It really bothered me, didn't want to breathe it in. But it was a really warm place where they put the bed at. I wasn't going to say a word about it, plus I was just another convict to them. They wouldn't give a damn anyways.

On one occasion, one of the COs came up to me and asked me if I did see the guys getting beat up during the night. I just said no, that I didn't. This was already the second time I was asked this, but it was a different CO that asked me. I did, but I wasn't going to tell him what I saw. This was his job, to stay in the unit to see this going on, not mine. Next time if he will be where he was supposed to be instead of hanging with his buddies, maybe he would see it for himself what's going on in the unit.

The CO said, "I know you stay up most of the night. You're trying to tell me that you didn't see anyone getting beat up?"

I said, "That's what I'm telling you."

He left me alone but tore my footlocker apart a lot of times after that. He just turned, walked away like I was going to tell him what I seen, get the same thing the other guy got. It wasn't by just one guy either. This CO gets to go home at night, but I can't. I have to stay up all night and watch my ass. This guy got beat up for a reason. It wasn't my business, and I didn't want to make it my business, and really, I didn't really care. I just want to do my time then just go home, start my life over again, and just spend time with my family I left behind.

One day I went out for a walk around the track just to see if I could clear my mind of my wife and the way I dumped my home off on my daughter to take care of. What helped me on so many occasions was the good times but was always interrupted by get home again. I just couldn't understand why I had to wait so long for my wife to try to get me another attorney. She just keeps me waiting; I know she's not even trying to get me out of this fuckin' place now. I just feel it in my heart. As I was walking around the track, this guy just came up to me and started to talk to me, asking me where I came from. I told him, and he said he was from the same area I was from. It was good to see someone from my area. He just started to ask me questions; we just exchanged conversation, then he asked me if I was in Concord long. I said for a while and that I was waiting for my next move. We just sat down and kept a conversation going for a while, talking about different places that we hung around when we were on the street. One of the guys that I weight-lifted with came up to me and asked me what the hell I was doing. I said, "Talking to this guy."

He looked at him and said to me he's was no good, then he said right to this guy, "Get the fuck out of here, stay the fuck away."

I said, "What's up?"

He just looked at me and said, "He's a fuckin' Didier, a kid rapist. Some of the guys were looking at you talking to that fuckin' asshole. You don't want them saying that you're in with that type of scum, do you?"

I just said, "I didn't know."

He said that he was looking for me in the unit, wanted to know where the hell I was, so he came out to the yard. He saw who I was talking to, put the guy right out there. He just said, "Watch who the hell you talk to. Stay away from most of these guys. Just hang with the guys you know so far, like us."

The guy just got up fast, started to walk away, and didn't even look back. It must have been true because he would have said something to defend himself. He said, "We looked for you in the unit after lunch. We knew you weren't feeling good, so we came out looking for you. Then we see you with a Diddler. Good thing we found you."

When we got back to the unit, the COs had a field day. They tore the whole unit apart, and this time they dumped all the lockers on the floors, looking for contraband. I guess drugs because two guys had just died on the track. They must have been looking for drugs, but of course, they won't tell you this. This was just part of a day in this place. It happens so often that you get used to it, but this time it was real bad. After this, we saw a lot of guys getting shipped out. It was just a matter of time before it was our turn to go to different prisons as I thought. We just said that maybe we will go to the same prisons, but if we don't, we can exchange our telephone numbers, addresses, so when we get out, we can get together again, have a few beers together, talk about the shit we had to put up with. I was on their list to go to Bridgewater Max. Of course I didn't understand and went back to the unit to tell the guys. They were surprised that I was going to a maximum prison instead of a minimum. They tried to explain it to me, but of course I just didn't understand what they were trying to explain to me, but the way I looked at it, I'd find out very soon. To me a prison was a prison. I just knew that I was going to be locked up. I just didn't give a damn anymore. I just wanted to be out of this fuckin' place, but it just looked like I was going to see this prison life for a long time.

I was calling my wife from time to time to keep her informed to where I was, where they were going to send me so she could get in touch with me if she had to. This was so the new lawyer that I gave her the name of could get in touch with me if she was able to get him to take the case. The last time I talked to her, she told me that she was going to Boston to see if the lawyer would take on my case, to see if I had a chance of getting out on bail, reduce my sentence, tell him it was my first offense. Before I was shipped out, I was able to get in touch with her, and she told me that she did go up to Boston to retain a new lawyer for me. He told her that it looked good. He would send someone down to my father-in-law's house to get a deposit to retain his services. When she told me this, this made me so damn happy, saying that it looked good. He would take on my case. I thought it was going to happen right away. I told my so-called jail friends about what my wife had told me, and they said it looked real good for me because the lawyers from Boston were really good. As I was talking to them, I found out that they were going to Plymouth Forestry. They were happy about it. They said it wasn't too bad of a place to be at. They were expecting they were going to stay behind the wall. They were going to a minimum, and I still couldn't believe I was going to a maximum prison when this was my first time in jail.

One of the guys told me that Bridgewater Maximum, where I was going to, had a good visiting room. It wasn't a real bad place to be for jail. Then I realized that it wouldn't be too far for my wife to come to see me. I then called my daughter and told her where I was going to be. Of course, she said that when I was moved, she would be up to see me. When she did come up, she hid some of my food outside so I could eat it on the way back to the unit. Then I told her that my wife got me a new lawyer. She was happy to hear that, and I told her that the lawyer said that it looked good for me. She told me that she wouldn't go back up to Concord to visit me because they strip-searched her by this butch-like woman. She searched her so thoroughly that it felt like she was raped. She was so embarrassed when she was done she just wanted to leave. Then after all that, they wouldn't let her in to see me because she had a piercing, which wasn't allowed in this jail. I wanted so much to see her, but this piercing kept her from coming in. One thing fuckin' COs can't understand is taking someone's family away can really fuck with a guy's head and especially after not seeing them for a while. In my heart, this is one thing that would have been good for me, helped me with the mental state I was in. To see a family member, this would have been great.

At this time I was just about begging my wife to come up to see me because I missed her so much. I just wanted to see her face. But of course, she gave me the excuse that she was on probation; she couldn't come into the prison. My wife did tell me that she was going to ask her lawyer to get her the okay to come up to Concord for a visit. What a cold-hearted person she ended up being. She always had some way of backing out of coming up to see me. This was a part of her that she kept hidden very well, and I was shocked to see it come out in her. But what I can't understand was why they let in one of the students that I taught at the school in to see me. He wasn't even family. I just couldn't believe it. While I was getting my visit from my student, I noticed a guy that killed a little boy with his friend, cemented him inside a metal barrel. I thought it was a plastic pool, but I was corrected by a CO that I talked to after I got out of jail, I think it was the little boy from the guy of America's Most Wanted. He was getting a visit from his family; they brought in a bunch of kids in with them to visit him. I just couldn't understand how they could let kids in to see a child murderer but not let my daughter in because she had a piercing. What a fucked-up place along with fucked-up COs. To me, I think the State should save their money and hang him by his nuts. Anything to do with kids, there is no excuse.

After a long while waiting to catch my wife at home, I was able to talk to her along with my daughter. They are the two people that meant the most to me, my daughter, my wife. If I was shipped to Bridgewater, I wouldn't be able to talk to my wife and daughter until their numbers could be cleared again before I would be able to call them and tell them where I was transferred to. The rest of my family didn't bother with me because I couldn't supply them with any money, which they all asked for all the time or fix their cars for free, so I was not worth their time. They would have been happy to get some of my wife's supply so they could sell it, but my wife would never give up any of that to anyone, especially now that I was in jail.

The superintendent came into the unit; I asked the CO in charge if I could have a minute of his time when he came around to where I was. The CO came back to tell me yes. I asked him if he could let my wife in to see me, but she was on probation. I asked if he could give her a pass to come see me, and he said for me to give the information to the CO, and he will look into it. The next day he sent word back to me saying that he never denied a visit from my wife, Right there I knew she was lying right through her teeth to me. She just made up this excuse to me because she was going out a lot with some of her girlfriends, so she said. I knew this through letters I was getting from someone on the outside that what she told me was bullshit. To this day I still don't know who it was sending these letters to me, but as time went on, they got very expletive on what she was doing. I kind of knew it was someone trying to piss me off. Of course, it did. This person said that he was able to follow her to a banded Fairhaven outdoor drive-in where she was seen getting out of a car half-naked to take a piss. Yes, naked. Now I know she was fuckin' some guy in the car to be naked. I feel the person that was writing these letters was one of the guys that she was seeing at the time because he was very explicit in what he was writing. I knew he wanted her to leave me, and in my heart, I knew it was going to happen. As I said, I don't know if he was the one fucking her at the time but kind of knew it was one of the guys she was seeing. I think he wanted me to confront her with it so she would ask me for a divorce. I guess this was so she wouldn't have to come up to see me anymore. I've gone out with different women, but she had something over me when she would tell me she was coming up to see me. I couldn't wait to see her. When I see her come in, I was just happy to see her. It was like she was on vacation and I was there to meet her. Even though I knew letters I was getting, I just couldn't let her know that I was getting letters from the outside telling me what she was doing. The reason for this is I thought she would give up trying to get me the lawyer to get me out of this place, and because I still love her. When I called her house asking for her, her fucked-up brother answered the phone and told me that she wasn't home, just said that she was out with her friend. Damn asshole. I was in jail, him not saying if it was a girlfriend or on a date with a guy, this was tearing me apart inside all fuckin' night. Just her brother telling me this was making me think that her so-called girlfriends were probably one of her fucking boyfriend that she was fuckin'.

I had to go to see the shrink again. I was telling her what I was going through, and she asked me again right from the start "What can I do for you?" just like before. To me this was a stupid question to be asking me again. I was there for her to answer my questions along with what was bothering me. Then she said, "There is nothing that can be done in your situation. You will have to find a way around it. Just try to stop thinking about what she's doing. Concentrate on where you are, not what she could be doing."

I figured this was what she was going to tell me anyways. The way I started to look at it now, it was just another day out of the unit. I just had to deal with the scum that I was in the cage with while waiting to see the shrink or doctor that I was there for. I did feel like saying to her, "What are you, some kind of asshole?" But you had to watch your temper and everything you said to everyone in a place like this. You can't even raise your voice because there was a CO right outside the door waiting for a flare-up.

It was getting so hard to find a place so I could write letters. When you find a place, there was always someone who had to sit right beside you. After being in a place like this, I always thought they were trying to read what I was writing when someone sat next to me. At this point I was getting really paranoid. This place was full of guys who didn't know how to read or write. I was asked by a couple of guys if I could write for them because they can't put a letter together. Plus they looked like they were dumb bastards to start with. A lot of them just printed; they didn't have a clue how to write a letter, so they asked me if I could start to write letters for them. They did tell me that they would pay me with something from the canteen. That's when something clicked in my head. I didn't have much money in my canteen, so it would really help. I started to learn. At this time I could really use it because my wife was probably using the money I left her for nose candy because my so-called wife wasn't sending me any money for a long while. What she probably thought was that the prison was taking care of all my needs, so she didn't think much about it. My so-called wife hadn't sent me any money for canteen for months, and that's a long time. She was probably spending on herself, thinking that it was hers, or again on cocaine, powdering her fucking nose with her boyfriend.

At this time I'm having a lot trouble thinking out most of the stuff I have to do in here because I'm very depressed. Everything is still cloudy to me all the time, and I'm always talking to myself. The thing that was taking up space in my head was getting out of here with the new lawyer that my so-called wife got for me, getting home to what life I had left, and try to fix things with my wife and daughter. Dealing with the noise in here makes it t so hard to think with all these fucking assholes talking over each other. This means the COs also. I really think that I'm losing my mind. Maybe I'll be heading to the nuthouse very soon if this keeps going on. Maybe it would be better for me, and I wouldn't have to think about where they were going to send me next. This being my first time in jail, it's just hard to understand these stupid bastards. When the Cos talk to me, they talk very slow, like I'm retarded, like they do to these stupid assholes. All I can do is look at them with a stupid look on my face, make them think that I'm dumb as most of these guys are. I look at them, just wondering about them. If I knew I could get away with it, I could get a gun, rid the world of ½ of them. I really think no one would miss any of them, especially the kid rapists, skinners.

I went to chow with my so-called friend Daunte, like always. The food was terrible as usual, no taste at all. I had to add salt and pepper to it to make it have somewhat of a taste. In here, salt and pepper is your best friend at dinnertime. Keep your eyes on it or it will disappear. We always tried to take food out with us, put it down our pants in plastic bags, said that we can make it taste better at the unit after we recook it and added rice to it. As I walked into the unit, the CO said, "Pack up, you're out of here." I asked the CO where I was going. He said I will find out when I get there. I looked at him and said, "What a fuckin' asshole." In a way, I was very happy but scared at the same time, hoping that the next place was better than this place but thinking that it will probably be a disaster like this place was. They did tell me that I was going to Bridgewater Maximum Prison, but you can't always believe what they tell you. I was hoping it wasn't Plymouth House.

I packed up all my stuff, mailed out letters to my daughter, my wife, and asked my daughter if she could call my wife to let her know that I was being moved to another jail, because she was never home. I said bye to my two friends and said, "Maybe we will meet again someday in the system." I told them to have a good meal with the food we just took from the chow hall. It was a long ride to get to the new location. I didn't know where I was, but I knew I would find out very soon. I had to use the toilet real bad as I did when I got at Concord. I knew better not to tell them because they would make me wait. The CO stopped the van, and I heard him walk along the side of the van and opened the doors and said in a real nice way, "Get out, you're here."

I looked at the CO and said, "Where?"

He said, "Here, that's all you need to know. Get in line, get ready to be searched."

This was in August of 1999. I was taken out, of course strip-searched. They take such a long time to look up a guy's ass. I don't think I could ever get used to a guy looking up my ass, but I did what I had to do. I'm put in here for a nonviolent crime. They put me through hell. What they have to do is drift off and put what they are doing in the back of my head. A lot of times they would start to hum the song "Cocaine" after they asked me what I was in for and then they'd laugh. They should have a special place for guys who get caught for nonviolent crimes, not get treated so bad because I know a lot of COs that also use drugs. But it's okay for them to do drugs as long as they don't get caught with it, but it's not whoever gets caught with it. Of course, it's not illegal.

I was there for a while when this Cape Verdean woman CO came in and said to me, "You're not going to stay here. You are going across the street to a minimum," and she walk me across the street. I did ask her where I was, and she answered me with no problem, talked to me like I was a person, and said, "You're at Bridgewater Minimum." She said it's very easy to walk away, but if you do, you will never see another minimum prison again, and that was her exact words she said to me. As I left the maximum prison, I was brought directly across the street. As I was crossing the street, I noticed that there wasn't any barb wire around the compound. I was shocked. She brought me to a room where I was strip-searched again. I was shown a room and was told, "This is your room." There were five beds, so it was a five-man room. Of course I had the top bunk like always. There was a window, light coming in, that was a plus. There was a guy in the room. He said that I could go outside, but before I did, I checked it out with the CO in charge first.

As I was walking out the door, I asked if it was okay. He just said, "Listen for the count." I didn't understand how you could hear count on the outside until I saw a bunch of guys coming in all at once, then I knew it must be count time; I also heard it, them yelling, "Count! It's count time!" I had to go directly to the room, I noticed that there were three white guys, a Spanish guy named Louie in the room. Of course, the fuckin' Spanish guy started to lay down the rules. This guy was a real piece of shit. All the white guys that were in the room at that time had just come in from being in the gym when count was called, paying no attention to what he was saying. Then when count was cleared, he came over to me and told me to watch out for the Spanish guy in the room because he worked with the COs. He was a rat. This guy told me that there were three guys in the room with him. He got them all lugged. This means moved to high security behind the wall. Again I didn't understand, until they said, "Where you just came from." I told the guy I didn't give a damn. It didn't matter where they put me. I was going to be in jail for a while if my next lawyer didn't get me out first.

Of course, the first week we almost had it out with the Spanish guy. We went face-to-face, and he asked me if I wanted to go back behind the wall. I said, "I don't give a fuck." Then he showed me a bedspring, and I showed him a pen. It stopped at that. He just turned to his bed and told me to leave him alone. But from his bed, he said how it was going to be. I said, "Who died and left you boss?"

He said, "I have pull."

I said, "What part of the COs do you pull?"

From that day on it was just dirty looks. He just did childish things to me, and all I could do was put up with it. The first thing I did was put for my phone numbers to be checked out, see if they would clear my telephone numbers so I could call my daughter and my wife to see if she got in touch with my so-called new lawyer. My wife got the lawyer for me, but I never followed up with it because didn't have enough time to do so. It was just a matter of time. It became very clear to me my wife, my best friend, was giving up on me. I would have done anything for her, as I did. I remember my vows when I got married very clearly; I thought it was for better or worse, as they say. She seen some of the worst; she didn't want to see any more. As for me, her face was full; she couldn't suck any more of me, so I was replaced. I guess she just had too much to do with her free time. I guess she didn't want to spend or waste any of it on me. She was just thinking of herself as she always did. Whenever I talked to her, she would say, "I called the lawyer, but he's at court all the time. When I get home at night, it's too late for him to be there, so I don't bother calling."

I just said, "I just want you to try to talk to him, see what he's going to do for me, if anything, and please try to get me the hell out of here." I was just about begging her. This place was better than Concord. I had somewhat some freedom, I was able to walk around the track without barb wire surrounding the place. It was a pretty big track, and it took a while to walk around the whole prison. As I walked around the track, I would see cars drive by, and I just used to say how much I missed driving my Corvette around. I just wanted to stay away from the unit as much as possible because of that Spanish piece of shit that was in the room and didn't want to go back behind the wall because of him. This slimeball just about never left the room but for a half of an hour to run around the yard. When he came in, he had an odor to him as a wet dog had otherwords he stank. I knew when he was in the room because when I walked into the room, I could smell his stink. I always carried a pen in case I had to stick him with it.

I would sit on the bench on the outside; I would just look around the yard, and all I'd see was more of the same garbage people running around playing games on each other, having fun without a care in the world. I just couldn't understand even to this day how it didn't bother these guys to be locked up. I'm not saying all the guys, but a very large number of them looked like they were having fun. I just couldn't understand. It was like they were on a vacation. All I thought about was going home, being with my family again, but I knew this wouldn't happen for a long while because no one was helping me on the outside. I mean no one. The most I could do was to write letters on the inside, but it didn't amount to much. Not many people wrote back. The only good thing about this place is that it had a laundry room, a cooking stove where you could cook some food on that; of course, you bought from the canteen or stole from the kitchen. That was a good thing, at least this took your mind off where you were at for a short time. I didn't know how to cook the food that they made in jail. It was nothing like what I cooked on the outside so I hooked up with some of the decent guys that I met in there, and they started to teach me how to cook in here.

One of the guys I hooked up with was a guy named De Jesus. Of course, he was Spanish, and this helped a lot because they just about ruled the stove when it came to using the stove to cook. In this unit at that time, there were more Spanish guys than any other nationality, and if you were white or black, you had a long wait to be able to use the stove. We had no knives to cut up the food we had, and he showed me something that I will never forget. He took the top of a can and folded it in half and used that to cut things up, and I never would have thought of doing that. After that when I ran out of laundry detergent, I took a tuna can and took a nail and banged holes in it and ground state soap up to use as detergent to wash my clothes. But this is something that you kept outside and would never let a CO see you using it because it would be back behind the wall again because they would think it was a weapon. One of the new guys that came in with me just got lugged. There was an empty bed in the room I was in, so I asked the CO if this other guy I cooked with could move into the same room as I was in, and to my surprise, they allowed it. I cooked with this guy all the time. It made it so much easier when it came to making food together, so now it was two of us using the stove. But it drove the Spanish guy Louie crazy, and he hated it, and he made life even worse for me just by doing stupid things when I left the room.

The other guys name was Johnny. I changed his name as I'm writing this. He seemed like a good guy. At last I had someone I could carry on a conversation with. I really needed to find someone that I could talk to because my last two buddies were still at Concord waiting for their moves to other jails, I think. Of course I asked him what he was in for, and he said, "Drugs, just like you." I got five years also, but I couldn't understand why he didn't get a mandatory sentence. He just said, "If you have money, you can change your sentence, but it's going to cost you big bucks." And he had lots of it. After hearing what he was telling me, I knew I really did the wrong thing. I was doing five years but didn't have a pot to piss in if I sold drugs like he did. Maybe I could have bought my way out of jail or had my sentenced reduced as he did. This guy John was from New Bedford also. He was a big drug dealer. He sold at a bar I knew very well. His rivals got mad at the amount of stuff he was selling and ratted him out to the narcs. I don't know why he was even selling drugs, because he had a great job, had a real beautiful wife. All I say is why. Besides, he was a pretty smart guy as well.

Well, again I had someone I could cook with. He supplied a lot of food we cooked. I didn't have to pay for food as long as I cooked it, and he could afford it because he made a lot of money from selling drugs. Even the job that he had would be waiting for him when he got out of this hellhole. Plus because he couldn't cook to save his life, he always ate out when he was on the street. He would buy the food all the time. He worked out of Boston; he worked on the trains, made real good money with his father just hooking up the trains. The company he works for was going to wait till he gets out. The boss told him his job will be there no matter how long it takes. I know I would never get the chance to get my job back as much as I loved it. The cops made sure of that by dirtying my name real good through the newspapers saying I was selling drugs to the students, because that's the way they are. Of course, the narcs checked into it and found out after interviewing all the students that they had no idea what I was doing, but of course they never put that in the papers.

As I was cooking one day, I had someone tap me on the back. It was another guy I met in my travels in another jail that I was at. This guy's name was Neff. I already knew what he was in for, what he did, and it didn't bother him in the least. He did the time with a smile. This guy took money from his mother-in-law, explained to her that he was going to invest it in stock market, make more money for their retirement, for them not to worry about it. He invested it in some stock deals that started to lose all their money. He took a lot of it out, put it into buying old cars, thought he could sell old cars, make her money back that he lost, and it got to the point that he just started to spend their money on all kinds of stuff he wanted and not thinking about it not being his money. So he just spent it like it was his own on things that he so-called needed, then he just had the old cars to fall back, but it got to the point that he didn't want to sell them; he wanted to keep them. So after a while he lost his wife's parents' money, which was their retirement savings, but he still had the old cars to put back together to try to make their money back.

He never told them about the cars, didn't tell them that all their money was gone for a long time until they started to ask him questions about it. When they found out, they pressed charges, and he hired a lawyer to see if he could get out of jail or beat the charges, but he ended up getting five years also but for fraud, embezzlement, had to do the time. It really didn't bother him being in jail. He really didn't care that he lost their money either. I guess to him doing time was better than paying the money back. The strange thing about it is his wife stood right by his side through it all. My wife knew about everything I did, of course, but said she didn't know a thing about it. She left me to be with a wannabe guitar player, a cokehead, and just let me rot in jail.

All the money this guy had he never put in a penny for any of the food we would cook in the unit, but he liked to eat it. He was a real cheap bastard. This guy would go for visits all the time, would smuggle in cigarettes from the visiting room, sell them in the unit for watches, all kinds of jewelry that the guys would have in jail when they came in. I couldn't believe the stuff these guys would give up for cigarettes. This stuff was real good jewelry. A lot of it was gold. He would put it on and bring it back to his father on visits so he could bring it all home for him. He said that he would sell it when he got home. This guy was even making money while he was in jail. The COs caught on to him when he started to bring in McDonald's food in after a visit because it stank up the whole unit. You knew what type of food it was when you smelled it. After that they started to watch him. He eventually got caught with three packs of cigarettes. Right after that they shook down the room I was in, thought I had something to do with it. The UPPS put me through hell because they thought I was part of it. Of course, he was lugged out of the unit and put behind the wall, but he probably didn't give a damn because of all the gold he got out of the unit. He made out real good. I saw it all before he got caught.

When I came back from the job that they assigned me, the unit was real quiet, then the end of the day came. When they all were back, it got real noisy as usual, but a lot quieter than all the other places I was at. The COs were just as bad as all the other places, all pieces of shit. I couldn't stand any of them. I would keep to myself and just talked to them when they asked me questions. One of the Cos came up to me when I was writing a letter and said, "Is this what you do on the outside?"

I said, "No, I ran a body shop."

Then he said, "Was it just part-time while you were selling cocaine to little kids or what. Don't think you're going to be just sitting around writing letters all day, doing nothing all day. I'll find a job so you don't have time to write so many letters." He came back to talk to me about an hour later and said, "I found a job for you. The grounds officer needs a guy. You know how to use a shovel rake, don't you?"

I said, "Probably better than you." What a look I got from him.

He looked at me and said, "We are not going to get along, are we? You start your job tomorrow, hard labor, I'll make sure of that."

I met the grounds officer the next day. Of course, what a piece of shit he was. He was a real slob, really fit the part as well. It was like he hadn't changed his clothes for a week. I said to myself, How do they place an ad in the paper when looking for guys to be COs? They must put in the ads: must be an asshole, a real piece of shit. That must cover it all. No other requirements needed. He started off on the right foot. He was all that, a real asshole. He started off by saying, "You're going to pay for what you did on the street, pay real good." I said, "Here we go again." He said this because he looked like he hadn't worked for a living in the last twenty years, fat, always sitting down, just yelling all the time and belittling you every chance he got, as all the COs did, so I was used to it. He started off by saying that I was going to be cutting the grass; we had to go to the cemetery first, clean up around the stones, and trim all the weeds because it was overgrown quite a bit after the winter. When we got there, we unloaded all that we had, rakes, mowers shovels, weed whackers. He said, "Just use all the things that we brought here to clean up the place, get it done today." What a mess. As I walked onto the ground, it was real soft, mushy, and you would feel your feet just sink into the ground as you walked on it. If you were able to stand the smell, which was real bad, throughout the graveyard, you had to remove the poison ivy all over most of the stones.

This place, as I remember it, was real creepy. It looked like something out of a horror story by the best horror story writer ever. I was shocked when the CO just left us there, drove off, and said, "I'll be back around lunchtime. This place should be real clean by then."

I said to myself, "Yeah right."

He came back, brought some food from the chow hall, and said, "Let's finish this off today. Get off your asses, get it done." Of course, what he brought us to eat was all shit food, but being in jail, you get used to it real fast or starve. When they gave this job to inmates, they called it grounds, supplied us with no boots or good shoes to do the job. When I got back to the unit, my feet were all wet, were covered with mud from walking around cutting the grass with the lawn mower, removing the ivy. When we left the graveyard, it looked a lot better than it did. All he said to us was that we could have worked a little harder, said to us this was supposed to be a quick job, not an all-day job. But the smell in the cemetery was real bad. It's something I will never forget, the smell, the feeling of my feet sinking in the ground. I was there all day long breathing in that nasty smell like something was rotting. Gee, I wonder what. Most of the guys liked it a lot because they found some cigarettes. They were smoking like champs and was able to get some back into the unit also and were able to sell them to make a decent canteen.

The next day when they called grounds, the CO was right there to pick up the guys to work what they called grounds. He started to assign all the jobs that the guys were expected to do for that day. Of course, I had the small mower to cut close to the building because the large lawn mower couldn't get in those places. When I got done edging around the buildings like I was expected to do, I brought the lawn mower back to the garage. He came right over to me and said, "What are you doing back? I know you're not done cutting the grass at the unit."

I said, "Yes, I am."

Then he said, "Right. Throw the lawn mower in the back of the truck." He said that he wanted to check out what I did and see if I did what he told me to do. We got back to the unit. He said, "I thought you were done? You're not even close to being done."

I said, "I did what you told me to do all around the building because the large mower couldn't get into those places."

He looked at me and said, "I wanted you to cut the grass, meaning the whole unit, not just edge around the building."

I then said, "You want me to cut all the grass?"

He said, "Yes. I mean the whole compound."

I said, "You know how long it will take me to do that with a small mower?"

He turned to me and said, "You have some place to go? I thought you have five years to serve."

Pure hate came to me at that time. I could feel my body heating up with hate, and he said, "Do you have a problem with that?" I just said no. He said to me, "That's what you're going to do every week, so get used to it." I just stood there looking at the field. He said, "If you don't want to do it, I'm sure I can find someone at the unit to take your place." I just started cutting the grass again. He got into his truck and drove off I guess back to the garage. I just went into my trance state then started to cut the grass again. I said, "It's better than being back at the unit." It was a beautiful day, nice, hot. I just let my mind drift off, wishing I was at home, cutting my own lawn, but no, I'm at this fuckin' place cutting the grass for these motherfuckers. While I was cutting the grass, all I was thinking about was hoping that my wife would wait for me to get out of this place, and we could make another go of it and really know that I would be a different person. It's so weird. Even after all she had done to me, I would still have taken her back.

This field was so large that you probably could land a plane in it with room to spare. This CO just brought out the hate in me, made me take a bad attitude toward him, just like the other CO I had to deal with. Damn it, just like all that I met so far. It was just like they made a mold of all the COs, and they all acted all the same, and they all knew how to bring out the hate in me that I had toward them. I had about a quarter of the grass done. I saw an inmate drive a riding lawn mower to where I was, and he said, "The grounds CO sent me here to cut the large areas because it will take you too long to cut with a small mower."

I looked at him and asked, "Were you cutting grass all day?"

He said, "Yes, why?" I told him that the mower that he was using was broken. I couldn't do this field with it until it was fixed.

He said, "Even if it was broken, there are three more just like this in the large garage, two riders that you stand on a plate in the rear."

I just laughed and said, "That ground CO is a fuckin' cocksucker."

When the CO came to pick us up to bring us back to the garage then back to the unit, he held me back and said to me, "Don't give me an attitude because I'll make life a living hell for you, even worse than you have it now." Then he said, "And don't look at me like you are ready to rip my face off. Take that look off your face."

I said to him, "I'm sorry, it's the only face I have, this is how I look."

When I got to the unit, I was reprimanded for what I said to the grounds CO. If I said anything like that again, I would get lugged behind the wall to spend my time till I got another move to a different prison. This fuckin' CO wasn't through with me as of yet. The next day came, and he put me on ground duty digging holes, picking up garbage around the unit, as he got into the truck. He said, "Leave the cigarettes alone or you will be lugged like the last guy that was doing this job." I started to pick up all the garbage. As I got to the Dumpster, I found two packs of cigarettes on the ground unopened. Right away I knew it was a setup; it was a plant. That's why I was put on grounds that day, because of what I said to the CO back at the unit. Between both COs fuckin with me, I know they were trying to get me back behind the wall, but they failed badly. To this day, I don't know if it shows up on my face, but I hate these cocksuckers with all my heart. What they have done to me I will carry this for the rest of my life as I know this because I'm writing about it even after I've been out for a while.

As I was walking around, I noticed across from the field where I was mowing there were three guys with two riding mowers, one trimming around the building with a weed whacker just where I was told to do a couple of days before. I just shook my head and just kept doing what I was told to do. It just burned me up inside. When I was picking up garbage on the side of the street another inmate walked over to me from the other side of the street where he was, picking up garbage, said that he wanted to change bags with me and gave me a new bag. I just took it and went on with what I was told to do. The grounds CO was sitting in the parking lot and had seen what was going on. He came racing over and said that it was lunchtime, for me to go to lunch and to come right back to the same spot that I'm at now and finish what I had started. I didn't even look at him; I just said, "Okay, I will do that." Off he drove, and I just left all the lawn equipment there and went to the mess hall to eat.

As I started to walk to the chow hall, I looked over and saw that all the holes that I dug a couple of days earlier, they were still there. There were no poles being put in their place, and he said that it had to get done that day. The grounds CO said that he needed the holes dug because he was going to put up another fence, and the poles had to be put in right away. Every day we worked for this CO, we would work sometimes a little after two o'clock, sometimes earlier. It depended on how he felt that day, I guess, and if he was going through DTs. Well, after lunch he came back to where he told me to go after I had lunch. He said that he had one more thing for me to do before he brought me back to the unit. I just said, without looking at him, "Okay."

He brought me back to where I dug the holes and told me to cover them back up because he changed his mind about the fence he was going to put there. He just told me to cover them up again. As I was covering them, he just stared at me while doing it and said that he saw what I did with the bag exchange, said that my so-called friend was gone, was now behind the wall, said he was wishing he could have got me too. I just did what he told me to do and shut my mouth. So I did all that hole digging for nothing. He just did it to bust my balls. As he was taking me back to the unit, there was another guy cutting the grass across from where I was with a rider mower. He stopped just to yell at him, told him to get the lead out, work faster. He wasn't going back till he finished cutting the grass, as he told me one time or another.

The CO turned, looked at me, and said, "That guy will do anything I tell him to do, will never ask a question, will never give me a dirty look no matter what I tell him to do."

I had no answer for him. I think he was waiting for one. I just said, "I'm not going to give into it, get lugged."

As I walked into the unit, the sergeant said to me, "You're still giving the grounds CO a hard time."

I looked at him and said, "I never talked to him all day long. Did he tell you that he tried to set me up with two packs of cigarettes today?"

He said, "I know, we got someone else for that."

Every one of these COs stick together even if they know the CO that they are sticking up for is an asshole. They just do it. It's just their way. They all just stick together when it comes to fucking with all the inmates, and they do this every chance they get. In a way I think I'm just like them because I think a good number of the guys I live with in here are fuckin' assholes. I think and look at a lot of them and feel the same as most of these Cos probably do. But the real big problem is that most of the COs are always trying to outweigh each other, trying their best, sometimes going out of their way just to fuck with some of the inmates. Also a very good number of them belong here. By the looks of it, a good number of them are very happy being here because a lot of them don't have anyone on the outside to tell them when to shit, shower, shave. A lot of them need this, to be told when they should take care of themselves. Why? Because a lot of them are smelly, dumb bastards and can't think for themselves and need to be held by the hand and told when and how to do things. The only thing they can do without being told not to do is jerking off to any paper that has a woman on it, even if it's a cartoon version. You wouldn't believe what these guys jerk off to in the showers. The only thing that is real bad is that I have no choice but to put up with their shit every single day and sometime over stupid stuff like the cooking stove, places where you sit. I just ignore most of them. I just look at them and tell them to leave me the fuck alone. That's what I want, just to be left alone, go into my own world.

Well, most of the guys I talk to in here come to me to write letters for them as they did in the other places that I was at. Sometimes it gets into conversations, and this is what they tell me. They start off by telling me how they got caught, what they did wrong to get caught, what they will do not to get caught the next time they do it. But the next time they do it, they say how they are going to make all kinds of money by doing differently, live rich for the rest of their lives, how they are going to fool the cops the next time. A lot of them can't even write their names or even write a letter, but they are going to fool the cops. (Yeah right.) These days, there are too many guys that just spill their guts when they are just brought into a police station, as my cousin always did. I don't even think about doing any other type of crime that way. To me, there will never be a next time for me to end up in a place like this. The only way I would end up in a place like this is if someone hurts my family, then it's a different story, but I know there will never be another cocaine case against me ever again. I don't even want to ever look at that shit again. It ruined my life. Don't get me wrong, in here I have met a lot of decent guys, but the assholes outweigh them by far. This is including the COs, in which I can't even come up with any names bad enough to describe them, so I just use what I have described them in what I'm writing.

I was downstairs waiting for the grounds CO to pick me up to go to work doing useless things along with getting humiliated every day, looking like those bobbleheads guys that people have in the backs of their car windows, in which the heads just wobble around when you drive. The grounds CO finally came to pick me up for work. Right off the bat, he said, "Are you ready to listen to me and do what I tell you to do or what.?"

I just looked at him with my body heating up, hate going through my whole body, and said yes, but I felt like saying to him, "I'd rather do what?" I looked at him and said, "I'm not used to this type of life, and I'm having a real hard time adjusting to it, but I'm here to work, and I'd rather be doing this instead of being in the unit." But what I wanted to say was, "I'd rather be here than being at the unit with all the scum."

He overheard me say scum and looked at me and said, "Who are you calling scum?" He started to slow the truck down, looked at me, then I said to him that it had nothing to do with him. Then he said, "Who."

I just said, "I'm talking about some of the guys at the unit."

He said, "You call them scum? And does that make you better than them?"

I said, "Damn right and I know this with all my heart."

He then said, "You're a fuckin' drug dealer, and you sell drugs to kids. Of course, you think you're different than them or better than them, which one?"

I said, "Both. I never sold any drugs to any kids. I wasn't a bigtime drug dealer as you think. It's more to it than you think, or even more than you could comprehend." I just looked at him and said, "I don't want to go there and don't really want to talk about it. I'm just here to work on the grounds with you and do what you tell me to do," and he then said, "Okay," and I added, "Sir."

He started to drive at normal speed, brought me to the back to the parking lot of the prison, and gave me two bags and said, "I want you to pick all the trash and put garbage in one and cigarettes butts in another."

I said, "Okay, will do as you tell me." As I looked around, this place was loaded with cigarette butts, and they were scatted all over the parking lot. I saw a couple of COs who were smoking put them out in coffee cups, but a lot were just thrown all over the ground. I put all garbage I picked up in the same bag and didn't do as he told me because I didn't want him to say that I was separating them to bring them back to the unit. Again I had to watch every move I made, and by not separating the cigarettes, I think I was just again thinking ahead. Again thinking that he is trying to set me up again. I didn't trust this CO at all and watched everything he told me to do. This CO was always smoking in front of me and just throwing the half-smoked butts on the ground and did ask me if I smoked and I said never. I said to him, "Can I ask you a question and without you getting upset with the question that I'm going to ask you?"

He said, "It depends on the question."

I just said, "Forget it then."

We were just on the way and ready to pick up the next guy and must have been bothering him bad not knowing what I was going to ask him, and he said, "Go ahead and ask me that question that you were going to ask me." I asked if we could pick up the next guy up first so he can hear what I'm going to ask you just so you wouldn't say I said something to you that you didn't like. We picked up the next guy, and I asked him if he could listen to what I'm going to tell him.

"I'll do the jobs you ask me to do, and I don't smoke cigarettes, so there is no need for you to think I'm going to smoke them or sell them." I told this CO that I just put in for a revise and revoke to see if my sentence can be overturned, and I don't want anything to jeopardize that, so I really can't do anything that might mess up my chances.

He looked at me and said, "I didn't know that you didn't smoke."

"I did tell you that, and could you stop trying to set me up? It's very noticeable." I looked at him and said, "I just want do my time and go home and stay out of the unit as much as possible because I can't stand being in the unit."

He said that he fucks with every inmate that works for him, and he will never change for anyone and then said, "You think I'm going to stop with you? There is no chance in hell I'm going to stop, so get used to it."

I said, "Okay, I just wanted to let you know I just want to work and try not to do anything stupid and try to get home sooner if possible, and I'm not going to fuck with you in any way."

He dropped the grounds crew at the unit, and of course he went into the office to talk to the other COs and was laughing, probably telling them how he's fucking with me, and it looked like they were all having a laughing fit. The inmate that heard the conversation I had with the CO said, "You're trying to converse with that fucking asshole? Don't even try, no one talks to him at all, even the COs hate him."

Every time that I got back to the unit, I would clean up and sit down and write a letter to my wife and daughter to let them know that I'm okay and to tell them stories of what goes on this place and sometimes I call them, but I'm always worrying about the bill of the phone calls I was making. I feel so lost it feels like I'm just wandering around to nowhere, more like I'm in a maze. I feel so lost, so useless. But this time I was sitting at one of their round cafeteria-type tables in the day room and didn't want to call my wife and daughter, but not calling them was like having a drug addiction. It's just something I wanted to do all the time. As I was sitting at the table, this young CO named Tweet came up to me and said, "The grounds CO hates you really bad, and he wants to get you out of this place because he said that you're a smart-ass. I also think that you are."

I then said, "Take me out of grounds and put me somewhere else because there are a lot of other guys that can work with that CO picking up cigarettes, digging holes, and covering them back up. So just pick out some stupid motherfuckers in this room to take my place, it won't bother me a bit."

The next day when the crew was picked up and of course I was dropped off at the same place and was told to do the same job, pick up garbage and put the cigarettes in a separate bag. But this time I did what he told me to do and put all the cigarettes in a separate bag; of course I was waiting for the IPPS to come bust me for doing this, but it didn't happen. As I was cleaning up, I saw another inmate come over to me and start to pick up around me. I asked him if the CO sent him over to where I was. He just said no, said that he was here to get some butts.

"I'm a smoker, and this is the best place to get them." He looked at me and said, "Do you take them for yourself?"

I said, "I don't want any of them, and if you want, you can take my bag, and there are quite a few butts in it. Just trade with me if you want. I'm a nonsmoker."

The grounds CO was just across the street in the parking lot, and I told him this, but he still wanted to change bags. Again this is what he wanted to see, another inmate switching bags with me, and I told him not to do it, and he didn't listen. Well, of course, he came racing up like he was a narc making a big bust. He got out of his van and said, "Don't think I didn't see what was going on and what you were doing by trading bags. This is the second time I saw you do this."

I said, "What are you talking about? If he traded bags with me, I didn't know about it. I put the bag on the ground, and what he did, he did it on his own."

He said, "It's when you put your bag down to pick up something else. I saw him trade garbage bags with you."

I told the CO, "I don't smoke, and to me, it's just garbage. If he traded bags with me, it's on him."

Then he said, "Now I know how the cigarettes are getting back into the unit. You two guys have a system worked out, and you thought you could keep doing this and not get caught." Then he looked at the other guy and said, "I've been watching you smoke all day long. Just kept an eye on you." He just looked at me and said, "You two get in the van. You both are going back to the unit and strip-searched, and if they find anything on either of you, you're gone. Whoever they find cigarettes on is going back behind the wall, gone, do you understand?" He looked at me and said, "I hope it's you, Mr. Smart-ass who has an answer for everything."

The CO at the unit asked me if I had anything on me in the form of cigarettes. I said, "No, and all the other stuff he's saying about me is just a figment of his imagination. The CO said that I was helping this guy who came back with me sell cigarettes in the unit. This is not true. He's just out to get me. He's just pissed off because I ask him questions about the jobs that we are doing, and he doesn't answer me, and I won't ask him any questions about the job again. Then I just do what he tells me to do for the rest of the day and don't ask him any more questions, just do what I have to do in the form of work. All he wants is a bunch of puppets for workers who ask no questions and just work with their heads up their asses as he has and don't really care if anything is done right. I think even if it is done wrong, it's okay with him unless he has a hair across his ass. I just think he enjoys having that power over all the guys that has to work for him, and it gives him a hard-on being able fuckin' guys over that fat drunken bastard."

I told the CO in charge, "I know whatever I say you're going to agree with him, so I don't know where this is going to get me but behind the wall, back to high security."

He looked at me and said to me, "We will see after I look at everything he will say to me."

I also told him, "I know he just wants me to get lugged out of here. I've been asking for a job change for a while now, and they just say that there aren't any other jobs available. I did ask him if there was a place in the mechanics garage. He said he will check and let me know, because you have to have a job to stay in this minimum."

Well, he said, "We have to strip search you, and we will go from there. If you don't have any cigarettes on you, we will get you a job change, okay. If we find any cigarettes on you, you're out of here, so if you have anything on you, give it to me now."

I said, "I have nothing on me," as I told him so many times before. They strip-searched the other guy and found cigarettes on him, and the other guy said that he changed bags with me, and I didn't know what he had done. He told the CO that he was getting for anyone in the unit who wanted cigarettes what they wanted in exchange for some canteen. When it came to me, I had my own way of getting cigarettes in. When I would find them, I would leave them on the outside, and when I went out for my everyday walk, I would sit on the bench and reroll them outside with the paper from the toilet paper rolls and stick it together with coffee creamer. Even before I was done rolling them, all of what I had was gone, and I would collect my fee in canteen at the end of the week.

As I walked into the unit. I just dealt with three guys and never had a problem with any of them. This day after I came back from my walk, the guy named Jeff that just came in and was trading cigarettes for jewelry was in the office handcuffed to the bench. He was caught with three packs of cigarettes and was lugged. For the time that he was there, he made out real good trading cigarettes for gold watches or anything made of gold, and I know when his time was up, he made a good amount of cash. The CO came up to me and said that they were waiting for an opening in the mechanic shop working on the transport vehicle and said that I would be there very soon and away from the grounds guy whom I hated so much. But little did this CO know I hated him just as much as I hated the grounds CO. Told me they were all the same. The grounds CO didn't say much to me from that day on. He just threw his little digs at me, and I wouldn't pay any attention to him, and I knew this went right up his ass, and the rest of the time that I was there, he kept me on the rider mower, cutting the grass around the unit. I just about never said a word to him unless I had to because I knew he would make a big thing out of it, so the less said, the better it was. One day he pulled right up to me and said, "Get into the truck. I got to take you home." I was done in seconds and just waiting to go back to the unit, thinking that my so-called wife had done something with the attorney and I was going home. I just can't tell you how excited I was.

The CO said, "You're in a rush to go back to the unit."

I turned to the CO and said, "You told me that I was going home."

He said, "Ya, the unit, that's home to you." This fuckin' asshole started to drive me back to the unit and said, "You will be home soon."

I really thought I was really going home. I looked at him and said, "That's not my home. My home is in Acushnet."

He said, "Well, that's not the home you're going to," and he started to laugh at me. On the way back, he asked me if I owned my home. I said yes, and he said, "You did well for yourself selling drugs to little kids." Then he said, "That's hard to believe that you own your own home. Did you make a lot of money selling drugs?"

Then I said, "That wasn't right what you said to me about going home."

He then said, "Now I know what to say to you to get you pissed off."

I just shut my mouth and didn't say a word until I got back to the unit. Then in front of the sergeant I told him what he said when he got me into the van. He looked at him and said, "Yes, I did tell him that he was going home, and that's where he's at." He made it look like I was really going home, and it was a bullshit lie, and the sergeant just looked at him. He looked at him and said, "All I asked him was if he owned his own home, and he said yes," but he never told him all the other things he said that I said. He was a slob and didn't take care of himself, and I knew he was a drunk because I could smell it on his breath in the morning. It stank real bad, like he drank before he came into work, and the van carried the odor of his breath and body odor. I guess they call that a booze freshener. I kind of knew he didn't own his own home because he spent most or all his money probably on booze, and he looked all that. But he did say something that hit me hard. He said, "At least I'm not doing time, and you're in here for the next five years."

BUSTED

I looked at him and said, "You're here till retirement." I know what I said to him went right over his head, and the CO behind the desk just started laughing at him, and it felt good for a change. I wouldn't have said it if there wasn't another CO present, and I'm very surprised they let me say what I said. Then the CO behind the desk said, "You don't work at grounds anymore. You start to work at the mechanic shop tomorrow. You got your job change." I was glad that they gave me a job change, and I was hoping that the guys at the mechanic shop were not like the grounds CO. I needed the job because I was making a whole eight dollars a week, and I needed soap and some food products so I could skip some of the meals that in my eyes were saying that they were not edible. I ate a lot of tuna and peanut butter and learned how to make a lot of rice meals that I still cook today, and people ask me where I learned to cook rice like I did. I just say "In jail," and they just say "Right" and laugh. Lot of people look at me when I say that and just carry on laughing. I really think they think that I'm kidding, but that's when it stops. After what I said to the CO from grounds, this CO named Tweet told me that they were thinking of lugging me but changed their minds. This was because of what I said to the grounds CO. This was the same CO who told me to watch what I said to the grounds CO and what I did when I was working with the grounds crew. A lot of the COs in Bridgewater didn't like him either because he was a drunk. It showed on him. After I got back from the mechanic shop and it turned out to be not that bad, but I had to keep in mind that they were not my friends, and they were COs and were all the same. They all stick together; I've got to remember that.

The day came to an end, and I just hated to work for these motherfuckers, and when I got back to the unit, I had mail, and I noticed that it was from the lawyer that my wife hired for me. It said that I was going to court at the end of the month. I was as happy as a pig in shit. I said, "This is what Boston lawyers can do." This was all I thought about all month long and couldn't wait to go to court. All month I was thinking that I was going home and he had found a loophole, and I kept saying, "I will never look at drugs ever again." I just want to live my life back and be with my family again, especially see if I could change my wife's mind about the guy she was seeing. I never told her that I knew about her messing around. I always kept it to myself until now. In my mind I was drifting off, thinking that I couldn't wait to hold my wife again and hug my daughter and grandson. So strange of me even after all my wife had done to me, I never let the bad things that she did to me change my feelings for her, stupid bastard that I was. Now I just ripped a month off the calendar. It seemed like it would never come to an end. I just thought I had a lot more to go. Now think about it and just think, if you were in jail and confined to one place as I was, you would also see how long it takes for time to go by, as I found out. It gets even worse, especially when you're in a fucked-up place like this and watching all these guys do fucked-up things to each other all day long.

Well, I watched day after day come up and go by, and when the day came, I was ready to go to court all dressed up and was waiting for transportation to come by to bring me into court. Of course, transport COs came in and handcuffed me by the rests and legs chains like I was a murderer going to the gas chamber. I was in a minimum prison. And I was no threat to anyone. I was thinking I was finally going to see the lawyer my wife hired for me. All I kept saying was, "He's from Boston and he's going to get me out of this place because he's from Boston." As I got into the car, I was told that I was going to Barnstable for the hearing, and the COs from the unit said good luck and started to laugh while looking at me. This was January 8, 2002. I was going into court for my revise and revoke and was hoping that they didn't give me more time than what I already had. The transport guy said, "You must have a real good lawyer because not many lawyers like to go to Barnstable for hearing." I asked why, and he paid me no mind, and it made me wonder why. Then they said, "Whoever goes to court in Barnstable always gets more time added to their sentence. They take no shit from anyone, and they pass harsh sentences just about every time, especially when it's a drug crime. You better have a very good lawyer." He asked me what my lawyer's name was. I told him, "Mr Bigfish," and he said that he was a real good lawyer. They said that they see him in court, and he was very good at what he does, and they have seen some guys just walk right out of the courtroom. He said, "Maybe it be you. Think about it. You could be at home with your family tonight, eating supper with them tonight."

I said, "I hope so."

These fuckin' guys are just like COs, and what they said was going through my head for a few minutes. Then it hit me. Were these guys just fuckin' with my head? I was going along with them because I wanted to go home so bad. At this time they could have said, "Your lawyer presented a good case, you can just go home to your family," and I would have believed them. One of them turned and asked me how much I paid him to represent me, and I said, "I just gave him five thousand to start with and will pay him more if he says I owe him more," and then it got real quiet. As we got to the courthouse, I couldn't wait to get into the courthouse, out of the car, and I had to use the toilet. I told the transport guys I had to use the toilet, and they said, "We have to bring you into the courthouse and into a cell to wait for them to call your case."

Well, I was there for a long time, and the transport guys came and said to me that the date was changed, and they were not going to hear my case today. They said the jail was notified about the change, and we didn't know about it until we were arrived at the courthouse. "We brought you into the courthouse because we went for coffee, and you had to use the toilet.

I said to them both, "You knew that it was going to be continued and didn't tell me, or were the two of you just fuckin' with me with the story you were telling me about the guy who just walked out of the courtroom." The two transport drivers just started to laugh and said, "Yeah." I just put my head down and shook it from side to side. I said that was a rotten thing to do to a guy. The guy in the passenger seat turned and said with a smile on his face, "That's just too bad. You may think twice before you do the crime again."

I said to myself, You piece of shit. I hope you die a miserable death, or maybe someone will cut your worthless throat or even better cut your balls off and stick your dick in your mouth. Pure hate was running throughout my body, and I couldn't do a damn thing about it. I watched them make a fuckin' joke about it. At that time, all my good thoughts went right down the drain, and I went right into depressed mood, but I still had so much hate going through my body, thinking I had to tolerate these assholes all the way back to the unit. What these guys did was make a big joke out of me.

As I was sitting in the back seat, I just stared at the backs of their heads and wished I could shoot them both in their head or wish the car would flip over and kill all of us. Then the driver CO would say on his last breath, "Looks like we're all not going to be eating supper with our families tonight."

Then out of nowhere, the driver said to me, "At least it was a day out of jail, and you went for a nice lone ride down the Cape." I said that I needed to use the bathroom, and he said that they don't let convicts use public restrooms while being transported and that I would have to wait.

The smart-ass passenger said, "I would let you use this cup to piss in, but you're handcuffed, and we are not allowed to uncuff you. We are just transport guys."

One of them turned to me and asked if they could stop at a Kentucky Fried Chicken place because he was hungry and then said, "Why am I asking you, you're a fuckin' convict."

One of the guys went in to get food for them to eat in the car, and as he got into the car and sat down, he said to me, "Bet you haven't smelt this in a long time. Smell it good because this is the closest you are going to get to it."

Oh, the smell was killing me. I haven't had any outside food in a long while like for at least a year, and the smell was like tasting it.

The passenger said to me, "I'll eat slowly so the smell lingers, and you really know what you're missing being in jail and won't do anything wrong ever again."

As they got finished eating, he turned and said, "I can't finish what I have, and I don't like the thighs and neither does my partner, and you can't have it, but look at it this way, at least you got a chance to smell it." Then he left the car and threw it into the garbage. He said, "The reason we do this to guys like you is because you will think twice before you commit another crime and remember this day," and he laughed at me. These motherfuckers were there for at least forty-five minutes talking and joking around and knew that I had to use the toilet, and they just didn't give a damn. They don't know what it's like to be in chains, sitting in one spot for a long period of time. This little episode will be with me also for the rest of my life and the cop's voice saying over and over again "Doesn't it smell good" and "Look at what I'm going to throw away." This is just some of shit you have to put up with when you're doing time in jail, and everyone thinks that you're a real bad person, but sometimes you get caught up in the mix.

When we got back to the unit, the COs in the office were laughing as I walked in and said to me that it was to be continued, and by the looks of it, they knew before I left in the morning that it was canceled. After that, I went to the restroom, and I called my so-called lawyer, and the secretary said that he was in court, just like so many times before, and he would be up to see me very soon, that he was working on a murder case. I got ahold of my daughter to see if she could get a real date and if he could answer some of my letters. I tried so hard to talk to him on the phone, but you only have so many minutes, and the phone hangs up automatically.

The next time I talked to my daughter, she said that my next date was on February 4, 2002, and it was on a Monday, but it was just for him to talk to the prosecutor about my case. At this time I was trying to get in touch with my wife a couple weeks prior to me going into court to see if she could find out what was going on with my case, but she told me that she was working a lot of overtime, and it was very hard for her to, but she will try. I kind of knew this was a bullshit story just to shut me up and knew she wouldn't even try and her intention was to let me rot in here. But who knows, maybe she was working overtime by taking her boss to bed, and I wouldn't put it past her to do so as long he would supply her with some cocaine. But she was free as a bird, and I stuck out my neck for her, and I got five fuckin' years. Instead of three, she got two years of probation and walked away free as a bird right out of the courthouse and went out for dinner with my so-called best friend John, probably to fuck him for coke. She was on the outside looking in, and that's the way she wanted it. She had no intentions of trying to get me out of jail. She just told me what I really wanted to hear no more, just to shut me up. My wife told me in a conversation that we were having saying that

God doesn't sleep when it comes to people in need. I said to her, "I sure hope not because I hope he sees that I'm doing my time in hell right now."

I was still getting letters from someone on the outside telling me the things that he was doing to my wife, that he just got through fuckin' my wife in this old abandoned Fairhaven drive-in. Then he brought her to a strip club, and they kicked her out of the place because she was too drunk and couldn't stand up and was making a fool out of herself. He said that whole week that they were together all they did was spend money, do drugs, and fuck. Then to top it off, he wrote that I had a good wife, and he was doing what I couldn't do for her, like fuck the hell out of her. It was hard to believe she was partying and getting high all week long, and she didn't get thrown in jail after the cops caught her in the abandoned drive-in so-called pissing in the woods. She must have had a real good probation officer because the way she was partying and getting high, she should have come up with dirty urine, but nothing ever happened to her the whole time she was on probation. For sure it would have come up positive, and if she got on her knees doing what she did best, it may have changed from positive to negative very fast. This was one of her good points and what she was very good at.

My daughter tried to call my lawyer, and he was in court, so she wrote him a couple of letters, and he said in the letters that my wife was working, and she would make an appointment with him to talk about my case. My wife told me that she tried to do so when she got home from work. He wasn't in his office when she got home. They told my daughter that my wife missed appointments all the time to talk to the attorney and canceled all the time at the last moment. My daughter gave the secretary her telephone number and said, "Please call me first. His wife don't give a damn. To leave it to her, he will rot in jail." He called and told my daughter that the lawyer will be in touch with me shortly to discuss my case and not to put him off like my wife was doing. This is why you need someone on the outside to make phone calls because they are able to stay on the phone if it requires you to do so. My daughter finally got ahold of my so-called wife and told her that I had to talk to her and, if she could, spare some time to come up to see me. She told my daughter she will try to make it up to see me as soon as possible, how hard it was because she was working a lot of hours. So I took a chance and called my wife, and she answered the phone. I couldn't believe she answered the phone, and I asked her if she could come up to see me. I had some things I had to talk over with her. She said that she would be up on a Saturday afternoon and because she slept late. I expected her to say that that anyways.

At this time I knew the guy who was cleaning the visiting room, and it wasn't that bad of a place for a visit. He told me if I wanted any money for the inside, to just tell my wife to put it in a soda bottle, and he will bring it to me after the visit but for a small fee. There was this one older CO named Chapman, and out of the entire time that I was at Bridgewater, this Co that I met while being incarcerated was the best CO that I met the whole time that I was there. He was the only CO I met while being incarcerated that I can remember who treated me like a person. He was a real decent guy. I would tell him about the cars that I had and mention that I owned a Corvette, and he said that he owned two, and they were old ones. We got along real good, and we talked from time to time. When I walked into the visiting room, the CO was shocked to see me come up for a visit because my visits were long, far between. In other words, I never got any. That day that I was called for a visit, he kind of knew that it was my wife that came that day because I talked about her all the time, and in my eyes she was the most beautiful girl in the world. Isn't it so funny we all think our wife is the most beautiful woman in the world, and he just laughed. As soon as we sat down, he came over and took a picture of us both and gave it to me because the COs took all my pictures out along with some of my letters, especially when my daughter sent them to me. This is how some of my letters stating how and when this guy was fucking my wife disappeared. These Cos would just go through your stuff anytime they wanted. A lot of time they would chuckle when I walked past them. At this point I just kind of knew that they read my letters when they went through my stuff.

After he gave me the picture, he went back to his desk and sat down. The good part was that there was no one else in the visiting room, just my wife and myself. I was so glad to see my wife that it got to the point that I felt weird because I just couldn't stop staring into her eyes. Of course it was followed by me telling her how beautiful she was and how I missed her. As soon as we sat down, I sat sideways on the bench, and my wife opened my pants and started to give me a hand job. I just couldn't believe this was happening to me, and boy, did that clear my head. I have been without a woman for over a year and don't swing the other way, so Mary's palm was the next best thing. I asked the CO if we could go in the back room where the bathrooms were, and he said that we couldn't go at the same time. My wife told me that she said that she would give me a blow job, and I was just about out of my mind to hear something like that. I more or less asked the CO in a different way if I could go to the bathroom and said she needed to go too. He said, "I can't allow that," and he was closing his eyes to what she was doing on the bench to me; it was obvious. I gave him no disrespect and just said thanks as I looked at him. He then said if I were not married that he would never let what was going on go on. "It was just because you had not seen her at all since you have been here."

We went back to the bench, and she finished what she was doing so well. When it was over, she looked at me and said, "Do you feel better?" She always had a great way of saying that. By a woman saying anything like that to you in jail, believe me, it turned me on, and by her saying that I suddenly started to get sad because she would be going and I'd still be here. The way that she said it to me, I looked at her in a different way because at this point I had seen a big change in her and just wanted to go home even more. I wanted so much to ask her if the sex comments that I was getting in letters from some guy on the street were true, and I said no, I better not, because she might come up again and give me another hand job. This happened twice while I was in jail, and the second time it was cut short because just before I was ready to blow a load, the captain walked in and said "What are you doing?' and yelled "Turn around! Face front!" I was so pissed off at this fuckin' asshole that it would be hard to put into words how mad I was. It was such a long time since I had the touch of a woman, and this asshole walked in and spoiled it for me. You will never know how much you miss a wife or a girlfriend until they are gone. I was so much in love with her as I was with my daughter's mother that it killed me inside when it was time for her to leave to go back to Tom, Dick, and Harry. In my whole life I never loved any other woman like I love my wife. She made me very happy because she was also my best friend.

Now that I'm older I think maybe losing both of them was because I wasn't supposed to be happy in my life. Well, she looked at me and said it was time for her to leave because she had a lot to do on a Saturday because she worked all week. I knew it was a lie but had go with it.

When I was on the street, I knew a lot of girls, and I could have gone out with a lot of them, but my wife had some kind of hold on me, and I guess that's what they call some sort of a curse. Even after all the bad she had done to me, I don't know what she had over me, but I will never know. I guess it was the love I had for her. It wasn't just the physical part I was in love with. I think it was her soul, or should I just say just her. She looked a lot like my daughter's mother when she was young, and when I met her, I felt like I was bringing back the past, and we got along real good, and she could make Christmas feel like it was a holiday again, like when I was young.

In another conversation I asked her over the phone if she tried to talk to the attorney, and she said that she left a few messages, and he never returned her calls. Right there I knew she was lying because my daughter had told me prior what the lawyer had told her earlier. When she told me this, I didn't know which way to turn and who to believe, the lawyer or my wife. I felt so helpless inside because I couldn't do it myself, and in here your hands are tied, so all you can do is the time. Every time she came up to see me, she would tell me that she was going to wait for me to get out of this hellhole and carry on our marriage, but as I looked at her, I noticed a coldness in her eyes, and I noticed that she took off her wedding rings. I asked her why she wasn't wearing them, and she said that she forgot to put them back on after a shower. I knew this was another lie because when she took a shower, which was very seldom, they were always on her fingers, and for her to take a shower was like pulling teeth a lot of times. Many times before I would tell her "Please take a shower," and her response was "I took a sponge bath."

After the visit, the sergeant came up to me and asked me how things were going at the mechanic garage. I said, "Real good and it's better than working at the grounds job."

He said that he noticed that I was a teacher at a vocational school and said, "This would be right up your alley to work at the garage."

I just said, "There will never be a good job like that again in my life."

As I talked I told him that I owned my own body shop on the street and had a good business and made good money, and he said, "But you're a drug dealer, what was that, a front?"

"If you believe that I was a drug dealer and working at a school, you're as crazy as the cops were."

"But you were caught with a lot of coke."

"You would if you had a junkie for a wife."

I refused the mechanics job before, and I had to take it this time to get out of the grounds job. Staying there would only get me lugged. I was at the mechanics shop for a couple of weeks, and there was an older guy there named Pick, and he thought he knew everything about cars, and he was trying to teach me the way he did the jobs and just wanted me to do the job the way he did the jobs. To him, his way was the right way and didn't want it done any other way. I was upset with this but had to do everything the way he wanted it done. Every job that I did he had to check and make sure I did it right, to make sure I didn't do something to injure a CO, and that was because I was an inmate. It was like I was a student of his, and when I got a job done, he would say that I did it too fast and had and always wanted to take it back apart and see if I did something wrong. What he didn't know was I would never do anything to hurt anyone in a car that I fixed even though I couldn't stand a lot of the COs.

It got to the point that I didn't care anymore. I just wanted to stay away from the unit as much as possible just because of the scum

I had to look at in the course of the day. I would lots of times just go and sit on the outdoor bench they had and just put my hands on my head and just say too many crazy people in here. I started to watch everything I did because if I fucked up, they would press charges, and I could get more time added to my sentence and get sent behind the wall, and I wouldn't get a chance to see my wife and daughter again. It was at least a month before I was able to talk to my wife again, and the reason for that was she was working real hard at her job and most likely on her boss as well. Her boss wouldn't let up on her, and I expected her to say that was the reason she wasn't coming up to see me. Well, that's what I was hoping it was. Her visits were getting to be less and less, from once a week to twice a month to once a month, and her excuses were more common. Then I asked her if she wanted a divorce, and she said no and we will be able to work it out. She was just going through a difficult time at work. I asked her if I could call her more, seeing that she wasn't coming up to see me, and told her I needed to at least talk to her. She said yes that I could call. That ended up to be a joke. This went on for a while, but I had to tell her what days I was going to call her, and she would try being home to take my calls. It took me a while to get a phone to be able to call her on the night she expected me to call. I really wanted to hear her voice because it was mesmerizing to hear it because we used to talk a lot before I was incarcerated, and that was about everything we usually did in the course of the day.

Now think about what I'm writing about and think about it. Look at what I'm losing along with five years of my life. Is it worth it? When I was able to get one of the phones, her piece-of-shit brother answered the phone, and he said, "She went out with her friends and didn't want to wait for a jail call from you," as he said to me before. I got a hold of my wife later in the week, and she said that her brother really didn't know where she was and just assumed that I went out with my friend. It took a while, and the lies started to get more obvious, and there was no stop to them, but of course you put up with them and keep telling yourself you can deal with them. A week went by, and I got a hold of her again, and she said that she was coming up to see me, and of course I couldn't wait and just forgot about all the lies she was saying. Of course, you were told that you were going to get a visit, and of course, the weekend couldn't come fast enough, and you start to count the days down and then hours as you do for your time you have left to do. Being in jail counting is part of doing time. It's either counting to go home or counting down for a visit. This can be a big deal for you.

Well, Saturday came finally, and you're waiting for your name to be called for a visit, and it seems like an eternity, and then you hear your name, and they say "Visit," and you can't walk fast enough to the visiting room because you don't want to waste a minute, and it feels like the faster you get there, the longer you get be with her or whoever. It's like you're going on a date for the first time and you just can't wait to go somewhere with the girl you just met and don't want to keep her waiting. I entered the visiting room, and to me she's the most beautiful woman in the room, as my daughter's mother was when I met her. At this time, all I could do was just focus on just her and nothing else. It was like I was in a trance. As I walked into the visiting room, my eyes were just focused on her. She was standing next to the vending machine, and she asked me if I wanted something to eat, and I just said, "Yeah." I didn't really hear what she was asking me, and I just said "Yeah," and I was just so happy to see her. I walked up to where she was standing, and I just wanted to kiss and hug her so bad it hurt. As I got close to her, she had a bad odor to her, and I came to a stop and kissed her on the side of her face.

As I got close to her, I said to her, "I can smell you."

She said, "I just started my period, and it's real bad this month."

I said, "Yeah, I noticed that. I've been with you for quite a few years, and I've never smelled it like that before."

She said, "Is it real bad?"

Then as she turned, I wiped my lips off and had a chill run though my body. It was like she didn't wash up after sex. What the fuck! I was like get rid she just had this bad odor to her and it smelled really bad I had to stand back from her. Then she said, "You're not just saying that to me?"

I said, "Why would I just tell you that right out of nowhere?"

Then she said, "You can really smell it?"

I said, "Yeah, it's really bad. After this visit, you should go and take a bath."

When you're in jail, you can pick up smells really easy because of the guys you live with who just don't believe in showers. To me, it smelled like she just had sex in the car on her period, and it got all over her before she came in to see me, and it was hard to believe that she would do this knowing she was coming up to a visit. As I sat down across from her, I happened to look at her fingers as I always did and noticed that her wedding rings were still not on her fingers again along with all the others rings I bought her. As I questioned her about this before. The first thing that came to mind was that she sold them for cocaine to take care of her habit. Or maybe her new wannabe guitar rock star probably didn't want her to wear them. I had to bring it up and asked her where her rings were, and she gave a lame excuse and said that she left them in the bedroom after a shower, and the way she smelled, I just said, "Yeah right." After she came in smelling like she did, I would really believe she took a shower and left the rings in her bedroom after that? When her brother took over her bedroom at her dad's house, if there was any left behind of hers, her scum brother would have sold it. My wife's brother couldn't wait for my wife to move out so he could move into her room, and he couldn't move in fast enough. This piece of shit could never make a life of his own because he was a leech and sucked off everyone he could, as his sister also ended up to be. I was with her for so long that in my eyes she could never do any wrong, and I just put the conversation behind us but had tears in my eyes because I loved her so much.

At that time I was so happy to see her and kind of knew it wasn't going to last but tried to make the best of the time I had left with her. But I did remind her that she would never find another guy to love her like I loved her and to think about what I just said to her before she made her final decision of what she was going to do as time went on. She was there for just about an hour, and she was in a rush, like she had someone waiting in the car for her or she had some place she had to be at, and she was very nervous the whole time she was with me. I think she came up with someone, and the person she came up with was waiting for her in the car, and he was the one who fucked her on the way up to see me. I think some of the nervousness was also the drugs she was still doing even after we got caught with that fuckin' shit. I was thinking that when she took a bathroom break, she was snorting coke. I wouldn't put it past her. She was still sucking it up because there was a crust under her nose and lots of tissues in her pockets and in her hands also at all times. If she did have a guy in the car waiting for her, I hope it made him feel good by fuckin' my wife before she came in to see me. May he and her go to hell because he could have waited till after she left the visit before he fucked her. I hope it made him feel good (cocksucker). She just said that she will come up again when she had more time, and she had a lot to do that day, and all I got to ask her was if she got in touch with the lawyer. She said no, that he was never there. In turn, I said, "Please don't let me rot in here." I looked at her and said, "I'm still your husband."

She said "I would never do that to you" and said "See you soon," and I know bullshit, and she was just sugarcoating what she was saying to me. I had to wait at least five minutes till they got an okay from the CO at the gate to make sure I didn't jump in her car when she was leaving. I rushed back to the unit so I could see her through the window leave the parking lot in her car and to see if there was someone else in the car with her. All I could see was her car leaving, and it killed me to see her leave, but the smell was still in my head, and it was just that odor that stood with me throughout the night. After she left, I was in a real depressed mood knowing that she fucked someone before she came to see me and then left as fast as she came, and I told her to leave some money in the soda bottle and place it in the garbage for me to buy something from the canteen, and the guy that cleaned the visiting room will give it to me. All she left me was three damn dollars, and I just said, "What the fuck I can do with three fuckin' dollars?" She had over three thousand dollars of mine, not including my checks. I gave her and just couldn't understand what the problem was. At the end of my time in this fuckin' place, she must have given me five hundred dollars in all, and I was doing the time for both of us. Now I wish I let her do her time along with me. I stuck out my neck and said it was all me and she knew nothing at all about the drugs they found because I couldn't see her doing time. When the cops entered the house and went into the cellar, there she was with coke all around her, and I told them that she knew nothing about it. (Right.)

As I was sitting at the table writing a letter to my daughter, the sergeant came to me and asked if that was my wife that came in to see me. I just said "Yeah," and he said that she looked and smelled like a whore, and he could have fucked her for a chunk of crack cocaine, and she would beg for more. I just kept my temper, my mouth shut. I said to him, "Do you know what I think?"

In a louder voice he said, "What?"

"I think you're a fuckin' asshole for saying something like that to me!" Then as I got up to walk away, I just started to mumble to myself, "I could fuck your wife as well and you are most likely a jip in bed and find me a better fuck than he could ever be.

I think he heard part of what I was mumbling and said that he could lug me for what I said, but no, he probably thought "I'll keep you here with me and make you sorry for what you said under your breath to me, and believe you me, you will pay dearly for that."

I just turned to look at him and said, "Why, because I said that?" To me it was just words, like guys did on the street to each other, but he was no friend to me.

He looked at me and said, "You're not on the fuckin' street. You're in here with me."

Knowing this CO, he probably asked her out as she was on her way out. That's if she didn't have someone in the car with her. I have the feeling that she would have said yes to him because she was a cokehead even worse than before I came in and could see it in her eyes. Well, the next day, this tall goofy blond hair CO named Tweet came up to me and said to the guy next to me, "You got to move to another room."

As soon as the guy moved out, they moved another guy in, and he was black and he said as he walked in, "Great, a white guy." Then as I was in my bunk, I saw two more black guys start to come in and said, "That's all I needed." That's when all the shit hit the fan. Then within a week, they put in another black guy in the room and moved out another white guy, and the guy that I walked the track with said, "What the fuck you did to make them do that to you?"

"Well," I said, "the sergeant said that he could fuck my wife in one night, and I said that I could do the same to his wife."

He turned and said, "Why did you say that? You know that they are always messing with you the guys."

They did the "Hey, bro" thing and then ended it all by calling each other niggers. Now this made four black in the room with me, and that was when I thought he was one of the devil's advocates that was moved into the room. What a payback this was, and these guys were as racist as they come, and I mean they hate white guys. This made life a living hell for me, and they call white guys racist (bullshit). Every word that came out of their mouths were "Hey, nigger" when addressing each other. These guys were nothing like black guys I knew or were like the black guys I hung out on the streets with. They were nothing like these dickheads. This last guy was the one that got the ball rolling with the black thing in the room, and I just put up with it because of the revise and revoke I still had to go to court for. Just my luck, he had a doctor's appointment the same day as I did, and he just so happened to be in the same cage with me along with some other black guys.

As we were in the same cage together, he walked over to this other black guy that was also sitting alone in the cage with us and said to him, "Hey, nigger."

The other black guy looked up at him and said, "What did you call me? I'm not your nigger. I'm African American, not a nigger, and save all your nigger talk for your so-called nigger friends."

I just couldn't believe what I heard. He looked at him and said, "That's the way you want it. That's okay with me." I thought there was going to be a fight, but he just walked away. This guy Trooper walked away like he was from the Neanderthal days (you know, caveman) and had a big lump on his head and just looked like he was deformed. It was probably from his mother dropping him on his head, and all he needed was for his hands to be a little longer and his knuckles would be hitting the ground. This guy was dumb as a stump. He had a new name for the word stupid, and I hated this cocksucker with all my heart. I wish I could smash him in the face. I'm surprised he has lived this long without being shot dead. When I was young, my dad had a lot of black friends, and they were always over the house. If we ever used the word nigger, that would be it. My father would have bounced any one of us off the walls if we ever used that term in any form in the house, without question. We were brought up the Old Portuguese way, and that word was a never used in our house. It was considered swearing in our house and was never to be used, and we respected that.

I did see that black guy that put the asshole in my room in his place in the cage again, and we talked, and he said that the reason he got into it with that guy that day was because he was in a bad mood and that he was no fuckin' nigger. As we talked, he did say he didn't like to be called a nigger, and that day he just didn't want to hear it. He asked me if I got along with that guy, and I said, "I have no choice because he's in my room with his three friends, and they are all like him."

He said, "Not all black guys."

I said, "Yes, all black."

He looked at me and just said that he didn't like to be called black. I said I never looked at the color until I came into a place like this. By me looking at a black man, I kind of knew he was black and never went any further than that. I was out of my room all day whenever I could. That's if I wasn't working at the garage. But as soon as they cleared count, I was walking the track because they were up all night and playing their rap music. It's like the COs gave them the okay to fuck with me. When I came in from my walk, the room would still be in complete darkness, and that's all day long because they would be sleeping to get ready for the "stay up all night" rap concert. The worst part was, the room stank like sweat real bad, along with that shit odor. At night when I went to bed, I would block my ears with toilet paper until I was able to get some ear plugs from the garage and put them in my ears, and I would place the covers over my head for the lights that would be on all night and did my best to go to sleep. This made me hate them all the more. The room during the day, because it was so dark you couldn't see from one end to the other.

I hated this black guy, Trooper, that I could shoot him, and it wouldn't bother me at all. At least in my eyes he was and is a piece of shit, and to rid the world of scum like this would be okay by me because he was a racist bastard. I came into the room and this guy Trooper was talking to another guy from the other side of the unit named Mendes, big tall black asshole as he was, and he was saying how much he hated white guys, and he didn't know that I was in the room until his buddy nudged him. Then he just happened to turn and see that I was in the room. His eyes, I thought, were going to pop out of his head. He said that he didn't care. I just gave him a stare, and the black guy Trooper walked over to me and said, "You better not call me a black ever again. Remember, I'm a nigger, not black," and walked out of the room. This guy really thought I was scared of him (not). As I said, I could shoot this piece of shit and cut him up into pieces and feed him to the sharks and then go out to eat a good dinner. That's how much I hated him, fuckin' scumbag.

At this time there were five black guys in the room, and one was sitting on my bed, and you just don't do that in jail, and I just told him to get off my bed, and he said, "I'm not doing anything."

I just said, "Get the fuck up," and he did. I said, "Find somewhere else to park your ass to sit."

These four guys were in the same room as I was for over a month, and that asshole Tweet came over to me and asked what I wanted, and I said that I wanted a room change, and he said that he would look into it, and of course I know he never did. He did come up to me about a week later and said that I had to watch what I said to COs when I speak to them because they could make life miserable for us. Then he said, "Remember you're in our house now, and you got to remember that and never forget it. Enjoy your roommates. I hope you're getting enough sleep, and I heard that you're starting to listen to rap music, enjoying it with your roommates. We picked them out especially for you, so sleep tight."

I said after he started to walk away, "Maybe we will see each other on the outside."

He turned and said, "What did you just say to me?"

I said, "I really hope that we can see each other when I get out."

He then said, "Is that a threat?"

I said, "Of course not."

This asshole was from Fall River, and some of the guys I talked to were from his area and told me that his sister was a fucking cokewhore as my wife was and was told by a couple of guys that they had fucked her and left her at the doorstep. Under my breath I said, "You fuckin' cocksucker. I hope you get hit by a car on the way home. It wouldn't be any loss to the world either." Every time this asshole was on, he made a special effort to walk by me and laugh and stare at me, and I would see him coming from the corner of my eye and paid no attention to him. Then that was when he would shake down my room and throw everything that was in my footlocker all over the floor. I started to learn to never let things like that bother me. I just picked up what he threw on the floor and remembered they were in control. It was their house. I just thought, What a fuckin' asshole. What pissed me off more was his black friends who were seeing him do this to me, making a joke out of it. These black guys just about never bought canteen because of all the special treatment that they were getting from the COs. After that I just watched what came out of my mouth and kept my comments to myself and remembered where I'm at. I had to remember that I was not on the street, and these were not like the guy's that I knew on the street, and none of them were my friends. What really made things even worse was that I was still fucked up in the head. I had to think before I responded to the fucked-up comments these guys make. You have got to remember the way to talk on the street is not the way you talk in jail. You have to watch what you say. The meanings are very different. After a while, I had to learn to ignore the black guys that were in the same room as I was. It was for the best. I really had to try my best that I could. That was hard for me because I also could be a jerk as I always was. I was trying to call my so-called lawyer just about every day and got real used to him hanging up on me and not responding to all my letters I was sending him.

I was talking to this CO, asked him if he could take a picture of my wife for me to have, he also said that he told her that he would take one next time she came up again at least once a month. They made sure that I couldn't touch her on a visit because they changed the CO with this other CO called Sagely, the property officer, because I think they knew about the hand job my wife gave me on one of the visits and probably had it on the monitors. Every time my wife came up to see me, she would tell me that she was going to wait for me to get out so that we can try over again, and this would make my day because I still loved her so very much. You know, even though I knew she was fucking on me, she was telling me all the time that she would never cheat on me, which made me think that she felt guilty. I knew how to put that aside, not put out here that I knew what she was doing, so I had to watch myself and try not to do or say anything stupid. It took me a long time to find out what kind of girl she was. She fooled me real well until we were separated, and I was sent to jail, then she showed me her true colors, but I always liked bad girls. They were always more fun, but you always end up alone.

Today I walked the track most of the day until they called count. Unless I was working, as I was walking, I was thinking of what I was seeing so I could write it in my letters. I wrote down just about everything I saw in this fucking place and all the shit that went on in here. I just did this just to pass the time until it became an obsession. A couple of the COs would ask me what I was writing about all the time, and I would say, "It's all about this place, and someday I'm going to write a book about this place when I get out, and don't worry, you will be in it."

He just said, "Yeah right."

I said, "Believe me, you will be in it."

He looked at me and said, "This is going to be your life now, and you will never be able to complete it because you will be back again, and this will always be your home away from home."

I said, "Look at me good because this will be the last time you will see me in this fuckin' place with this scum." I wanted to also say real bad, "Including you fuckin' COs. I'm not just talking about the inmates."

He said, "You better watch what you say."

I just said, "What are you talking about?"

The CO said to me, "Didn't you hear me before? Watch what you say." Then he walked away.

Now I am writing the book that I said that I was going to write, and I hope he gets one and reads what fucking assholes that all the COs were to me and other guys who were at Bridgewater, named Chapman. He doesn't deserve to be called an asshole. One time when the CO shook down my room, I noticed that a lot of my letters were missing when I got back into my room. I just knew the COs either took them or threw them out. After that I started to mail out everything I wrote during the day and just thought just in case they were reading them, and I wouldn't put it past them. It became a rule that I made to make sure when I finished a letter I mailed them out as soon as I was finished with them. How I knew this is some of the COs would come up to me and would say, "You must think that we are real assholes," with their feet on the bench that I was sitting on. While he had his foot on the bench that I was writing on, he did say to me, "What makes you say that we are nothing but assholes?" And they'd just give me dirty looks and walk away. Now at this point I kind of knew that they read some of my letters and was waiting for what I was going to get out of it. I waited a week and nothing happened, so nothing came from it.

At this time my wife hadn't sent me any more money in a long time, and I was not going to beg her for it either. Even though it was my money from the start, it became her money, and it was probably up her nose by now. So I would have to find ways to make money in here so I could get the things that I needed, especially footwear for the shower because the inmates would piss and shit in the showers. I also needed some food because of the garbage that they would serve us to eat; they must have had a market on mac and cheese. Of course I never ate any of it the whole time I was in jail, not even once in five years. It got to the point that I found my own hustle and would sew pants, make lifting straps to lift weights, along with making cards and rolling cigarettes from what butts the guys would find and bring to me to roll whatever made me a canteen. Because the money I was making at the garage just wasn't cutting it, the eighty-five dollars that my wife was sending every six months just wasn't enough. I started to save all the money that I made at the garage so I could buy a TV and a pair of sneakers. My sneakers and shower shoes were being held together by me sewing them together with my sewing kit and the use of some paper clips. As I said, and believe me, you need showering shoes before entering the showers because all you would have to do is breathe in and smell and you know you would need shoes. The reason you really need shower shoes is because the showers are always blocked, and the guys are always shitting and pissing or jerking off in them, so you need this most of all because you stand in that water that they do this in because the water doesn't go down. When taking a shower, I have seen everything relating to a woman right down to a K-Mart flyer in the showers stuck to the walls that guys jerk off too. I've also seen guys get smacked for using other guys' pictures that they left in the showers even if they were from flyers. I just can't believe the stuff I've seen going on in this place. It's just a different kind of world.

    I was able to get my so-called wife on the phone, so I asked if she could spare some time to come up because I had to talk to her about the attorney again and the letter he had sent me. To my surprise, she told me that she would be up to see me. My wife did tell me that she would be up at the end of the week. Well, Saturday came, and she did come up, and I waited so impatiently for my name to be called. When they did call my name, I still couldn't walk fast enough to get to the visiting room. When I entered, I knew she kind of knew I was of course glad to see her, and as I walked fast up to her to kiss her, the smell came off her breath again. It smelled like she just gave some guy a blow job and was very strong. I just looked at her, and she said, "What?" It was like she didn't know she would get cock breath from doing what she just did. I just backed off and started to tell her about the black guys that wanted to be called niggers. That was what they wanted to be called, and she said, "Don't you do that." I said that I wasn't. Well she came in, and this time she didn't smell bodywise, but her breath could knock you out, and she was dressed like she was going out on the town after she left seeing me.

BUSTED

While she was there, she was acting like she was too good for me, and I told her just to knock it off. I just got mad at her. I told her, "Just remember when I first met, and you were pregnant and looked like shit, and no one wanted to help you, not even your family, but I did, and helped you through school and married you. Remember who you're talking to." I told her not to let anyone read my letters and to save them all for me for when I got out. She said that she read them all and put them away. Yes, she put them away so good that someone was able to send me letters stating what she was doing and where she was going. Then I told her, "Make an appointment to go and see the lawyer and see what he can do for me, and stop fuckin' around and try to get me the hell out of here. If it was you, I would make time for you." It was like she never was involved in the coke we both got busted with. I just started to stare at her and realized that she was looking at me as if it was my entire fault and I belonged where I was.

It was just like the same old shit. She listened for a short time and was gone in about one hour. I never smacked a woman before, but I wanted to smack her in the back of her head to knock some sense into her head. In the whole time I've been married to her, I never hit her, but she needed to be knocked on her ass. What I was hoping for was to hear that some girl at the bars that she was going to would beat the shit out of her. It was like she just hit the lottery for big bucks the way she was acting and the way she was dressing. When I met her, she was making ten dollars an hour and was doing something she probably loved doing, washing guys' dicks. If I let her do the time that they were going to give her, she would be in Framingham sucking off some CO for a hamburger or a stick of pepperoni. The pepperoni would be used to satisfy herself after the CO left or, even better, getting strip-searched by some horny piece-of-shit CO. Yes, it's true; it happens. I have clippings of all the stuff that I write about, and that would be her bedtime horror story, to get raped by a CO. It would be something that she would remember for the rest of her life, but again she might have enjoyed it. But again she'd probably be a better person also if she were to experience what I was going through in this damn place for herself, then maybe she would think differently. On so many occasions, she would tell me that being in jail would make me a better person and to pray to God to help me. All this place did to me was fuck up my head and make me hate being around people and then hard to find employment. She never really knew what I was going through at this time, and she never will. So her fourteen visits really didn't amount to anything but make me think that she cared for me, but it all was just a put-on, like our marriage was. After talking to her about the lawyer, at this point it was useless, as I kind of knew it would be, and of course, I was back to square one and wondering if she would try to contact the attorney after our talk. What I didn't see was that her face was full, and she was really kicking me to the curb right after she threw me under the bus. Well, of course, I was back at the mechanic garage, washing my laundry there because I could save money using their soap and stealing socks from their rag barrel, washing them and trading them at the unit for canteen because the property officer very rarely gave anything out and said, "Buy it with what you make." The scum dog property officer Sagely thought everything in the property office was his and it was stuff he bought with his own money. I think me calling him a scum dog covers it all. The COs always searched us when we would come back into the unit after the jobs they got for us but never checked how many pairs of socks we had on. Whenever I came back into the unit, I always brought back triple pairs of socks to sell so that I was able to make a decent canteen. But Sagely kept his eyes on me because of all the rats there were in the unit that were telling him what I was doing. There were a lot of guys who couldn't get new pants from the property officer so they were walking around with pants that I patched. It was like bringing back the hippie days with a lot of the guys wearing patched pants in jail. When Sagely saw that I was at work, he did his room searches of my room and checked and took anything I had too many pairs of and took it away, but I wouldn't care. I would just get more from the garage. But the worst part of it being in this jail was when you got back from work, the CO would strip-search you, wanting to look up your ass for cigarettes or weapons. To me, I think they were wasting their time with me because I wasn't sticking anything up my ass, as I told them many times before. But why did they want to look up your ass all the time I will never know. I guess for cigarettes, it couldn't be for anything else. The way I look at it, to put cigarettes up someone's ass, to bring it in that way and have someone want to smoke them, I say good luck and let them smoke them.

I know the black guys in my room were some of the guys that were ratting me out because that's just the way they were because I saw them getting canteen bags from guys who recently got lugged. Mostly this guy Trooper, the one who wanted to be called a nigger, was the one who got the canteen bag from the lugged guys. I had no problem with that at this time, so what I did in that case was not to bother with him at all, as I did most of the time. I've always had black guys as friends, and I will never change the way I am no matter what. I hope this guy Trooper buys a copy of this book so he can realize what I thought of him. It's not good at all. But now thinking about it, I hope the words are not too big for him and he can read this because he was a real stupid bastard. Maybe after he read what I wrote about him or have someone read it for him, he will know that he's no damn good and he definitely should kill himself. In my heart I hope he never tries to breed because all he will do is bring another fucked person into the world. I really mean breed because to me he was and always will be an animal.

At this time I wasn't getting any money from anyone in my family, and that's of course including my wife. Once in a while I could get something from my daughter, and I would call her up and yell at her and tell her to stop it, and then she would. She was paying for the house, and that was more than enough. At her age, she did great. But when I was on the street, I would help everyone in my family whenever they needed something, but when I went away, they just forgot me, but I struggled and did it all by myself. I got myself into this mess, and I got myself out of it, and with a fucked-up head. Maybe that's why a lot of guys wouldn't fuck with me, because I was so fucked up in the head and wouldn't take any shit because I just didn't care what happened to me. I was still seeing the shrink, and she wasn't doing me any good, and she was just paying her debt back to the government probably for her school loans she took out, because she was real bad at what she did. The biggest thing that was bothering me was the black guys that still stood up in the room all night long and played their fucked-up rap music in the room from a speaker they put in Pringle cans. These cans were used for more than one thing when you're in jail. The black guys were still staying up all night and just to piss me off, and this was because the CO told the guys in the room to mess with me. This was the CO who said my wife looked like a whore, and he could have fucked her if he really tried. This is the one who started all the shit in the unit between the black guys and the white. He didn't care he went home at night. I wasn't sleeping most of the night, and they would sleep most of the day and get on my case to clean the room when they got up, and I wasn't going to do it when they decided it should be done. These cocksuckers wanted to make me their slaves and do there bidding, and Trooper's sidekick friends were this black that called himself Smooth, another piece of shit who wore sunglasses all the time even when it was dark and thought he was the best thing that hit this side of the world.

One day I was going to take a shower, and as I was going in, the guy Smooth was coming out, and he had a towel wrapped around his head and damn sunglasses on his eyes, and he walked out of the shower like he was a woman and just smiled and walked by. I just said, "What a strange bird," but he said hi to me like we were friends. He wasn't hostile to me at all, but I was waiting. He was just an asshole when his sidekick Trooper was around. Now I wonder if he took his sunglasses off when he was showering. I guess I'll never know. I put up with this shit for just about a year, and there wasn't a day that CO Tweet didn't come by and say something disrespectful to me about the black guys that were in the room with me. When I would say or call them something like fuckin' assholes, he would run in and tell them, and they would do something to piss me off other than what they were already doing. I would see CO Tweet the next day and say to him, "Are you trying to start shit in the room?"

He would look at me, just laugh, and walk on and say, "I didn't say a word to them."

BUSTED

There were so many times that I saw COs start trouble with inmates and edge them on to the point where they were going to fight with a CO, and they would call in the rest of the COs in the unit to lug whoever out. But when it came to lugging an inmate, it was best to call the IPPS to take care of the shit the COs most likely started. In jail, it's a no-win situation for inmates, so even if we thought we were getting fucked over, there was nothing that can be done for anyone. It got to the point I just learned to shut my mouth because the COs had you where they wanted you, and after a while they would go beyond the point, just fuck with different guys as they did to me. I was their main target, and they fucked with me as much as possible because of what I said about the Sargent's wife. They enjoyed watching me suffer after they put those four racist black guys in the same room as I was in just to have them fuck with me at random. At this time I was trying to find a way to get myself lugged to get out of that racist black room that I was in, and now I wanted to real bad before I did something stupid, but I didn't know how to do it. The only thing that was on my mind was doing something that wouldn't hurt my case if I brought it back into court for my revise and revoke.

Every program they had I would join, but the only problem was that they were all church programs, anger management programs, and horticulture, and I did them just to get out of the unit. There weren't too many more programs for me to do. I did just about all of them. All they taught you was how to be a puppet to COs and do what they said and don't give them a hard time, learn how to take their shit, as I did all the time. But I did what they told me to do with a very dirty look on my face, and to them that was enough. The medical doctors were the worst I had ever seen, pure fuckups in every way, and they really didn't want to help any inmates at all, and they were always pushing you out the door as soon as possible. I would see them and tell them that I had a cold, and they would tell me that it would go away in a week and to buy all the medications that I needed through the canteen. But I would see them just to get the medication off them, and most of the time they would say "Buy it through the canteen," and sometimes you would have to wait a whole week to get the stuff you needed. It's like they are telling you to suffer. The State put you in this hellhole, and they should take care of you the whole time you're here, if not put you in a program on the street and make you pay for it if it has something to do with drugs abuse. The whole time that I was there, I never had a decent day unless I had a visit, and that was just about never, and I did the time all by myself. I did about 98 percent of my time in jail alone without any visits from my family or friends.

As time went on, I got used to it very fast, but it was very hard on me being cooped up like an animal. The only letters that I was getting were from my daughter or from the bar of overseers for legal matters discussing matters with my so-called great lawyer from Boston who convinced my wife that he could get a time reduction in my sentence. All I got from Mr. Big Fish was the great big pond and little pond stories about different big fish lawyers. He then told me that's why my lawyer in New Bedford wasn't that good and could never swim in the big ponds that Boston lawyers swam in. He was a good storyteller, wasn't as good as he said because what he ended up doing was holding on to five thousand dollars of my money for five years with all kinds of promises. I have some news clipping saying how he fucked over big-time people also. I hope they find ways of having him disbarred forever or hope someone gives him a payback. The other thing that I was hoping for was to hear they found him in the ocean somewhere because of all the big people he fucked over. But being in jail, I did learn different trades, like how to commit different types of crimes, how to break into homes, make bombs, how to break into safes and teach you how not to get caught, but I don't think that was a good lesson because they wouldn't be in a place like this if they were right. Did you know that you can make a bomb with just rolls of caps by sticking a needle through the heads of the caps then rolling them up tight with a fuse or a heated wire and a battery also with a little extra and I will never say.

After having a conversation with some of the guys they would say that they knew how they got caught and how they could do it the next time and not get caught. I just listened to the great criminal mines and didn't pay much attention to them, but this was what I heard from jail to jail, how they could do the crime and get away with it. I did talk to a lot of intelligent guys that got away with crimes and were just ratted on and was doing their time but had all the hate like I had stored up inside them as well. While I was listening to these guys, I would be thinking of my so-called Boston lawyer, hoping that he could get me out. I would never touch or look at fuckin' cocaine ever again, and that's for the rest of my life. The time that they had me in Dartmouth Correctional was enough time for me to say that I will never return. That's how fast I learned my lesson, just by being in a place like that. Just like all the movies you see on TV and them saying I don't belong here, I kept telling myself the same thing, and to this day I still say the same thing being out. I still say that I didn't belong in jail for that length of time. If I knew what kind of a sentence it carried, I never would have bought so much of that shit. I always thought they called that entrapment, always thought that police couldn't do something like they did because it was illegal to do so. Oh, it slipped my mind the police can do whatever they want because they do no wrong but love to hear when one of their own gets busted. Both the dealer that I got my drugs off and the cop who shot my dog must have made some sort of a deal because I never saw the dealer who sold me the cocaine in jail. It could be because I was told that he died from some sort of disease. I just hope he suffers as I did and rots in hell because that's where I was, in hell. The other guy who turned me on to him was the one whom I first started to buy cocaine from. He was the one who told the cops where I lived. Well, I found out that he went to New Hampshire and got into a hot tub and cut his wrists and bled out, and all I got to say about that is that he will have company, and good riddance to two rats. I hope he kept his wrists in the tub so no one had to clean up the mess. The way I was going to do it was with a gun I had, but it misfired, but my back was to the pond. When it comes to drug crime, they are too harsh with the law. It's a nonviolent crime, and they put guys in the same place all mixed together with murderers, bank robbers, skinner dialers, and so on, all violent offenders. I guess if you get caught with weapons, it's a different story, because if you have a weapon, it's a closed case because they just shoot you and that's the end of that, and that's what most cops do. Most of these narcs are as crooked as most criminals, but some of them can be somewhat human if they try but don't unless it's their family. They should give the power to the judges, not to the fuckin prosecutors. Make them work to put you away, and the judges would know what sentence to hand down to each and every person convicted for drugs. On every drug case that I heard from guys in jail, they all are different from each other. If all the courts look at is that its drug crime. There were so many guys that I've talked to while being in jail that were taken away from their families because they got caught with a small amount of drugs and put away for five to fifteen years or for just possession of drugs. If you're in government or in law enforcement, they find ways to brush it under the carpet, and you hear about it all the time. You hear it once and never again. This is like they say, it's who you know, or even better, who you are. I have some of it in clipping I got from the newspaper showing how these things get brushed under the carpet and still have a lot of my information that I got out of the newspaper and hated to give it up to the guys that let me read it. Even after you have read it, it tends to stay with me long after I've been out of jail and right to this day, but in my mind, I'm still in jail.

Just got back to the unit from the Mickey Mouse job at the auto garage, and I decided to write my everyday letter to my wife because she was in jail with me twenty-four seven. Meaning she was in my thoughts constantly. I guess this is what they call a one-way love affair, me loving her and her loving whoever she happens to be with and not giving me a second thought. As I was sitting at the table in the dayroom, I noticed a guy who just came into the unit from behind the wall, ducking under the window, and I was watching him very carefully. I saw that he was looking out the corners of the windows. In the dayroom, we were able to walk around the unit freely because we were at a minimum prison, and I was wondering why he was doing this. I was unable to keep writing because he was mumbling to himself as he was going from one corner of the window to the other, looking out. I started to watch him very closely, and he started to say to me, "They are out there," and he said that he could feel it, and "They are coming to get me real soon."

BUSTED

I said to myself, "Oh shit, this guy is a nutcase, and he's right beside me," and started to say I think I have problems this guy was full-out nuts. I thought I was going crazy, but after watching him, I realized I was not as bad as he was, and I was thinking, *What's next to come?* This guy was brought in a couple of days prior. I saw him from time to time, but to see him do what he was doing was a start to crazy episode in the making. When I first saw him coming in to me, he didn't look that swift at the time they still brought him in. The moment I saw him start to do crazy things, I got up real slow and moved to another table a good distance away and watched him real closely. I didn't know what he was capable of doing. Plus it was a show, and you never know what could go down when you see shit like this. In this unit, there were so many ways to make a weapon, and it can be hidden on your body really easy. I didn't know if he was carrying any. When things like this happen, you just stay away and watch the show. But if the COs see it, they call count and everyone returns to their rooms, and usually the one who's fucking up always stays behind. When it came to me, I had a bedspring in the sleeve of my shirt and never left the unit without a pen in my hand and had other weapons hidden around the unit. You kind of knew where to stick a guy where you could fuck him up or sometimes just to tell them to fuck off. This place is nothing like the real prisons, where these COs would shit themselves as soon as they entered a real prison. I can just imagine one of these asshole COs looking at an inmate in a real prison and telling them, asking if he wanted to go behind the wall again. Yes, a lot of the COs that I have encountered in all the places that I've been at are as scared as I was when I entered jail. Now getting back to the nut in the dayroom when all the craziness with the new guy came in. While all this was going on, the COs were real busy bullshitting and drinking Dunkin Donuts coffee, and I guess they weren't watching the monitors.

There were other guys sitting in the so-called dayroom, and they were making so much noise and just didn't see what I was seeing except the two other guys that were sitting at the same table that I was at, and they thought it was funny, but I didn't. Well, not too long after that, they called count, and every one returned to their rooms and waited for count to be cleared. Well, when I returned to the dayroom after count, I didn't see the new guy anywhere, and I went back to finish my letter that I was sending to my wife because I wanted to send it to her that night. I spent as little time as possible in the room because of my black roommates and because when I was in the room, I would just stare at them and had hate written all over my face. Plus they made me hate them because of the rap music that they played and would put the music up even higher when I came into the room, and it went on all night long. I hate all four of the black guys that they put in the room with me. I just can't stand any of them, but most of all the black guy named Trooper. This dickhead was the one I hated the most of all not because he's black but because he's just plain scum. I always carried a weapon with me when I entered the room at all times, just in case I had to use it on this fuckin' guy Trooper. It was a sharpened bedspring that I slid into the sleeve of my jacket or my shirt at times along with my trusty pens. Yes, writing pens. I wouldn't think twice to use it on that fuckin' guy, and I know if they were to bring me into court for stabbing this guy, I think I would win under self-defense because of all the threats that came from his mouth, which never scared me in the least. You should never place four raciest black guys in a room with one white guy, ever. It's like striking a match in a fireworks factory. Today I think back and know how messed up in the head I was and can't believe how out of controlled I was. I just about could have snapped at any time myself. I guess it was because I had believed that the new attorney from Boston was going to get me out of jail, and I could go back home to my wife and daughter.

    In jail there are no speakers in the radios, TVs, and we would take a Pringles chip can and pull a headset apart and put the speakers in it, and it would make it sound like a regular speaker and with four guys and all of them tuned to the same station. It was real loud, and one of the songs that they would play over and over again was some song named "Check Who." They would all woo to it (assholes). But at the end of their concert, they would have to put the speakers back into the headsets because if the property officer seen it, he would take the headsets away. We would do the same to our hot pots. We would take them apart and wire them with a paper clip or a piece of wire that I sometimes would get from the garage and put it across the restore so it would heat up and boil so we could cook spaghetti and other foods that needed to be boiled.

    Where there is a way, there is a will, and you got to find it when you're in a place like this and the reason why you can't have a boiling hot pot is because you might want to throw the boiling water in an inmate's face if you wanted to fuck him up real bad. There was a new guy that just came into the unit, and he was so lucky to get the grounds job, and he would go to the parking lots and pick up drugs and cigarettes and bring them back into the unit. When I was doing it, I would bring it in closer and closer every day until it was so close that the person who wanted it he could retrieve it himself with no problem. Of course after, he paid for it. I told the guy how to do it and keep him from getting in trouble and make a good canteen but told him not to get involved with drugs, and of course he did after a while and got ratted on and lugged. Some of the guys would go to the far end of the field and smoke and do nutmeg. They said it got them high. I could have but was clean the whole time that I was incarcerated and just had my share of drugs and just don't need it in my life anymore because I had lost too much in my life by being involved with drugs. It got to the point that when I walked into the room, the music would start, and now that I was in the garage, I was able to get some earplugs and didn't have to use instead of toilet paper for my ears and when the guys in my room noticed that I got earplugs, they got real pissed off. I just used the ear plugs just when I had to be in the same room with them for long periods of time, like when I had to go to bed, and that was always early. The way I thought is if I went to bed early, the next day would come and it would be another day I would be able to cross off my calendar. Every time I lay down to try to sleep, my wife and daughter were always on my mind nonstop. It was like torture to me. When you're in a place like this, you think of different ways to cope with time when you're in here. During this particular night, I got up to use the toilet as I always did, and when I entered the restroom, the nutcase that was in the dayroom was in the men's room, and he was stark naked and was jerking off in the bathroom while looking in the mirror. I just couldn't believe what I was seeing, and he turned to me and said, "Are they out there and are they coming to get me?"

I just started to say to myself, "Oh shit, this guy has more than a screw loose," and I thought I had problems and left very fast. Just then I can't say the other things that were going through my mind at this time while being in the same room as he was. I looked at him and asked him, "What are you talking about, and who do you think are coming to get you?"

He just said, "You know, them."

I just walked out and went over to the CO's window and said, "There is a nut in the restroom jerking off and asking me if they are out there." The CO asked me if I told him that they were out there to get him. I just asked him, "Who are out there to get him?" As I turned and started to walk into the restroom to take my piss, I heard the CO that I was talking to say, "He's doing it again." Then I noticed the COs come out of their office and go into the restroom to try to talk to him. I was in there, I was trying to take my piss, and they yelled at me to get out of the restroom. I just wanted to see what was going to go down, what they were going to do about it or do to him so I could write about it. Of course it must have been like work to them, and they called the IPPS in to take care of the problem for them, and he was out in a flash. Why they brought in a guy like this in I will never know and don't really care. The IPPs are what they call inner perimeter police, and they come in all dressed in black like a hit squad and think that they are all of that but are just wannabe cops and couldn't cut it as real cops on the outside, as I overheard the Cos talking to one another. They flunked out of real cop academy, and all they could become is a correctional police or cops or whatever they call themselves. But if you're a little smarter than the average CO, you can be a CO storm trooper, or IPPS, as what they were called. This could be why they are always in a pissed-off mood, because they are just a little smarter. All I can say about them is that they dress real good and have swelled heads and are bigger dickheads than the regular COs, but they can make life a real hell for you whenever they can, and I think it's part of their training that they took to become COs or a storm trooper dressed in black.

At this time the black guy in my room that I really hated was egging me on, and I just sharpened my bedspring and stuffed it up my sleeve in case I need it to stab this black guy named Trooper in his fuckin' face. I'm looking at him as I'm writing a letter, and he's talking to the sergeant who said that he could fuck my wife because she came in looking like a call girl, and they were looking my way, so I know they were talking about me. Now I know for sure he had something to do with mixing these black guys in my room to make life a living hell for me. The sergeant still had his sidekick Tweet, or should I say his sweetie because he's a real kiss-ass CO and had to be told what to and how to do a real follower. The other Cos would just laugh every time he walked by me because they knew what he was saying to me when he walked by me. I had to go through this from the day the black guys were put in the same room as I was till the day I was lugged out. This black guy Trooper thought he scared me, and he is so wrong. I'm just scared that I'm going to hurt him real bad. Because of the hate I had for him, I could stick a pen or something similar into his fuckin' neck or his eye and end up getting more time added to my sentence. I'm trying so hard to not to let him bother me, but he's always sticking pins in me, and this is just a figure of speech. When it happens, he's going to be real surprised when he fucks with me and he goes down with a fuckin' pen in his fuckin' eye. They don't realize how fucked up in the head I am, what I'm capable of doing. This place is doing it to me. If I start with him, I know I won't stop there. I'm going for the rest of the guys in the room. They are going to get the same. When I totally lose it, and I'm going after the rest of the guys in the room, then they will be running around like the three blind mice after their leader is down. This is just some of the shit you have to deal with in here, and the COs put guys up to it and promises them lots of nothing, and I so damn stupid they fall for it. If they say there are no racist guys in jail, they are crazy, and the black guys are ones that are the most racist of all. The blacks guys that were in my room were the only black guys that gave me the most trouble the whole time I was there. I put up with their shit every fuckin' day. But

I did have my arguments with the white guys, but they were always the white guys who wanted to be black. These are the ones that the blacks guys always wanted to throw under the bus. I still have some black guys in here that pay me with canteen to write letters for them, and they all belong to Bible class, and I get along real good with them, and they did see what's going on and just stayed out of it.

Well, it's early in the morning, and the CO just came in to bring me to the garage to do a brake job, and my mind wasn't really up to it, and I told him this, and he said, "Well, I bring you back to the unit." Then I told the CO I'd do the best that I could do because I didn't want to go back to the unit because I had in my head to hurt the black guy in my room, and I was afraid I'm going to hurt him real bad, so it's best to stay at the garage. The other reason was that I was having trouble with waiting for the week to come to an end because my wife was coming up to see me. This is one of the reasons why my mind wouldn't be on the job that I was expected to do. To this day I really don't think my wife knew how much room she took up in my head and never will. I just wanted to see her face real bad, and that was the only vision that I could see at that time. I could just hear it over and over again, her telling me that she was coming up to see me. Well, I took the van apart, and the brake pads were all worn-out, and there was nothing left to them, and the CO ordered new pads to put in, and he took it for a ride, and he came back real fast and said that there were no brakes at all, and I must have done something wrong, and he almost drove off the road.

I really didn't want to do it, and he said, "Just take it apart and see if it needed new calipers," and so I did, and when I did, I noticed that I put the pads in backward. It was metal against metal, that's why it felt like there was no brakes. I just can't believe I did such a stupid thing and had never had done anything like that ever before, and there were no brakes on one side. The garage mechanic came over and asked me if it needed new calipers, and I said no and that one of the pads was cocked, and I couldn't tell him that I messed up because I would have been lugged. I couldn't have this because I would have missed my visit with my wife, and this was what I was thinking of when I was doing the brake job. One of the worst things was the thought of me losing my wife, and that was always running through my head day after day. This always put me into such a deep thought and depression thinking of her and the things we did, and I think this was what was putting me into such fog. In my whole life I never thought I would let another woman fuck up my head as bad as my daughter's mother did, but it was happing again. My mind was getting so bad and I was hoping it wasn't going to be permanent and thought that maybe it could be brain damage due to this place. It also was the trauma that I went through when I was in Concord. It was like the lights were on, and no one was at home. It was like my mind was just keeping what I needed to just survive. I started to do things that I did on the street, like cut my hair once a month started to cook more often, just more of everything, and I tried to stop thinking of home and see if this would help me. I was never incarcerated before, and I was having a real hard time adjusting to where I was. My appearance was real bad. I had long hair and beard and just looked real bad and hated my life and just wanted to die.

When I was at the garage, I was sticking pins in my legs to feel pain and thought so many times of drinking bleach that was in the garage because the thought of being in this place for several more years was killing me from the inside out. I was still writing lots of letters to my wife and lawyer and noticed that my wife was just about giving up on me. She was having too much fun out there, going clubbing. Plus I was still getting letters from someone on the outside telling me this. I figured all the letters that I was writing to this so-called big fish lawyer that my wife hired was trying to get me out of this hellhole, and I was starting to get my doubts about him, and there was nothing I could do about it. This lawyer had all my money, and my wife had the rest of it, and what I left her was probably up her nose because she was partying hardy out there. I had no one else to help me out there, and my wife wasn't thinking of me, and to this day she had good intentions of just letting me rot in here. But what can I say to this day God doesn't sleep. I hope he sees everything and what comes around goes around, and maybe she will pay for what she had done to me by letting me rot in here. When I thought it was going real bad for us, I would write her and ask her if she wanted a divorce, and she said no and that she would wait for me no matter what or how long it took.

When I talked to her on the phone, she answered and again said that she didn't want a divorce. It made me happy, but then again I really knew it was bullshit. While I was talking to her, I then asked her if she could come up to see me again, and she said that she was very busy, and all she can do is try to make time to do that. If I had a pile of cocaine, she would be up in a flash to suck it up, and I still had a lot buried at my home that the cops didn't find, but if she found it or if I told her, she probably would be dead, and then I would be in here for murder. As soon as I talked to her about the divorce, a letter came in the mail, and it was telling me that she was going out all the time with some long-haired, guitar-playing wannabe rock star. He put into her head that he loved her and told her to ask for a divorce from me so he could marry her, and she was so stupid and she fell for his bullshit stupid bitch. I had to start to ignore the letters and concentrate on her trying to talk to the attorney to see what he could or couldn't do for me so I could try to fix this problem that my wife and I were having. She went up to Boston to talk to this lawyer in my behalf because I thought she really wanted me out of jail, but after that talk, she didn't call him and never went to see him when he called her. I kind of knew she didn't give a damn. Now I think about it and I wish I never met my wife and I never would have fallen in love with her and I never would have ended up in this place, fuckin' junkie bitch. Now I can't believe that my friend George brought her over to my house that day to drop some weed off with me and pick up an order. He was one of my friends that I got stuff for; he brought her over that day so he could pick up some coke so he could fuck her. After that night she just kept coming to my home without him. The only reason for that was because she told him that he got her pregnant and he was dodging her. What I noticed about her was how she was able to figure me out, I mean my ins and outs, and she was real good at this. She kind of knew when I would leave my home to go out, and she would hunt me down until she found me. Once she figured this out, she started to come over before I left, just started hanging around until she became part of my life. Well, that's all in my head, and I'm trying to concentrate on trying to get out of this place which I knew I was going to. I kept calling my so-called wife and told her if she could give the attorney a call and tell him that he could take my Corvette as payment to get me into court to reduce my time. I was waiting for an answer from my wife in this hellhole, hoping that she would put a little effort into helping me get out of here. I just couldn't wait to call my wife back in a couple of days to see what the lawyer had to say about taking my car for payment.

Well, when I got to talk to her, her telling me that she would call the attorney, I just couldn't believe that she put that off. After talking to my daughter on the phone, I found out that she called the lawyer, and she asked him if my wife called him. He just said, "No, at all." At this time if I had a million dollars, I would give it up to get me out of this place. This is how much I wanted out of this nuthouse. My wife told me that I should think about what she was saying and just do my time, for the second time, and I would come out a better person and just remember what I was in jail for and to teach me to never do it ever again. What a fucked-up thing to say to me, and there she was out there snorting the shit up and fucking her cokehead boyfriend who ended up leaving her and then dying of prostate cancer. After talking to her on the phone, she started to tell me being in jail would make me a better person. After that I was really depressed, and I went to bed early, cursing her. The black guys were of course playing their rap music loud and of course making lots of noise just to mess with me, and all it was doing was getting me real violent inside, but I kept it inside of me. Now that I'm out of this place, every time I hear rap music, it still gets me violent and starts to make me sweat. I either change it if I can or leave where I'm hearing it playing and give the people dirty looks that are playing it. To this day I wish I sold the cocaine for a profit so I would have been able to afford a real good attorney and get the hell out of this nuthouse. Like they say, money talks and bullshit walks. I thinks that's how it goes.

Of course the morning did come, and I did finally fall asleep, and I went to breakfast as I always did real early or you don't eat, and I went out to walk the track because the blacks were always sleeping till noon. The room was as pitch-black usual. It was about 8:15 a.m.

on September 29, 1999, and I heard a lot of noise. When I looked out the window, I saw that the unit was being surrounded by a large number of COs dressed in brown uniforms closing the unit off. Then they came in a storm and tearing the whole unit apart and just starting to dump everyone's lockers in the halls of the unit. What a damn mess, and I just couldn't understand what they were looking for or doing. I did find out that they were trainees, and they were doing a training exercise to become CO, and the unit I was in was being used for this training exercise. We were all put in the dayroom until they were finished fucking up everyone's room. When we were able to go back to our rooms, there was so much stuff missing, like all my stamps, some money, anything that was worth anything was gone. I had found a lot of my stuff in the next guys' rooms, and good thing I had my name in them, so he gave them right back. I don't even think this trainee knew what they were doing, or maybe they really want to look good in front of the COs on duty that day. Of what I saw they were all going to be great COs because they all looked like their heads were up their asses, just like the ones that were already on duty.

After they tore the rooms apart, they made us go back to our rooms to clean up the hallways and rooms. As we were cleaning, the so-called sergeant's voice came over the intercom telling all the inmates that we were to stay in our rooms, and we were not able to leave at all no matter what. He also said that they were not done doing what had to be done; they will tell us when it was over. Shortly after that, they said that we would have to give DNA samples to them so they could check if we had done any other crimes in the past. The best part was them telling us that we would have to pay for the test or get lugged, and a lot of guys started to say that they were going to take the lug. Everyone started to yell saying that it wasn't right, and they were not going to pay for the test, and the Cos said that they were going to take the test or get sent across the street to Bridgewater Maximum. The ones that were doing the yelling and saying they were going to refuse the test were put in another room to be lugged, and they really didn't give a fuck as I heard them yell out. We were allowed to come out to the so-called dayroom again as they were doing the tests. I started to see guys getting brought into another room and strip-searched and blood samples taken, so I think these were guys that they really wanted from the start because they were the only ones tested. As I was sitting at the table, a guy that I wrote letters for came up to me and started talking to me and said that he was real scared to take the tests. I asked him why, and he told me that he was in for ten years for attempt of murder, and there was stuff that they didn't know about him. I said, "How bad can it be, and what did you do that you're so scared about?"

"Well," he said, "I was involved in white slavery, drugs, and transporting young women across the border and pimping them off and was never caught for it."

I couldn't believe what he was telling me, and he kept going on, and I said I know they must have my DNA on something. I really wanted him to stop telling me the stuff he was telling me. I just didn't want to know what he did on the outside. All I wanted was to be left alone. I was also scared because I was new to all this shit. This guy said when he was doing that, he was using a different name at that time, and he was scared they might find this out. I didn't want any more time, and then I just said, "Stop telling me what you're telling me. I don't want to hear anymore." I just looked at him and said that was enough. I looked up and noticed that a CO was just looking at the both of us and watching me write, and I was putting down everything he had said to me and said to myself, Oh shit, what if they confiscate this letter, what kind of trouble can I get in? So I just tore it up into really small pieces and flushed it down the toilet. I just wanted to finish the other letter I had written and put a stamp on it and mail it out because I didn't want them to think I was writing down things that he was telling me or what was going on at that time. I really think if they knew what that inmate was telling me and things he had done, all I can say is "Oh shit."

As I was sealing the letter, the CO that picks up the letters came in, and I mailed it out and was just thinking if they thought that I was writing down stuff that inmate was telling me that he had done. It's so weird how most of the stuff guys in general told me just found a place in my head and stuck there. I was glad I ripped the letter I was writing of what that guy was telling me.

The DNA thing went on for most of the day, and out of nowhere we were told to return to our rooms and said that they couldn't do what they were told to do because it was against our rights. Then one of the CO said to me, "You don't have any rights while you're in jail as far as I'm concerned because you're a criminal."

I say that's bullshit, and they just had a few guys with bull's-eyes on their backs, and they wanted to know the full amount of shit they had done and made it look like it was for everyone. They told all the guys that they had to destroy all samples because they said that it was against our rights. I never got a chance to give them a sample, and it wouldn't have bothered me a bit except if they reused a dirty needle, and I wouldn't put it past them. All the trainees returned to their vehicles like robots and went back to where they came from, and it was like nothing had happened that day at all. In the course of the week, they did lug a couple of guys, and those were the ones they had in separate rooms when they were doing the DNA test. I noticed it, but most likely no one else was able to put two and two together. That's because most of the guys in the unit were dumb bastards. I figured this was going to be my way out of the unit because after thinking about it, I would never have let them take any blood samples from me even though I didn't have anything to hide, and drugs was the only thing I was convicted of.

As I was sitting at one of the tables in the dayroom, I was sweating a lot because had a lot of clothes on in case I got lugged because it takes a long time before you get your property from where you get lugged from, so you put lots of cloths on so if you get lugged, you have clothes to wear at your next stop. The only thing about high security was if I went behind the wall, it would be harder for my wife and daughter to come up and see me. I really thought I was going to get lugged for sure, so I did as other guys told me to do and just doubled up on all my clothes and wait. Just being in jail for a short time, I learned to watch and listen to guys talking to each other just to learn what to do in times like this. Really at this time, I was a real green bean and really didn't know which way was up. I didn't know what to do when this shit went down. I really didn't know if this was true or not but did it anyways, but in time I found out that it was true. Just like you don't call someone a punk or even say "fuck you" to anyone because you have to remember you're not on the street. Guys take it seriously. If you happen to do so, the next thing you know, the guy disappears, and they go to their room and do what they call strap up; they double up on clothes and put their boots on. Just to spell it out, they are ready to fight and get lugged just for using words that you use on the street every day of the week but don't use in jail unless you really know the guy.

At this time I really needed visits, but I didn't know if I was going to get any because I didn't get many visits from people on the outside and not even from my own wife at that time. I did most of the time all by myself. I was mean and going nuts. But in my head everyone I loved were doing time with me because they were always on my mind, and all you do most of the time is think of everyone you knew and did things with.

Well, they just called count, and we had to return to our rooms, and the black guys in the room were picking up their things that were on the floor, and of course, I got the look like I didn't belong there and just gave them my normal dirty look. I heard the guy that I hated say they must have had a treat because he hadn't washed in a few days, and when I was in the room, he smelled all that, and his buddies put up with it because they were scared of him, but not me. Piece of shit. I just wanted to smash him in the fuckin' face. I was hoping that they would call count cleared, and all this bullshit would be over so I could go outside and get away from these fuckin' black guys. I just hated to be in the same room with them. These guys were pure scum of the earth. When I was in the room, it was just when I had to be there or had to sleep. Other than that, I was outside walking the track or at work. I took a course in CPR, and if one of them fell to the floor, I wouldn't even go to help them. That is how much I hated them because they made life a living hell for me, and I would enjoy seeing them kick off racist bastards.

Again I asked for a room change, and he looked at me and said, "Why would you want a room change? You have such great bunch of guys for roommates." Again the CO said to me there was no chance of that while I was here and to stop asking for a room change because it was not going to happen. I just walked away before I said something that would get me into more shit, and I still would ask them every week for a room change and thought they might get sick of hearing it and give it to me. Now I was sitting at a round table in the dayroom writing a letter. Sometimes I would just go into a trance and have visions of me stabbing the guy in my room named Trooper several times in the chest and enjoying watching blood gushing from his body. It would be sick thinking this, but thinking this would make me very happy. In my mind, I would get off on it. But then I would wake up from the trance, and I would be in the world of prison again. But sometimes it felt so real to me, but then I'll realize that it was just daydreaming in the dayroom. This guy doesn't know how close he came to being stabbed to death, and I had a weapon on me at all times. This is how much I hated him and still can see his face if I really try. I'll always have hate for him. All that I can hope for is that someone will take this fucking asshole out when he gets out of prison, and it would make me very happy to know this because of the hell he put me though. I started to think about what I was daydreaming about and realized how a man's mind could get really messed up in a place like this; there is no one here to help you.

I watched this guy Trooper come out of the room, and my eyes were locked on him. I started to think and then started to laugh about it and knowing that he was really just a low form of life, and he wouldn't be worth killing, and he will never change. He's just an ignorant bastard. Just thinking about spending the rest of my life in a place like this was just too much for me to comprehend, and I'd rather cut my throat or, as my so-called rat friend did, cut my wrists as I know I would have done if they gave me ten to fifteen years to life. (For what? Drugs.) This would have been the next thing. I would have also tried using a gun but it failed at the pond I was at. People in government do far worse than what I was accused of, getting life sometimes and getting out in a couple of years. It's just not fair. I guess this is how the COs are trained in a correctional institution to mix and mingle with the guys and move guys that don't get along together so there is a fight, and they end up committing each other. The CO's job is to belittle you whenever they can so you can do something stupid and end up getting more time, and this is like job security for the COs.

As I look at it now, I realize how bad they really fucked with me by mixing four black guys in the same room with me. You should never mix certain guys together like this, knowing that there will be trouble, especially four racist black guys to one white guy, and I will never forget the COs that did this to me. The COs are even worse than the cops that are on the outside because they are programmed to mess with your mind. They are very good at that. The cops mess with you to get you in jail, but COs mess with you day in and day out, and it's like a game to them. In the whole five years that I was on the inside, I just met one CO that was a real good guy, and his name was Chapman, and the only one that treated me like a human being, and I will never forget him and hope he is well. I was stuck in the room with this fuckin' black guys, Trooper and his sidekicks, or should I say his followers. As I was looking at him, I just had a shit grin on my face and was contemplating how good it would be to hurt this guy day in and day out. I could do this with a smile on my face. Sometimes I would listen to him talk and realize everything I said to him when we were arguing went right over his head because he was as dumb as a stump. He looked over and saw that I was staring at him and walked over and said, "They put me in this room to fuck with you," and I said, "Do what you have to do and you're still not going to get this single bunk that I have." I just looked at him and said, "Just keep your distance from me along with your followers and I will stay away from you. The cops on the outside couldn't get me to rat and tell them where I was getting my drugs from, and you think a fuckin' CO in here are going to break me? Not even you black guys are going to break me, so try your best."

When I would have to talk to any COs or the blacks in my room, it wasn't for long periods of time because they lacked intelligence. You know, it was really hard to commutate with them because it was too hard for me to learn to talk stupid. I flunked that course, but learned it good while in jail. The black guy Trooper, when he talked to me, it sounded more like a grunt or a slither and in a low voice and with a black gangster way of talking, and to me he is the type of guy who gives good black guys a bad name (piece of shit). This guy told me that he wanted to go back behind the wall, and he wanted to take someone with him and told me that he chose me, and I said to him, "I really don't give a damn."

The next day, I was brought to the garage as usual, and when I walked in, I noticed that there were two garage COs working on a car together and said to myself, "It's taking two of them to put an alternator belt in a car. What a joke." And then they just walked away. I just walked over to see what they were up against and used a jack and a two by four under the tensioner and put the belt on, and they came back after their break, and I was sitting down, and they asked me if I could do it, and I told them that it was already done. They asked how I did it by myself, and I said that I used a jack under the pulley and it went right on. He looked at me and said that it was good to see me back at the garage and the reason for that is that they can sit in their office and let me do the jobs for them. The head mechanic that was in the garage was old, thought he knew it all (asshole).

In the past, they would pay their inmates with doughnuts, and they would be happy as a pig in shit except for me. He asked me, and I said, "No, thanks. I don't work for doughnuts." There would be fresh doughnuts from that day, and they would never offer me any of them from that day. But if there was a doughnut left over from the day before in the garage, those were the ones they would offer me, the hard ones. The only reason for that is because they wouldn't eat them. He said that he was surprised and asked why. I said that they were hard, and he said that I should be glad to get them, and I said that I didn't want them from the start and always told them to throw them out. I said that I was doing this because they sent me here, and it made me think about when I would be doing this in my own garage on my own cars.

The older CO I called Prick came from lunch one day, and he asked me if I wanted a calzone, and I asked him what a calzone was, and he said that it was like a wrap. I said that I would give it a try, and then he said that I would have to eat it in the restroom. I said no, that I would go to lunch at the chow hall before I would eat any food no matter what it was in the restroom and told him to throw it out.

He said, "Even though it's outside food, you still won't eat it?"

I told him again that I was not going to eat food in the toilet, and he said that he was not supposed to give me anything from the street. I turned to him and said, "Where do you think Dunkin Donuts comes from?"

Then he said, "Just go behind the truck and eat it."

Then I said okay. That day after when they sent me back to the unit, I was able to get in touch with my wife and just about pleaded with her to try to make an appointment with the so-called lawyer she got for me and see if he tried to push my revise and revoke through, and she said that she would give him a call. I still was writing a lot of letters to the attorney, and I got one back but never explaining what he was going to do for me, and all I got was just double talk in his letters, I guess just to keep me quiet and to make it look like he was doing something for me. I did get through once in a while and ended talking to the secretary, and all he told his secretary to tell me is not to get into any trouble and just walk away because it would hurt my case. It was easy for him to say; he's doesn't have four black guys in any room he was in. Now the black guys were now tag teaming, and there was always one in the room when I was there, fucking with me and still giving me a real hard time, and I didn't want to take any shit and just walked the track and went to bed even earlier.

Every night I went to bed with pens by the side of my bed and a lock inside two socks under my pillow so it wouldn't rip through just in case they started any shit. I wouldn't think twice to smash any one of them in the head with my lock sock and stab any of the other motherfuckers with my pen if I had to. I sent all the stuff that I went through in letters to my wife and to my daughter so that they would know what I was going through and how many times I asked for a room change and how many times I was refused one. I did this just in case I hurt one or more of these motherfuckers, and believe me, I did have good intentions of hurting any one of them that really fucked with me. All any of them had to do was put their hands on me, and that would have been it. It would have been real bad. I still can't explain it. I just wasn't in my right mind, and it just wouldn't clear up. I just didn't know what I was capable of doing to any of these black guys, and I really didn't give a flying fuck either. Every time I looked at any of them, I had hate in my eyes and throughout my whole body. These COs never let up on me. They were always fuckin' with me, and the worst thing they did was strip-search me in front of women COs, and on many occasions when leaving the room where they stripped me, I would hear them laughing afterward. I'd feel so embarrassed because of what they did to me. Every day that I would get up and I would think, Is this the day that I'm going to get killed, or will it be me hurting someone real bad because of my big mouth? Especially when I was arguing with the black bastards who slept all day. When they were sleeping, the shades were down. I came into the room, and I couldn't see any daylight at all. I really did take chances by turning my back on them, and I did this on too many occasions, not thinking, and going to sleep at night with them still being up, but I really didn't care if I was stabbed during the night or even if I kicked off. It would have been a favor to me. The new thing that they were bitching about was me not cleaning the room again, but how could I when they were always sleeping all day long, and why should I. They messed it up. I was never in the room and was walking the track all day long.

In my whole life I've never seen so many stupid people in one place before, and I had to deal with them day in and out. One of the guys that I cooked with got cocky with a CO, and they moved a black guy in his room also, and to top it off, he was gay, and he was always saying stupid stuff to him in regard to sex. This guy that I cooked with, his name is Pete, and he told me, "Now I know what you're going through." Of course he also hated the black guys that were in my room. He kept on telling the COs that he didn't get along with the black guy in his room also, and he had hepatitis C, and he didn't want to catch anything from him. The CO said, "Deal with it." This was in February 26, 2000, after he complained about the black guy in his room. The black guy was caught having sex in the gym with another guy, and he was lugged out of the unit.

Pete came back from work, and he was as happy as a pig in shit. He came out of his room with a big shit grin on his face; I just said, "I wish the same could happen to me." With there being four black guys in my room, there would be no chance of that happing anytime soon. Well, the way I was always asking for a room change, the guy Pete waited till the end of the day and asked the night CO, who really didn't give a fuck, if he could move a guy in his room that just came into the unit, and he said yeah and to let him know who he was so he could change it in the book. Then he said, "As long as it isn't your next-door buddy. You know who I mean." (Meaning me.)

I wasn't the only one that was singled out in this unit. There were others before me, and this was a way to make guys fight so the COs could bet on to see which one would win. No matter what, one guy would be out of the unit after or both. I still ask God from day to day to please take my life and take me out of this place. I looked for stuff that I could drink while I was in the garage that would poison me, but I didn't want to take something that was just going to make me sick and not put me out for good. Because living this way was really too much for me to handle. What a waste of life. I was supposed to learn something from this. I was still sticking needles in my legs so I could feel pain so I would think of the pain and maybe I wouldn't think of my daughter and wife so much and where I was. Most of the guys that were in here were pure garbage people, and that's including the COs, but not all the inmates are, but a very large number of them are. I really think they enjoy being incarcerated. The hard part is finding someone that you can carry on a conversation with, and this could help me a lot with dealing with the fucked-up guys I had to deal with. Sometimes they would let me clean the COs training hall, and I would dump all the barrels and sweep all the floors and clean all the weight benches and pass the mop around. I would take my sweet time doing it so I could use the weight benches when the COs left to get us the dog food from the chow hall.

One day I was dropped off at this place they called Warren Hall to clean, and this is a place where the COs trained, and as I walked by a stairway, there was a gun on the bottom of the stairs with ammunition, and I just couldn't believe what I was looking at just left there. I wanted so much to pick it up and shoot myself in the head, but then I thought this must be some sort of a setup and just walked away. I'm glad I didn't because I would have missed helping my daughter bring up her kids that I love so much now. Nothing would have made those fuckin' COs really happy if I did what I was thinking of doing at that time. As I was cleaning the hall, I went by the stairs that the gun was on, and a CO was coming down the stairs, and he asked me what I was doing in the hall, and I told him that I was cleaning the area. He just looked at me when he was picking up the things he left on the stairs. Again of course, it was the gun I saw earlier when I came in earlier. I can just imagine what must have been going through his head when he saw that I was there to clean and he left his gun where he left it (see again intelligence). In his head I guess he didn't think there was going to be any inmates in the place that I was cleaning and just left his stuff where I could see it. Just imagine if a real asshole inmate got hold of it. Good thing I wasn't some kind of a real nutcase, and he wouldn't be around to tell anybody the stupid thing he did by leaving a weapon on the stairs with ammo unguarded. That gun should never have left his side no matter what (fuckin' asshole). When I was there and done with what I was expected to do, the CO would come and pick me up, and on one occasion, he had to go back and get some paperwork he left behind, and when he came back to the van, he asked me if I spit in his coffee, and I said no, but he still threw it out the window and said that he didn't trust me. By him saying this, he put sick thoughts in my head and said that's something worth doing to these asshole COs, and this would bring some satisfaction to me for the rotten shit they pull on me. So now to all the COs that transported me from place to place, I always thought about spitting in their coffee cups because of what the last CO stuck into my head. Now as the thought ran through my mind on numerous times, I said to myself, "That's for treating me so bad. Drink up, enjoy it, motherfucker," and I just wanted to do it to the ones who treated me real bad but couldn't bring myself to doing it. Now if it was the ground CO, I would have pissed in it if it was in my head at that time.

When I got back to the unit, I washed up and was getting ready for chow and just started to do my everyday thing and started to write a letters of course to my so-called wife, and as I was writing it, I realized that I wasn't getting any help from her at all and started to drift off into my so-called clouded world again and realized that she didn't marry me, and she really didn't love me but really married the drug that she was stuffing up her fuckin' nose and realize that's the thing she really loved, so she wouldn't have to buy it. Out of all my family, my daughter, Lisa, was the only one who stood by me the whole time that I was incarcerated. I did all my time all by myself as I said, and all I had was just my dreams and hopes, even that fell through as time went on. But it came to my attention that no one in my family really gave a fuck about me, nor did they send me a dime the whole time that I was in jail. I learned to rough it out all by myself, but in my heart they were there but just in my head, and I really learned if you want anything done right, do it yourself. I would think a lot of times that if I was to get out or if I did all my time, I would love to hook up with my wife and treat her like the whore that she really was and maybe she would like it better. In my whole life every woman I ever went with, I always tried to make life as best as I could for them, but now I realize that you just can't change the label that God puts on you when you're born. I see so many guys come in, and it looked like they ruled the world, you know, the bad so-called motherfuckers when they were on the street. Now they are in here, and so many of them but not all are in Bible class and praying to get them out of jail. A lot of them think one year or sometimes a little more is the end of the world to them. These fucking guys are getting good time, not day for day like I have to do. They are all fucked because of the time they got. (I wish.) I'm not saying all of them but a hell of a lot of them, a good majority of them start to carry a Bible around with them, and I found out that it's just a gimmick to look good for the parole board to tell them that they have mended their ways and are into God now, and they realize what they did was wrong. (Bullshit.)

I would see a lot of guys sending cards and letters to their families and wives because they treated them like shit when they were on the street, and they did this so they wouldn't abandon them while they were in jail. I was just in the beginning of my sentence, and I knew in my heart that my wife was going to leave, and I tried so hard by sending cards and letters to her to see if I could melt her cold heart that she had from the use of that shit cocaine, getting fucked over by the guys she went with. My friend Pete said to me in a conversation, "If your wife doesn't leave you and sticks by you like my wife has done three times in a row, she is a keeper and never do her wrong and stick by her no matter what unless you don't love her. If you're just stringing her along while you're in jail, like most of these guys do, you're no damn good, like the rest of these guys."

I started to write letters for a lot of the guys in here as I always did, and they got me canteen for writing for them. On one occasion this one guy I was writing a letter for told his wife that a guy was about to be released from jail that he knew. He was enclosing a picture of him. He told her that he was in the same room as he was, and he told her that he was going to send him by the house and for her to take care of him. It took me a little while, but I caught on. I told her that he was a good guy and send some of the money to him in jail. I asked, "Why are you sending a guy from this place to your home?" and he said that he pimped off his wife so he can get canteen in jail, and if it came to it, he said he'll pimp off her kid too because it wasn't his kid. I just couldn't believe what I was putting down on paper and sending off to his wife, and she was doing it, and I just couldn't believe what I was writing to his wife and telling her saying that he's a good guy. Now how could a guy do such a thing to his wife, and how could she do something like that. Call me stupid, but I could never do such a thing to any woman. He told me that his wife worked in a bar, and that she made just enough money to pay for the bills. This would be extra money they both needed. He said when he's out, he'd take care of his wife and kid, in those exact words, and she can't send any money from what she made, so she pimped herself off to guys so she could send him money for his canteen. I didn't comment on what he was telling me to write to his wife, but he did ask me, and I said if she was willing to do that for him, it was okay with me.

I gave my wife money before I came into this place so I wouldn't have to take any of her money she worked hard for. Well, at least I think she did, but now a lot of things come to mind now after writing this letter for this guy, but I had to get those types of thoughts out of my head. But when my wife did send me money, even though it wasn't hers, usually what she sent me was always chump change, and it felt more like an allowance. After that letter I wrote for the last guy, the thought of her fucking other guys for cocaine the whole time I was in jail was taking more room up in my head. I couldn't get it out. One of the times my wife came up to see me, she acted and talked like her shit didn't stink and she was better than I was. She looked at me like I was a criminal in her eyes. All the guys that she was going with on the outside, I should have tried to pimp her off, and she probably would have liked it. In one of the letters that I was getting, it told me that she was hanging around with motorcycle guys at the time because she did ask me if I knew a couple of them. I have this feeling that the guy that she was going out with was the one that was sending me the letters that I was getting, but every one that I received never had a return address, so it was from the unknown coward that had no balls to let me know that he was fucking my wife. I think he was doing this because he wanted my wife to go ahead and divorce me, and now that he's dead, I will never know if it was her motorcycle guy or the guitar wannabe rock guy that was sending me the letters. But now all I can say is fuck it. Whoever sent me the letters, I was in jail, and he had to realize that there was nothing that I could do about it. I never brought this up at all because I wanted to keep her on my good side because I thought she was trying to help me get out of this godforsaken place. But I was just blinded by all the bullshit and lies, and this was something that my wife was good at, lying. I know I could never treat any woman like she treated me.

Before she met me, her last boyfriend would let her go out with different guys and just convince her that they were just dating so he could go out with different girls while he was seeing her. After they were done with different fuck partners, they would meet at this coffee shop, and they would talk about who they just had sex with, then get back together and talk about it (sick). So now I know she was fucked in the head right from the beginning to do something like this, and I found this out from her own mouth one night a year after we were married. To learn about this after we were married was a fucked-up thing to tell me, but what could I do but accept it and move on. But she did say they would break up with her boyfriend before she did this, and then they would get back together and talk what they did. I knew I didn't marry a virgin, and I went through the same shit with my daughter's mother, pimping herself off at this bar in Westport, but we were not married, so I guess in her eyes she was single. I guess all the weed I was smoking at the time I didn't pick up on it until a friend named Bob saw her at this bar and told me what she was doing. Of course I didn't believe him after I asked her. During that time in my life, I was just thinking with the wrong part of my body, as I always did, and as long as was I getting it, I didn't see anything she was doing as wrong. I was getting sex all the time and thought that she would never do that to me until she kicked me out, but my love life was never the same after that. In my head I thought I could change my wife's ways, but I was wrong, and I guess once a whore, always a whore, and the worst part of it all was, she was a cocaine whore fucked for drugs. It took me a real long time to find this out, and she put on a real good act, and it fooled me till I saw her throw a guy up against a building and grab him, and this was just before I was sent to jail. Then people just started to tell me stories about her when I got out of the small sentence I spent at Dartmouth Correctional, and it was so hard for me to believe, and it took a long time before it hit me because I just didn't want to believe it. When they say love is blind, my name was right in the beginning of the stupid list, and I still thought I could change her (asshole), and I was still in love with her and couldn't believe I could still love her.

At this time I just did almost anything to get away from the scum in the unit. I had no problems with the guys who robbed places, accused of attempt of murders, and drugs, as long as they had some brains and didn't do things to kids or women. Don't get me wrong, I did meet a lot of decent guys, and they just fucked up as I did. I enjoyed hearing a lot of stories from different guys from time to time, and I'll mention some of them as I go along. Just looking around from day to day, I just feel like I'm in a mental institution and kept saying what a fucked-up place to be in. I'm living it. From the first day that I entered jail, and believe me, you just can't stop looking around. It's just crazy, as I was feeling at that time. I remember it all and relive every day of my life now, and it will be to the day I die. The biggest assholes were the COs, the wannabe cops. It seemed like they had to prove something to each other and see whom they could fuck with from day to day, as they did to me. They would take inmates, mix them in with guys that would make them fight one, and then they would step in. What fuckin' dickheads the Cos were in all the prisons that I did time at. My friend that I had on the street named Al brought a couple of COs by my home one time, and I recognized them when I saw them when I was incarcerated. These guys would party just like anyone else, drink and snort coke and do whatever they could get their hands on. But the ones I met never wanted to give out their names and hid what they did very well until they got drunk. Then they would start to spill out their guts and say, "I hope I don't meet you on the inside," and I paid no attention to what they were saying until I asked my friend Al what they did for a job. This is when I found out that they were COs, and after that, I tried to stay away from them and got mad at my friend Al who brought them over my house and told him that they were just like cops to me. When I was on the inside, I did see some of the ones that were partying over my house, and they looked like they did nothing wrong and acted like they didn't know me and didn't stick around long.

In all the time that I was incarcerated, all the COs that I met were the laziest motherfuckin' doughnut-eating, coffee-drinking motherfuckers that I've ever seen in my whole life. They did whatever they could to keep them from doing their job and let things pile up and wait for the inmates to come in and push it on us so they wouldn't have to work. Most of the inmates would work like heck for doughnuts, and the COs always had those inmates on hand, but not me. After watching what a lot of the inmates did with those hands, I'll wait till I get out to eat a doughnut. Well, turkey day is here, and it's one of the holidays that I miss the most, and I would spend the whole day with my family, and I did most of the cooking, of course. When you're in a place like this, you try to make the best out of something bad, and it is real bad in here on every holiday. Well, one of the guys that I cooked with in the kitchen told me how the COs load their cars with food from the kitchen, and when turkey day came, I saw him loading turkeys into the trunks of COs' cars. When I say load them, I mean load them, and I paid no attention to it until my friend told me about it, and that's when I saw it happening on every holiday. This was in Bridgewater Minimum.

They say most if not all inmates are considered bad, and what does that make the COs when you see them telling the inmates to load their cars with food that they are stealing from the kitchens? I get it, they are making the inmates do it so they are not actually doing the stealing. When you see this going on, and I'm in jail and convicted for doing a crime, and we get our faces rubbed in it day after day on what we did, but it's okay to load their cars with all the food that they are stealing from the kitchens. I just forgot they are doing time because they are in the same place as us, but the only difference is that they get paid for being thieves and are able to go home at night. I guess this is what they call fringe benefits, and this must be in their contracts when they get the job working for the prison system stating that it's okay to remove over stock food from the prisons, and it's not considered stealing; it's considered overstocked.

There was a high-ranking woman CO who worked in the training hall in Bridgewater called Warren Hall. She owned a restaurant down the Cape, and she would bring lots of the food from Bridgewater kitchen to her restaurants to serve to her customers, and I know this from hearing other COs talk about it, and of course, that's still not stealing. I was always eavesdropping to hear shit like that but made it look like I wasn't paying any attention to what they were talking about. The Spanish kid (Jose) told me this also because he saw it happing on many occasions because I told him that someday I was going to write a book, and he asked me to make sure that I put this in it because he took me seriously. I'm writing this now because of my aunt that lives in Florida. She told me that I should, and now I'm doing it just so people know what goes on in the jails and how they treat guys who are incarcerated.

The training that COs get should be based upon your record and how many times that you have been incarcerated, how you handle yourself while you're in jail, act toward authority. They don't give a damn who you are and what you are in for and treat you in the most disrespectful way they can. They have to realize that undressing an inmate in front of woman COs is real bad and isn't considered a big joke. They have to understand we are human also. Just took the wrong turn in life, as a lot of people do. When this happens to you, just do it, and I would just look up at the ceiling and just do what was expected of me and try not to let it bother me. I just got used to them, listening to them laugh when you leave the room. Of course you're embarrassed. They tell inmates to do what they tell you to do or get sent behind the wall, and when you're in a maximum lockdown, you can't go outside and walk and get decent visits like you do in a minimum. Everything is a lot better when you're not in lockdown for twenty-three hours a day, and that's all day long. But when an inmate gets real pissed off, as I am all the time, it gets to the point that you just don't give a flying fuck after a while. It really takes a toll on you, and after a while you don't really care where they send you because you adjust to wherever they send you, and you just say fuck it. It's real good that I could control myself, but some guys just lose it and go nuts. That's when the COs jump you or just send out for the IPPS. Most of the time they send for the IPPS because the COs start the shit to get inmates pissed off, then they back off and let the IPPS handle it. They don't fuck around. They gang attack you, cuff whoever, and ship them out to a maximum prison, and when they call the IPPS in, it's a no-win situation because they hate to work also. You do get into a lot of fights, and it's usually for stupid stuff, but you have to cover up real good because of the AIDS, and this is one thing you don't want to get over a stupid argument. I just go with the flow and stay to myself, and I'm not here to make friends. I just want to do my time and get the hell out of here.

Right now I'm just looking out the window and waiting for the winter to break because everything looks dead as I feel inside while watching the days, month, and years go by very slowly, always with my family on my mind. While you're doing time, you tend to drift off and go into your own world and just don't give a damn what happens. All I thought about was going home and how the two lawyers that I hired fucked me over and how I still had feelings for my wife and how much I loved my daughter. But the worst part was remembering over and over how I got here. It was just a repeat nonstop thing that went on every day I was in this fuckin' place. When you're here, you don't learn a damn thing but how you can commit different types of crimes that you have heard from different inmates from time to time. One inmate told me you always got to find out different ways to better yourself, study the jobs you do, and try not get caught at it.

This is the shit I have to live with and listen to all the time. I just say get a real job and stop coming back here, what they call correctional facility (short for jails). What they do to you is a form of brainwashing and try to erase all your thoughts and keep telling you to forget what you did on the outside and that this is your life now till the day you die. Then they keep telling you that your living in jail is your life forever. And a lot of guys believe it and tell you over and over again that you will be back. There are no programs in this place but anger management and church and jobs that COs don't want to do because it's beyond them and because it involves work, and this is what they avoid as often as possible. They don't want you to succeed; they want you to leave with your mind fully erased of thoughts and become clueless, and this is one of their programs that is mandatory that you learn before you leave here. Out of all the programs that they do teach you, and I forgot to put it down, was this one that you have to take while you're incarcerated: how to be dumb as a stump so you can return to jail so the COs have job security. Most of the COs takes this course before they start the job. When the COs get tired of what they are doing, they edge an inmate on so that the inmate turns on them, and they end up getting hurt, and they get out saying that they are emotionally damaged and can't do their job anymore. If people only knew what they do to guys that are in jail, the public would never believe it, so this is why I'm putting this in. I just can't believe what they put me though and how it affected me to this day. I will never come back to a place like this. I would rather die first before I would come back, and the only way would be if someone was to hurt my family, and still I would not come back if you know what I would do.

I don't want anyone to think that all black guys were bad. I did meet a lot of real good black guys in jail, but the ones who would address themselves as niggers were all racist assholes as the ones I had in my room. I was still messed up in the head and was still in a fog, and this guy Trooper had no idea how close he came to getting stabbed in the eye with a pen. He pissed me off one day so bad that I was standing over him one morning and wanted so much to stick him right in the head or eye and didn't and just went out and walked the track and put it behind me. This guy made life in here a living hell for me the whole time he was in the same unit as I was, along with his followers. As I walked the track, I would be talking to myself and calling my wife all kinds of names because she wasn't putting any effort to try to help me get out of jail. She was just letting me rot in this place and wasn't sending me any of my money to buy things I needed while in jail. I never told her that I was cursing her because I always thought that she was trying to help me, but in my mind, I always had doubts and then thought that you need all the help you can get from the outside. Being locked up in a place like this is just a waste of life, and you don't get anything out of it but hate that just builds up inside of you and just think about everyone that put you in this place, and what really hurts is my cousin was one of them. I can't understand how this pays back society for the crime that you did by taking five years of your life from you. All this does is break up families and put them on government assistances. How is this paying back society for the so-called crime that you did? I think that working it out day for day would be harder on a person than serving it in a jail. Now think about it, making the taxpayer pay for your time that you're spending in a state prison when it's your first offense. I could have worked for the town that I convicted in for half pay, plus use my trade to repair all the town's vehicles.

Along with some of the nasty letters I was getting I think from my wife's boyfriend and from some of my so-called friends, all the letters were saying how my wife was seen at different bars and clubs and was just thrown out of a bar for being drunk and disorderly. In one of the letters, I kind of knew it was from her boyfriend telling me that she was giving him blow jobs every night, and he probably got my address from one of my letters that my wife left on the table when he was over her father's house. To this day I think the sex letters that I was getting was definitely from her newfound rock star guitar player asshole wannabe boyfriend, and he was just rubbing the sex stuff in my face just to piss me off so I would divorce her. Being in jail and getting letters like these all the time was really taking a toll on me. I just didn't want to believe it, and in jail I couldn't do a thing about it but let it weigh on my mind, and I curse both of them for it. When I met her, she was pregnant by another guy that I knew, and she just started to come by my house day after day and complaining about how my friend dumped her when she found out that she got pregnant. He just saw her once on a one-night stand. She thought he got her pregnant. I thought to myself it's impossible to know that soon but didn't comment on it. She kept saying that she knew he got her pregnant after he had sex with her the first night. She said that she felt it forming inside her right away. Right there the flags were up, and I didn't see no damn way she could have known this unless she was psychic.

    My so-called friend called me up and told me that he thought she was nuts, and he was trying for a while to fuck her, and that's all he wanted and then didn't want anything more to do with her after that. When we dated, this is what he told me. She said only if he could get some coke that night. When I talked to him, he said that he never bought or ever gave any coke to any girl that he ever went out with. So that was lie number one, and like all the rest she told me, it went right over my head. I was so stupid when it came to women and always believed whatever they told me. Well, he got his way and got the piece of ass he wanted. When he woke up the next morning, he showed her off to his father while she was sleeping naked in bed, and she had no idea what he had done. After he told her that he didn't want to see her, she started to come over my house so much that when my girlfriend drove by and saw her car, she broke up with me thinking that I was fuckin' her. I told my future wife this, and it didn't even faze her in the least. She just said she looked young enough to be my daughter. She had the baby that she was carrying aborted, and after that she really started to hang around like a weight around my neck. On quite a few occasions, she was over my house before I could even try to leave. I really wanted to see if I could get back with my girlfriend, but it never happened.

BUSTED

After a while I started to take her everywhere. I went because I just couldn't shake her off. She was just was there all the time. After a while I just got used to her tagging around, and when I went out to eat, she was there, and I just forgot what she had done, and I just started to get along with her and got used to her hanging around, and she just started going everywhere I went. On one occasion she asked me to go to New Hampshire, and I hadn't been out of the city in a very long time, but it was raining real hard, and I said to myself, it's going to suck. We ended up going up in a rusted, bold, tired old Subaru, and when we got there, it was really raining still. She just said it will be all right. We got a room, and the next day I opened the shades. I just couldn't believe what I saw when I looked out the window, and that was all it took. It was so hard to believe that I could fall in love again with a woman like this after my daughter's mother, and it was a long time since I felt like this again, and it was so hard for me to accept. Just then I looked at her as my best friend. In the whole time that she was with me, which was three months, she never asked me to get her any coke, and then one day she did, and I said, "That's shit," and she said, "Just a little," and that started the ball rolling. The guy that I was buying the coke from I knew him as a kid. We went to the same school, and we would hang around with each other once in a while along with his brother as kids. At this time a couple of guys would come over, friends of mine, and ask me if I could get some coke for them, and I didn't think about it being illegal but just got it for them because they were my friends, and their wives liked the product also. Well, she would see this and ask me for some every time I would get it for them, and before you knew it, she was saying, "Can you get some for me like you did your friends?" I was so blinded by the fact I didn't see what was happening to her for a while, and then I noticed that she was getting very cold toward me, to just about everyone and just keeping to herself except my friend named John.

Some of my friends were telling me that the weight was getting to be a real problem, and it was under, and I just said that I wasn't taking anything out, and it was as I got it. I called my friend and asked him if he checked the weight of the stuff that I was getting, and he said that the weight will always be right on the mark. I noticed that there was money that was starting to disappear, and the coke that I was getting for friends was under and they would bring a scale when I got it for them, and it would be right on the mark. Then I set my wife up and told her where the stuff was, and I was going out with a friend and would be back in a while. When I came back and reweighed it, I then knew why it was underweight and was wondering where some of my money was going. Before I knew it, I had three friends asking me for it, and this just helped me pay for my wife's habit, and that was a thousand dollars a week. After a while this was the only way I could afford her habit. I would break it up into smaller packages so I could keep track of what she was doing and what my friends wanted and started to hide it from my wife because she was stealing it beside what she was doing.

I started to count them in front of her so she would know that I knew what I had so she would stop stealing it. This is when she started to take a little out of each one to see if I noticed. It took a while before I really knew that she was stealing a lot of it from me, and it wasn't for at least a month before my friends started to tell me that their stuff was really under. I told her about it, and she just said that she never touched it and that that my friends just wanted more, and I just gave her the look. It stopped for a while, and it didn't take long before it started to happen again, and I started to get mad, and I just said "fuck it" and told her that she had a problem and that she had to stop because I didn't want to do this anymore, and she said, in these exact words: "This is the only enjoyment I have now and will slow down, I promise."

This was the week that I got busted. This was March 18, 1997, and a so-called friend named Bob set me up for the bust and was asking me all kinds of stupid questions over the phone and said that he wanted some coke, and no one ever did this before because this is one thing I told my friends not to do. He came over, and I asked him what the hell he was doing asking those questions on the phone. He said he didn't mean anything by it. So I went to get it, and I had some stuff hidden in an exhaust pipe and had it hidden away from my wife. He looked at me and said out loud, "You hid it in an exhaust pipe under the porch?" and I just looked at him and told him that was all I had at this time. Then I said to him that this was going to be the last time that I was going to be doing this, and I just didn't want to do this anymore. Then I asked him again why he was asking all kinds of stupid stuff on the phone, and he had no answer. The whole time that he was in my home, he was acting strange while he was sitting in the chair, and I just felt there was something up and strange with him. He left, and I told my wife about it, and she said not to worry and it was just me. I then said, "He never comes on a Tuesday. It was always on a Friday for his girlfriend," and she just said, "Just forget about it."

That week I ordered some more off my friend Larry, and it took a long time to get in touch with him, and when I did, I got some for myself and my three friends. It was just eight ounces a half a pound, and my wife told me that I should get more because I told my wife that my friend was going to stop selling it, and she convinced me that I didn't get enough and we were going to run out, so I ordered another half pound, and this included a lot of my friend's money. I didn't need it, so I buried it until my friends wanted it, and I didn't want it lying around the house, so I buried it in my yard and just kept enough for my wife's nose. But I had to make sure that it was broken up because my wife didn't know when enough was enough. My wife was tall, very thin, dyed blondish hair, good-looking, but if you look at her fast, she looked like Olive Oil, Popeye's girlfriend.

My cousin came by and I told him that I was done with the product, and this was going to be the last time that I was going to get any. Then out of nowhere, he then said to me that he wanted to know where I had it buried in case anything happened to me. I couldn't understand why he would even ask me that unless he knew something was going to happen. I trusted him so much that he was the only one who knew where it was and just where I had buried it. After that we went down in my basement to smoke a joint, and I gave him some coke as he never would do when he was selling it and a joint. It wasn't long after he left he called, and it must have been at least twenty minutes and said that he got pulled over by the narcs, and they searched his car and found nothing. He had just left my house with something that I gave him. It was the narcs that pulled him over, asked my cousin where he was coming from, and he said that he just came from his cousin's house. Then they asked him if I had any drugs in my home, and he said that he didn't know. That's what he told me he said. When he was talking to me, he said that they were on their way over my house. Then I said that I had to hang up because a cop car just pulled up in front of my house. As I looked out the window, they pulled up in just a regular police car, and as I opened the front door, they rushed in. The head narc asked me if the dogs bit, and I said I didn't know. When someone was rushing in, I tried to get the leash, but by the time I got to the closet door, the cop had shot one of my Dobermans in the head. When she got shot, she ran down the cellar stairs and went under the cellar stairs. As they rushed down into the cellar, my wife was powdering her nose, and they caught her doing the product. When the cop discharged his weapon in my front room to shoot my dog, my wife was right below where he was shooting. What if he had missed? It went through the floor. This bullet would have hit my wife for sure. Today the mark where the bullet went through my dog's head and into the floor is filled but is still visible to the eye. I just looked at the cop and said, "You didn't have to do that," and he had this grin on his face like he enjoyed what he had just done. This was the first week of spring, and the last weekend that I was free for a long time. The weird thing about it was the cops knew just where to go, like there was an X to mark out the spot for them. Or maybe by someone who knew where the Coke was, and the only one who knew where it was buried was my cousin Charlee Rat. I told the cops that my wife didn't know a thing about the drugs and had no knowledge of the amount I had. She was just a user. (What an ass I was.) Now I'm in this place with a bunch of asshole COs who are probably no better than I was.

These COs think that they are gods, and they abuse me all day long just for the fun of it and get their rocks off because the power of the state gives them this right. In this place, there is nothing to do but think about what you're in jail for and your family. This is one thing you just can't stop doing. It goes on day in and day out. It's like watching the same movie over and over again. I was saying to myself, "This will be the last time that I am going to get the coke that I got, and it is the last time." I didn't want it to end this way. But now that I think about it, that was the last time I ever touched that shit, and I thought about how much I lost messing with that stuff. I remember it very clearly. The way the narcs raided the house is how I said it was going to happen. I tried to tell my wife that this was the way it was going to happen, and she just didn't want to listen.

Now here I am looking out the window at Bridgewater Minimum and just thinking what people are doing out on the outside, being free and not having someone telling them what to do. I'm so lost without my wife because we did everything together, and we were very seldom apart unless she was at her hangout called the Dog House. While I'm looking out the window, it's in February, and everything is dead, like the way I feel inside, just dead thinking about how messed up my life is and having to deal with the scum in here, and I'm including the COs also. To me a good number of these guys are the lowest form of life; I could give a good shit for any of them. I put them in the same class as the black guys who want to be called niggers now in the room that I'm in. Now don't get confused, I'm not talking about black people, just the ones who want to be called niggers, and I just can't understand it. Why would they want to be called this?

The year just changed, and it's the year 2000, and I'm hoping that the summer gets better and I can get out of this fog that I'm in. I have so much hate in me that it would be hard for me to put it into words; that's why I don't. It really feels like the winter will never end, and what a long year it was being cooped up like this. Well, spring is right around the corner, and it's coming close to the day I got busted. As I was walking around the track, I noticed that the flowers were starting to come up, and I started to think about my apples trees in my yard. I'm reading from one of my letters I had sent home, and it's Sunday 8:45 in the morning, July 2, 2000. I have a news clipping from one of the newspapers, and it's saying that a former principal is getting three years' probation for possession of heroin in New Hampshire by a federal judge. How come he was able to do this and didn't get a mandatory sentence like I got. Maybe it's because it's in a different county. I have more than one of these stories that I wrote about in my letters I sent home, and I guess it's about who you get for a lawyer. I would love to put the attorney's and the judge's name down and what a good job the lawyer did to a first offender. He got me five fuckin' years. This was after my lawyer told me three but didn't remember telling me that. Now as for me putting down any names, I don't know but I will just say the lawyer who represented me got busted with a kilo and never got any time, what does that tell you. Again it's who you know or who you give up to pay your debt to the courts after getting in trouble for possession of drugs. They should do something with this mandatory sentence. They are unfair and bad for the inmates and bad for society because you're going to be really messed up when you get out and you don't know which way is up and have to readjust to being back in with society that you were taken away from. Taking people away from society and families and locking them up for long-term is real bad for society and for inmates. They tend to fall back on social programs, and again it's the taxpayers who are the ones who pay for it while they are in jail but pay for it again when they get out. Think about it.

    I was still working at the auto garage and was able to keep my hands on tools. Even though I hated the guys I worked for, I was working on their transport vehicles. It was what I did on the street and in the school that I worked at, so it came easier. The guys in the garage were lost and were like all the rest of the COs, lost and without a clue. Maybe they were good at one time but were far from that now. The cars that I was working on were easy cars to work on. Most were Chevys, and those were the ones that I worked on most of my life. The only problem was that my mind was always someplace else and thinking about home, on the street, and my family, and it was real hard adjusting to prison life. It got to the point that I was just about begging my wife when I could get in touch with or call the lawyer to see if he was going to try to get me out or let me know what was going on. My first attorney told me to get in touch with him so he could put in for a revise and revoke, and he was just like the new attorney we hired, never there, and if he was getting my phone messages, he wouldn't even respond with a letter. Then I realized it was a waste of time. I was all by myself doing time and had no visits at this time; I was stuck in my own world dealing with all the shit that came my way. I just about spent all the money that was left in my canteen account. What money I left with my wife before I came in was most likely gone as well. By now she was having too much fun outside; I was soon forgotten. Like they say, out of sight, out of mind. Now when I was telling her on so many occasions about the way I was living in this hellhole, how bad it was, she just carried on with her life like she was blocking out everything I was telling her. Now for all the bad things that I ever did throughout my life, I was paying for it all. Just living with all these fucking assholes that I was in jail with day in and day out was one hell of a payback. The probation officer that was handling my wife case must have known that she was getting high but was very easy on her. The reason I say this is due to all the things that I was getting in letters saying what she was doing when she went out clubbing. If I know her like I know her now, she found a way to get around the drug testing because for sure she would be in jail herself. But there was something about my wife. She was able to dress up real good with no makeup, nail polish, nothing that would be outstanding that would make her out to be a drug addict. This was just another way she cried out to the courts just to get what she needed to save her own ass, get her probation plea from the courts. She fooled them like she did me. Now I think about it, I wish that she got time like I did; then she would know what I went through, and she wouldn't have sent me letters saying that it will make me come out a better person. The best part was when she told me to find God while I was in jail. He will help me handle the guys that I'm in jail with. I still say that God does not come into a place like this because I could never feel him in my heart the whole time that I was incarcerated. Plus there is too much deception in this place.

After I do my time in this place, I will never stick out my neck for any girlfriend or anybody ever again. I feel no woman is worth the time I spent in this hellhole. Damn it, where are all the good women in this world. I feel so much like a fool. The reason I told the cops that she didn't know anything about the coke was she looked so fragile, and she was my wife, and I thought that's the way it should be. The one day she spent in the county jail, a black girl took her jacket and bullied her all night long, and she's really scared of black people. When her father came to bail her out and she walked by me, she gave me a dirty look, and if looks could kill, I would have been dead. The thing that hurt the most is that she left me there and didn't even try to bail me out. I told her what was going to happen before this happened, if we got busted, but all she had to say was she wasn't ready to quit doing coke. I know she worked out some sort of deal with the prosecutor because she never lost her license and never did any time, just got two years' probation, and that was a joke, but she still had to look toward judgment day. When she was asked about the drugs, she told the narcs that she knew nothing at all about the drugs that were found in the house, and that was her bullshit story. Let me tell you, she knew everything that there was to know about it, even the guys I bought it from. She even made a few pickups for me from the guy at the bar my friend owned because she was that anxious to stuff it up her nose. The other thing was she never wanted to wait. She was always thinking that I was going to run out and wanted to make sure I didn't. One of my best friends was a big guy over six feet tall, dark hair, but was a gentle giant really. A good natured guy but loved his coke. John would come by just about every week just to hang around with my wife and I on the weekends. He'd say, "Let's drink a few beers and do a couple of lines and smoke." It came to the point that it was the weekend, and of course, I would go along with it after working all week. I mostly smoked pot and drank, and my wife and friend would do the coke, but as long as he was putting it out, she was sucking it up to save what she had. I would look at her and tell her "That's enough," and she would totally pay no mind to what I was telling her.

    But of course as time went on, my wife would say, "Come on, do some with me and we will have so much fun in bed," and that was all she would have to say to me. She would tell me that she wanted to start off by giving me a blow job after I put coke on it. Boy, there is almost nothing like a good blow job from a woman who wants you to put coke on your dick. That was all the question I wanted to hear, her telling me she wanted a cokesicles. After that, that was all she would have to say to me. I would be like putty in her hands after that. I didn't have any answers or questions that I wanted to ask her. When I found out that it would make me stay awake longer, I thought, Great, I can get more done in my garage and make more money, and it would make life more comfortable for the both of us. This lasted for a while until I started to realize that it was taking a toll on me, and I started to mess up in the garage.

One night I just finished doing body work on a car, and all I had to do was paint it, and my wife called me in, said that was enough for that night, and I went in. The reason for that was because she ran out of coke and wanted more. I also did some more coke that night and had the car that I had to paint on my mind and went to bed just to hear her start to breathe real weird in bed. So I got up and was getting dressed to go outside, and she woke up and said, "Don't go out to that garage," and of course, I said I won't. Of course, I waited for her to fall asleep and went out to the garage and started to mix the paint and the second coat of paint. I put on the hood of the car a long line of snot coke that ran out from my nose and made a large ring on the hood of the car. Of course, I wasn't using a paint mask. The line of snot was still hanging attached to my nose. I just snorted it back up into my nose, but it left a large ring embedded on the hood of the car. I called myself a load of names, and I tried to cover it up but couldn't and went back into the house to think about the mess I made, only to make more work for me the next day. My wife got up and said, "You went out to the garage, didn't you?" I said yes and told her that I messed up, and she said "I told you so," and to hear that from my wife was enough. That night, I told her that I was going to stop doing lines then said, "That's fucking shit." That was my exact words, and I said that it was time to stop, and her answer to me was, like, "I told you before I'm not ready to stop," and that she had it under control. It was real messed up when I got caught with all the coke. All my so-called friends that I used to have stood far away from me and didn't return any of my calls even though I owed them some of the product the cops took from me. Not one of them sent me any money, not one cent, and all the ones who owed me money never gave it to me and never even sent me a letter the whole time that I was incarcerated. Even the ones that owed me money for fixing their cars never paid me. I did see a couple of them when they let me out on bail and said that I could use the money that they owed me, and they said that I was out of business and that they didn't have to pay me anymore.

Well, it's time for count, and I have to go inside for the rest of the night. I hate going inside because of the black guys I have to deal with, including the fucking COs, and they tell me that they fuck with me because I'm a cocky motherfucker, and they can't stand the way I look at them. I just came in from the outside for count, and these are some of the things that I was thinking about while walking around the track, which I do every day to keep me from getting in trouble and remembering to watch what I say, most of all to the COs. At this time I have to stay out of trouble and watch out not to get lugged, as my attorney kept telling me because it will mess up my chance for a revise and revoke when I go back into court again. I said I had to remember to call the lawyer today and not let the black guy get to me, watch what I say to the COs, and think about how much I wanted my revise and revoke to go through and hope for a reduction in my sentence. The only person that was trying to help me some was my daughter, by staying in my home and paying the mortgage to keep me from losing it and having a place to come home to. I tell her it's like an investment for her future and tell her that I will leave it to her when I die, and I think that's a damn good deal, but I hate it when I tell her that someday I will die, as I told her mother the same at the age of twenty-five.

All my family's birthdays are coming up, and I got to either make cards for them or buy them through the canteen because I try never to forget them, then maybe I hope I'll get some letters from them no matter what as long as it was mail. I never forget my family even though I will not get a card from any of them. I know this because I didn't get any letters from any of them at this time, and being in a place like this, getting a letter is like gold to any of the guys in here. I'm looking outside, and I'm looking at the snow coming down, and Christmas is right around the corner, and it's killing me like it always does, and I'm going to miss four of them; I know this in my heart. When I was walking the track, I was able to let loose and show my feelings and cry because a lot of times I'm thinking about my family that I miss so much. The worst of the worst is not being able to put up a Christmas tree and go out and buy things for them. I'm the only one who holds the Christmas spirit and goes all out to buy things for my entire family member and gets nothing in return. I tell my daughter not to get me anything because she was the only gift that her mother had ever given to me that meant the most to me. My present from her to me was never taking any of her kids away from me because my love for family was everything to me, as my mother always said and told me to carry on.

All that Christmas means to me in a place like this is another year I can cross off the calendar as it's still an everyday thing for me to cross the days off every night, and then it hits me. I have less than four more years before I get out, and that killed me inside knowing this. I just want this nightmare to come to an end, and I'm not learning a lesson by them putting me in a place like this. It just makes me very bitter and hate a lot of the people who put me in here, fuckin' hypocrites. I've had time to think about it, and I think it was unjust, and I hate the court system and lawyers; then I just curse the lawyer who got me the five years. I know I can never own a bird or any animal in a cage ever again. Just the thought of seeing it in a cage will kill me inside because that's the way I feel inside. The most common thing I think about is killing myself, and this is always on my mind, but I think, what would it do to my daughter, and how would she take it? Now as for my wife, she wouldn't really give a flying fuck because I now realize she married the product, not me. When it disappeared, she disappeared also.

Right now I know I'm really fucked up in the head, and I know this because of my thoughts and how I'm thinking and all the stuff that goes through my head. I know what I'm thinking are crazy things and are things that I would never think about doing on the street. It's really bad in this place and all the other places that I've been at. They treat you like you're an animal, and they enjoy it, and the madder you get, the worse they treat you, so don't let them know it's bothering you. I hate these COs more and more each day that goes by, and they all know it, and when I look at them, it's like I'm looking right through them. I think they know it because it shows on my face because I have that look.

The CO just brought me back from the garage. After chow and count, I'll go to the greenhouse to earn good time because I heard from a CO that the mandatory sentences might be changed, and we will be able to use the good time that we earned, but maybe he's blowing smoke up my ass. Who really knows in a place like this (craziness). To me, anytime I can cut off my sentence in a place like this a plus, and to get out sooner by doing jail programs, I'm all for that.

As time went on, I got into all those stupid programs that guys do. I found out that what that CO told me was just bullshit, and he didn't hear any such thing, just another way of messing with me. I was telling another guy about what the CO told me, and of course, it got back to the CO. He shook down my room, and he ripped it apart, and it was just in my area, and threw all my stuff all over the room, and of course, this is when you realize that you have to watch who you talk to in a place like this. Fuckin' snitch. The black guys that were in my room went through my stuff when I was at work and stole a couple of bags of potato chips, and I told them that I want them back when I came back from my walk. When I came back to the room, I noticed that the bags were there, and one bag was open, and in front of them, I opened the bag, threw the rest of the bag right in the garbage. The guy who took the bag of chips said, "Why you dumped out the rest of the bag?"

I looked at him and said, "After you put your hands on it, it's garbage to me."

It was okay. I found ways to get them back. When I was walking the track, I found some dog shit, and I waited for that guy Trooper to do his laundry and threw the shit in his laundry when it was in the dryer and then sat back and watched. When he went to fold it, he got so pissed off and turned and looked right at me, and I just smiled. I never told him that I did it, but I think he kind of knew it was me because I had the look, you know, that shit-eating grin on my face that just about gave me away. This was a lesson to learn. Never tell guys that are in jail with you anything you don't want to get around unless you really know especially things you don't want the COs to know. Of course, wouldn't you know, he was one who ratted me out to the CO. Look what just happened. It didn't bother me what I did because I did my laundry at the mechanics garage, so he couldn't do something to my laundry, and we just had this hate for one another. Well, of course, I had to go to work, and I was thinking that he was going to do something to my stuff in the room, and when I got back, there was shakedown going on in the room again. As I walked in, I said, "Here we go again, another shake down." You have to stay out of the room when they are doing it. While I was sitting at one of the tables in the dayroom, they were taking the black guy that wanted to be called a nigger all the time. When I saw they put the cuffs on that piece of shit Trooper, I looked at him, smiled at him, and was so damn happy that they were lugging that piece of shit. He just happened to glance at me on the way out, and I said to myself, You never got me lugged beside you as you wanted to do. After that day I never saw that piece of shit again, and I'm real glad because I hated that slimy bastard. If I could have hurt him real bad and got away with it, I would have been really satisfied, for what he put me through.

After Trooper was lugged, the word nigger was seldom used around the unit again the whole time that I was in Bridgewater Minimum because he took the word nigger with him. When it was over, I entered the room, and the rest of them were all standing around, and one looked at me and said to me that I must be happy now that Trooper's gone, and I just looked at them and said, "Damn right. That guy was a piece of shit in my book, and I couldn't stand him." He just looked at me and stared and got up, and I said, "Go ahead, you will be in the hospital tonight," and he noticed that I had a pen in my hand and backed off. He looked at me and said that I had to go to sleep sometime, and I looked at him and said, "I know and that works both ways, and nothing ever happened or came from it." Even though he was gone, I didn't change my routine and still did the same thing I always did, walked the track and went to bed every night early after count, waiting for the next day so I could cross it off my calendar. The next day, the IPPS came in and shook down the whole unit. Of course he was a snitch, and he told the IPPS about everyone that the guys were doing in the unit. When the IPPS entered the room that I was in, they tore it apart again. My stuff was all over the room and all down the hall and in the next guy's room. I went to the next room over and asked Peat, whom I got along good, if any of my things were in his room. Of course it was. At least this time I got all my stuff back because the leader of the black guys was gone. When I went to the auto garage the next day, I was strip-searched as soon as I got out of the van right out in the open. When they got done with me, I looked inside the garage and was looking out the window, and the guys that were from Plymouth Forestry were getting strip-searched right in the open. As I was right in the street in front of this bigwig named Karen, she watched them while they were being strip-searched.

At the time of this incident, three of the guys from Plymouth ended up getting lugged because they were caught with cigarettes that were left for them to pick up. It's so fuckin' stupid. They're outside, it's their lungs, so let them smoke the shit they found in the street or what someone left them. It's not inside the unit. They were stripped while cars were going by, and there were three bare-assed guys standing there with a woman watching it all go on. I hope she got off on it too, looking at three guys with their dicks swinging in the breeze. Fuckin' bitch just had too much power. One of the COs that was in the garage was also watching and said, "That woman Karen is and always will be a bitch." I would use the real word, but I really didn't know her that well as he did, so I will use the word *bitch* instead of *cunt* but not in front of a CO. The crazy thing about it is that they were smoking outside, and what makes it so right for the COs to smoke but not the inmates? I'm not a smoker, and if it's so hard to quit, why do they think an inmate can just quit like that with no problem? Is it because we are in jail and this makes it easier for us and the guys that are in jail to no longer have a craving.

My best friend at the time was this guy named John, and he was helping me with my wife's problem by purchasing some of the coke and probably tapping my wife along with it, like an extra bonus for helping me with the price of the coke. He really didn't know how bad my wife was with the coke. He just kept feeding it to her even after I told him to stop. I just told him that she was doing a lot of coke, and

I really couldn't afford her habit on my own. I think he was buying it for himself but said it was for his wife also. Every time he came over, my wife was right there when he was picking his share of the stuff. My wife was probably hoping that he was going to do some with her. When he was checking it out, he would try some of the product, and he would always ask my wife, "Do you want to do some?" My wife would jump at the offer always. I took her aside for the second time and told her to stop it, and she was just too stupid to realize he was just offering it to be kind or a payback for having sex with him. I really don't know, and I will never know because my so-called best friend doesn't talk to me anymore. But of course she was just being selfish, thinking of herself, as she always did, wanting to save the coke she already had stashed away and see what she could get for free off him. With my wife, the more she had seen, the more she wanted, and a half of an ounce to an ounce a week just wasn't cutting it for her. Every week that my friend John came by, she wanted some of the coke that he was getting so again she could save what she had for herself.

When the cops raided the house, she was downstairs in the cellar, sitting at the table, powdering her nose, and I would have paid anything to see her face at that second. I can just see her now saying that she had nothing to do with it, all the coke that was in front of her. I can just see it now more clearly, my wife spilling her guts out and telling the cops whatever they needed to know and of course saying that she knew nothing at all about the drugs. Probably thinking that the narcs were going to let her go. What a joke. These are the ones that guys should call them dicks instead of the cops because that's what they are. Most of these narcs are the most crooked cops that are on the force along with being thieves that took a lot the stuff that was in my attic, and it wasn't drug-related items. When they were done tormenting my wife they placed her next to me at the kitchen table. I looked at her when she was close to me and told her to remember what I had told her to say, that she knew nothing about what I had and what I was doing with it. My wife was surprised when they cuffed her and arrested her along with me, and she looked up at the cop then glanced at me and said, "What are you doing?" She ended up going to the same place in New Bedford as I did called Ash Street Correctional, and it killed me inside when they did that to her.

When I was able to read the newspaper, the narcs said that I was supplying the whole East Coast with cocaine, and that was news to me. During the time of my arrest, I was driving two old cars and owing a mortgage while working at a school for chump change, and that was just enough to pay the mortgage every month. All the money I was making in my garage was paying for car insurance and my wife's coke habit, and I was working nonstop all the time, getting very little sleep, and it got to the point that I was even nodding off at work. If I was taking care of the whole East Coast, I'm sure I would have had a safe house and never would have found what they found. Living where I was living, if they found something, it would have been a very small amount, and I would have been living the best way a person could live. I would have been living high on the hog, as they say. This means very well, no joke intended. My house would have been paid, and I would have had houses in different people's names and a real big shop, plus driving real nice cars and not working for peanuts at a school. It's just that I loved the job and the kids I was teaching. But the narcs just needed that pat on the back and say that they just broke up a large cocaine ring. The best part was telling the newspaper that I was selling cocaine to the students at the school that I was working at and whatever they could conjure up to make them look good for the DA's office. Narcs are nothing but hypocritical scumbags, and without their rats, they couldn't do their jobs unless they were kicked in their heads about something. They do things just like everyone else but hide it real good, and every once in a while, they got to throw one of their own to the dogs to make it look good, but they are well off when it's ready for their retirement. But whoever they throw under the bus, they are usually a nobody, and it goes to court, and you never hear about it again. A lot of these Cos are as bad as the inmates, and of course in their eyes, they do no wrong.

When I'm in the garage, I hear them talk about each other, when I'm right above in a loft in the garage of course while I'm looking for parts. I just listen to them talk, what they say to each other. I'm in the corner of the garage at this time. I'm watching the door where the

COs are hanging out in. I'm just doing nothing and just sitting here, trying to figure out different ways in my head to do as less work as possible. I was still in a minimum prison doing a job similar to what I did in my shop, at the school that I was teaching at. What I was always thinking about was how stupid I was trusting my cousin the way I did, feeding all that coke to my junkie wife. I'm the one doing the time for it, while they are as free as can be. I need to call someone in the family to see if someone can send me some money so I can buy some shoes because I'm sewing what I have together with a sewing kit I bought along with paper clips just to hold what I have together. I'm hoping to get the phone tonight, hoping that there are not too many scum dogs waiting for the phones so I can call my daughter. I can't wait to hear her voice; it makes me feel a lot better. Again don't get me totally wrong, I met a lot of decent guys in jail, and they were not all bad, and a lot of them didn't belong in jail, as I know I didn't but I'm here. I've got to do the time they gave me to do and that's that (assholes). But for the whole time that I was in jail, I was always put in the wrong place at the wrong time. I was always hoping that my Boston lawyer could get my sentenced reduced. In my whole life I can say I never ratted on anyone in my whole life, never could. I'll take all the names that I did business with to my grave. I got caught, so I'll do the time. More than I can say for the fuckin' guys I bought my drugs from, and I know that two of them are dead, so I was told, or being protected by the police, but who knows. I hope they rot in hell for what they did to me.

Well, my cousin Charley Rat is showing his age, and he looks real bad. He is not in good condition. I hope he suffers like I did in jail. The rat bastard, but if I had to do it again, I never would have taken the rap for my two-faced wife who left me to rot in jail while spending the money I left her. She was fucking whoever she wanted while I was in jail. Now, if I knew what kind of woman she was from the start, I never would have taken her act. She fooled me good. She probably was having sex with different guys, as it said in the letters I was getting, for drugs.

Well, the trainees came in, and looking at them, they don't know which way is up. I see that they are fuckin' up like the rest.

While this was going on, a bigwig CO named Karol is watching what they are doing. She is nothing but a name, but all the COs are scared of her; they make sure they get their shit together when she's around, but she's just like the rest, a do-nothing at all, just like the COs. She just walks around the unit like she has a stick up her ass and she has no place being in a place like this, yelling at the guys to clean up their areas. These Cos are just dumping inmates' things all over the floor and walking all over it. All she is doing is saying to inmates that they have too much of everything and have to reduce what we have. While this is going on, there is a CO walking behind her just going through your stuff, throwing it out. Most of what you have even after its been approved by the property officer, there she is throwing it out. She has guys strip-searched while she watches, then disappears into the office to talks to the COs in charge. Then she comes out and says to us, "Clean this mess up," and she is gone.

As I'm just getting over what just went on, the young CO named Tweet yells over the intercom while laughing, "Drool is being served in the chow hall, so go and get it." He was right a lot of the times; it was a lot like drool, and the smell of the food was real bad most of the time. I couldn't eat it. But a lot of times I had no choice but to eat some of it, but I bought a lot of tuna fish through the canteen, cooked at the unit a lot because the food was that bad. I threw up a lot of times, but after a while you tend to get used to it. There were quite a few Spanish guys (I think that's what their nationality was) but got along real good with them. These Spanish guys were the ones that taught me how to cook good rice meals in jail, and it was hot food, better than what came out of the chow hall. In my travels, I met an Italian guy who's family owned a restaurant, and he showed me the real way to make spaghetti. He knew how to mix different meats together and spices to make it taste great. I'll never forget what this Spanish guy named Jose told me. "When you cook the way I'm showing you, remember everything must be made with Goya products." This jail had a stove to cook on. That was a real plus, but you had to wait a long time until it became available. We still used our hot pots even though we had a stove, but we would have to rig them to boil. That was something that we were not supposed to do but we did so we could cook spaghetti. This was done by crossing the resistor with a paper clip or a piece of wire. They didn't want them to boil because you could boil water and throw it in a guy's face if you wanted to get him for something he had done to you.

The COs were always watching me when I cooked because the black guys would rat me out when I cooked in a hotpot, telling the COs that I had a hotpot that boiled. So I started to use my hotpot to make food when they were out, so when they came back into the room, they would take the wire out, and it would be the way they sold it to me. I went through this every time I cooked food in the unit, and I guess the reason for this is because I guess they knew I wouldn't hesitate to throw it at them if I had to. The CO that messed with me the most was the CO that said my wife looked like a whore, and he made life a living hell for me the whole time I was there. This was every time he was on. When I would be out walking the yard, that would be all the time I really thought that I was losing my mind because I was still in a fog. I had so much trouble keeping things straight in my head; it got worse when I would look at certain COs. Sometimes when I was in my room alone, I would think of different ways of killing the black guys in my room, and then I'd think they are not worth it. Then I thought, well, maybe when I get out. Then I thought of being in here for the rest of my life, and then think none of these guys are worth it. To me I would be better off dead. This is why some guys say, "I'm not going back," and kill themselves. But the messed up thing about it is they take people with them when they decide to kill themselves. Why?

It's morning, and I'm sitting in the place they call the dayroom, waiting for the CO to come and take me to the garage to work, and I'm just looking around and realized I'm in a nuthouse. The guys were all watching kids programs on TV, and they were commenting on them and how they could improve the shows. Now I'm talking about kid programs. Now I know I'm I going out of my mind seeing this, then I started wondering, Can this be true? This place will do it to you or fuck you right up worse than what I am now. More than a quarter of these guys don't belong here, and the rest of them belong in a mental institution, on medication with real heavy doses; they are fuckin' nuts. Then when they ship them out, boy, I know a couple of COs that they could throw into the mix. Well, my ride just got here, and I was the last to be dropped off, and I was in the front seat now. They just lugged the last guy, so I moved up. Everyone wanted to be in the front. To me, I didn't really care, but it was better than smelling the stink of some of the guys that didn't wash up. I do admit it, smells can really get to you especially when it's early in the morning. It can get real bad. As I was in the front, I was looking out the window, and I realized why they all wanted the front seat, because you're able to see where you are heading, where you are going. But I always drifted off, just enjoyed looking out the window, but still I was able to smell the stink the other guys put off.

While I was looking out the window, I was thinking of my home and family and how I got here, like I always did. Of course talking to God, asking him to help the lawyer get me out of here. I didn't know if the CO that was driving me could hear me, because I was mumbling. I was asking God to help my lawyer get me out of here. It must have sounded like I was chanting it over and over again. But it was to myself, under my breath, not out loud. I just think about it now as I've been writing this, and thinking this brings me right back there. I was really losing faith in the lawyer I got because every time I called him, he was never there, or he was in court or I just get hung up on again. I never got any letters from him stating what he was trying to do for me. He had never made any effort to come to see me as of yet. All I ever got from any form of conversation from this Boston lawyer was in the beginning. That was about the big fish that practice in Boston courts, the little fish that practice in New Bedford because they were not good enough to practice in Boston. As I just got to the garage where I worked on the cars, the CO was told to bring all the guys back, and just before I entered the garage, he called me back and said, "You got to go home."

I heard that real good. I jumped right back into the truck and though I must have gotten word from the courts saying I was out of here. I was going home. I hoped they weren't fuckin with me again. But I noticed that the CO was going to all the other stops before he dropped me off. I asked him, "Didn't you say that they wanted me back at the unit to go home?"

He looked at me and said, "Yeah, the unit is your home."

I just looked at him and said, "That's not my home. My home is in Acushnet, not here."

He then said, "No, the unit is your home." He started to laugh. I always put up with this asshole, but I just had enough. I just looked at him and said to him, "Let me tell you something."

He said, "What?"

I just said, "I'm not in here forever. I will be out someday. I'm not doing life, as I told you." This young CO lived in my neck of the woods, as they say. As I was talking to him, I said, "Maybe we will run into each other someday."

Then he really looked at me and said, "Is that a threat?"

I said, "No, maybe we can go for breakfast someday. You will think different of me. We can talk about old times."

After that he never messed with me again and transferred to somewhere else, and I never saw him again. I was not here to humor anyone. I'd take all the jokes, as bad as they are, but they don't realize that I was the one who was doing time. That's bad enough. I didn't need any more grief added on to that. At this time, I really felt useless and worthless. I didn't know what to do, and I was having trouble remembering what family members looked like. It felt like my mind was being erased. But working at the so-called garage did help me take my mind off it for a short time. Then when they brought me back to the unit, I got out of the van, got my daily strip-search, and returned to my room. Then it starts all over again the next day.

While I'm working I'm so surprised that I never hurt myself because of the way I was thinking about things on the outside, all the time. It goes on all night long as well. I'm always hoping that my daughter is okay, is keeping up with the mortgage so that she's not on the street, all the bills that come with it are paid. The guy that she's living with is a real piece of shit. He hits her all the time, but she takes it because he's the father of her son. My daughter's boyfriend tells her he hits her because sometimes she gets out of line, and she needs it to straighten her out. I hated this guy the first day I met him, and I told my daughter this, but her answer to this was that she loved him. I just wanted to make her happy and shut my mouth, but I wanted to beat him up. When I called her up one day, while talking to her she told me that my wife was up in the attic going through boxes that I put up there. That's because I told her that there was some coke in the pockets of her jeans. I didn't think that she would fall for it, but she did. She went to the house, walked in, and paid no attention to my daughter. She just went upstairs and was looking through all her clothes for drugs. It must have been hard when you have to pay for it yourself or do whatever she had to do to get it. I did have a lot of coke that the cops didn't find, but I flushed it down the toilet when I got out of jail. I had a lot of it still buried in the yard, in the attic also, in an oil pan that was on a motor in my garage. When my wife moved back in with her father and left me in jail, I had no need for the coke that the cops didn't find, so where it was, that's where it stood the whole time I was in jail. I could have used some of the money but didn't want anything to do with that shit ever again after getting five years. It just goes to show you my wife married the drug, not me. She really was a coke whore and would do anything for it even when it came to leaving me rot in jail. I didn't want anything to do with that shit ever again, so I told my friend John about some I had buried next to a tree. I know he dug it up and took it. He said that he would send me some money but never did.

Well, I'm sitting down and writing another letter to my so-called wife, doing so because I remember my vows, for better or worse, and I'm trying to make the best of the situation. I was always stating that I knew that the COs started fights between inmates, and I have a news clipping from an August 1999 newspaper to prove it. It came from a magazine called Esquire, and the guards got away with all the fights they set up between inmates. They listed that several prison guards would make inmates fight to their deaths, but in this case, it's not that bad here, but they do bet on inmates that they place in rooms together to fight. They do bet on who's going to come out on top. This was in most of the places that I was in. You the public are not to know that this shit goes on because it's a correctional institution. The guys in here really pay for the crime that we do, but all they are doing is making us into mumbling fools. I think this is why they put all these black guys in my room with me. I almost came to the point of almost stabbing one of them but didn't. I proved to them all that I put up with all their shit that they did to me, glad I didn't fall for what they wanted me to do. The black guy that I was going to stab ended up getting lugged before I ended up doing something stupid. As I'm reading my letters, I also wrote about these Spanish guys that were in jail with me and just sometimes they would talk to me. On one occasion while I was cooking with one of them, he was telling me what he was doing time for. What he told me was that he was doing an eight-year term for having sex with his mother. The other guys he was in with would trade their family member among each other; they had similar terms. I just shut my mouth and didn't comment on it even when he asked me what I thought about it. I just said to each their own. I just thought that was the best way. I didn't tell them what I really thought. Sometimes I just can't believe what I see and what I hear. The whole time that I was in jail, I learned more about crime, how to do it, then I ever knew about it in my whole life. It's like taking a course on how to commit crimes. I couldn't even try to think about using any of what I learned in jail because I would rather die before coming back to this nuthouse with these guys. Again I wouldn't give these COs the satisfaction of seeing me come back to jail, throwing it in my face, them saying "I told you so," then them saying "You come back here, you hear."

I got up in the morning, and it was Saturday 2001, and I have to spend another day outside because the room that I'm in really stinks badly. These black guys haven't taken a shower in a while, and it smells like ass. I don't know if they are farting or just smell like shit! I don't talk to any of them, but one of them asked me to write letters, make a few cards for his family. He does it without the others knowing, said to me that he had nothing to do in what they are doing to me. I'm able to block most of it out, just do my own time because my mind is so fucked up, and I just don't give a damn what happens. As I'm walking around the track like I always do, mostly thinking, missing the school that I was teaching at, I was learning a lot as well as the students were. I was very grateful for that. These teachers were the smartest people that I knew at that time, were into what I was doing my whole life. I was honored to be able to teach at such a great school as New Bedford Vocational High School. I'm looking at myself, realizing that I'm in a place that has just no programs at all but anger management, alcohol twelve steps, gardening, and how to become a good work slave for the COs because they were allergic to work. I'm walking around the track as I'm thinking this, and I'm really hoping that someone would come up to see me. I could really use a visit. I'm so lonely it's tearing me apart inside. All that I've done for my family you would think that someone would feel something for me being in a place like this, at least converse with me one way or another. Again I'm outside walking the track and just thinking of what conversations I had with my wife and some friends. On one occasion, my wife told me what one of her boyfriends would do to her. He would get mad at her, break off with her, and just go out with a different girl, tell her to do the same. He would tell her that she was as cold as ice. Then he would go back out with her. They would tell each other what they did with the other people that they were seeing (sick). One thing I can say is that I was in this place for sixty months or two hundred and sixty weeks, even better eighteen hundred, twenty-nine days, but who was counting. All my family was doing time with me the whole time I was here. Every time I was able to get the paper, I would read it real good, hoping that I would see one or all the cops that raided my home in the paper in the obituary section, but no luck, but I'm still hoping to see if any of them would get shot during a raid and died (rats). I did read that a couple of the cops did get busted for drug violations on a New Bedford waft that was on the waterfront on Homer's waft, and I'm wondering if it was some of the stuff they took from my house, but of course it will get thrown out, swept under the carpet or whatever term they use. Most of the cops who get in any trouble usually will walk because they were cops, especially if it was by their own guys. The narcs were real cutthroats. But it goes to show you they even rat on each other. All I've got to say is, how does it feel, realizing now that even your own kind will turn on you? There is one thing I would like to know, and it's where all the wallpaper paste went along with all the baking soda that was missing from my house. It was what you showed it to my wife saying that it was cocaine. It probably used to cut the stuff they took from my house, used it to cut down some of the product they took from my house because the percentages were not the same as they put in the warrant. But who can say the police do nothing wrong because they are cops, so people think, but just remember they are human also, and that's when greed sets in. It's just the thought of money, and if you don't think so, watch Training Day, the movie. It's true and it's just like that. The stuff that I had was no 14 percent or even 32 percent, and it all came from the same batch that was outside, buried in my yard. At least this was what the place they sent it to be tested at. When the guy sold it to me, it tested at close to 80 percent. When the cops tested it, it was 32 percent and 14. What's up with that.

My wife told me to call her today. It was April 23, 2001. It was about eight thirty at night, and she said that she was going to come up to see me this weekend. Again I couldn't wait. I was counting the days. Well, this was the third time I called, and no one answered the phone. She must have gone out with her girlfriends (right). At this time I was starting to believe the letters that I was getting from an unknown writer, her newfound boyfriend. I just didn't want to believe it even though it was as plain as day. I never wanted to believe that she was seeing another guy or even guys because I was so fuckin' thickheaded. When I asked her, she would tell me no. I didn't want to believe it when she said that she was going to wait for me to get out. I think that she was just telling me something that I wanted to hear. Of course I believed her like an asshole and went on believing her, telling myself that I hope she wasn't just blowing smoke up my ass. After a while, I would think and say she would never do that to me after all I've done for her. (What a jerk.)

Well, the weekend came. I got up early and was just waiting for my name to be called, just looking at the clock, and I knew she always got up late as long as I knew her. It was about two thirty in the afternoon when they finally called my name. I rushed to the visiting room, as I always did when she came. Of course I was real happy to see her. As I walked up to kiss her, again she had the smell coming from her mouth. Her breath smelled like she just gave someone a blowjob. I stopped, and I kissed her on the side of her face. As I talked to her from across the table, the breath was telling me that for sure she gave someone head. I was so disgusted when I smelled it and knew what she had done. My wife did ask why I just kissed her on the side of her face; she never got an answer from me. I just couldn't understand how a grown woman could do something like that to her husband who was in a place like I was in. What, she didn't think that I could smell the smell that was coming from her? What a stupid bitch. Didn't she realize that not having sex in jail that I wouldn't pick up on that? So fuckin' stupid. Worst of all, this was the second girl that did this to me in my life. My daughter's mother did this to me also when she was pimping herself off at a bar in Westport. I kind of knew that she was still doing coke because she had a crust all around her nose, had tissue in her hands, and was doing the wiping as she always did. After that, I just knew it was just a matter of time before she would stop coming up to see me. I knew at that time she wasn't going to help me get out of this place. I did ask her if she was seeing anyone else. She said that there was no one else. All she was doing was going out with her friends clubbing. The worst part was, she looked at me in the eyes and said that she would never cheat on me. I knew right there that she was lying right through her teeth, then she said that she would tell me this because of me being all alone in the place I'm at. I never told her about the letters that I was getting in jail telling me that she was messing around but just the time that she was caught in the back of an old drive-in, and all she said was that she was going in the woods to pee. I'm really expected to believe that bullshit story to pee. There were all kinds of restaurants on that road, and she went to pee down a dark road. She did ask where I got that story from, and I just said that she had told me. She said that she didn't remember telling me that but never denied it either, so it must have been true. You can't let things like this bother you as it did to me. This stuff really fucked up my head, and I carried it with me most of the time that I was incarcerated. I gave the control of all my money to her. I did ask her how my case was going, and she said that she just spoke with the lawyer. It was going to come up to where I was to discuss my case with me. He had just filed the paperwork to my case. It looked real good. I knew she wasn't doing a damn thing for me because my daughter called. The lawyer said that he hadn't talked to my wife at all since she gave him the money, but my hands were tied, and there was nothing that I could do but time.

It's so hard watching everyone you love just disappear from your life when you come to a place like this. Sooner or later it happens to everyone who comes into a place like this. When you're in jail, the lawyers know how much time you have on the phone. They put you on hold until your time runs out, and there goes your conversation with your lawyer. I did ask the COs if I could talk to the superintendent to see if I could use a phone to talk to my attorney. The CO said, "No fuckin' way. You're here to stay, so get used to it." Then he said to me that the COs were not done fucking with me as of yet, and I had a long way to go before they were done, and I gave him my usually dirty look. The names they call you from day to day are real bad. You have no choice but to put up with it. Every single day these fuckin' COs are trying so hard to push your buttons. Sometimes I would just love to stuff my fist just under their Adam's apple or as hard as I can in the stomach. Pieces of shit. What I put in the beginning of this story about early retirement is what most of these guards look forward to after getting hit by an inmate, and they do a great job to piss off inmates. I did notice that there were a lot of guys that were doing less time for violent crimes, playing with little kids, beating up women; they get out sooner than guys who are convicted for drug crimes. What's wrong with this picture. These guys are earning good time, going out on the street, making money on job that the institutions are getting for them so when they get out of jail, they already have a job. These guys are able to make money from the start if they keep the job they got while they are in jail. When the jails do this, the inmates are able to keep their sanity and are able to get involved with all members of the community. As for myself, I have to learn to get along with people all over again on the outside because I'm not able to leave the compound, and I know I'll have a hard time adjusting to people again. This means that I don't get involved with people from the outside in any way except for the COs who do their best to brainwash you the whole time you're in jail. Doing the mando sentence the courts passed on me was so very wrong. Not letting me go on the outside to work to help my family with bills was not fair. I was in here for a nonviolent crime. I was getting nothing at all out of this but learn how to count time on a calendar and learn and hear all different ways to commit crimes. I hated authority figures at this time. What I learned to do was hate more and more the judges, prosecutors, and the fuckin' narcs the whole time that I was incarcerated. I was never like this before. I guess this is why they call it a correctional institution. All you learn is different ways of committing a crime so that when you get out, you have different jail trades in which to make money. Now when I get out and get a job, I know I will hate the boss within a month I start because they will remind me of the COs that I had to deal with while I was in jail. Now I'm hoping this piece-of-shit Boston lawyer who won't take my calls and won't answer my letters after I got letters from him saying what he can do for me. Lawyers like this Boston lawyer start off by telling you that they are going to get you out on bail, but they make sure they get every penny that you have first before they do anything for you. The whole time that I had this lawyer, he has done nothing at all for me so far, and I've had him for at least two years. The whole time my daughter was in contact with him and the messages that he was leaving just stated that he needed more money for what he's done. That was nothing at all.

While I was in jail, I saw a couple of COs that would come over my house with my friend Al to do coke, smoke weed, but of course they were already drunk. I did see them while I was in jail, and they ignored me when they saw me and just walked away. When they were down in my cellar, they would sit down, and I would listen to their stories about different guys that they had to deal with while they were doing their jobs, how they fucked with the inmates every chance they got. Now I'm one of those guys, and they really fucked with me. In my whole life I never thought I would end up in a place like this, but here I am. When they saw me, they looked at me like they didn't know me. They thought they were better than me by the looks they gave me. Every time I saw these two COs, they were really messed up. These are the guys that should be drug tested in random drug testing. If I was to see these guys on the street right now, you put them right in front of me, all I would see was that they were COs, feel nothing but anger, and that would be it. If they were right in front of me now, I probably couldn't recognize them because of the hate I have for them to this day. Plus to me, a cop is a cop, and a CO is a CO. It's just the clothes that they wear, and that's all I see now.

The whole time that I was in Bridgewater, I was in that sort of a fog that even I couldn't understand. No matter what I did, I just couldn't shake it off. I just couldn't think straight. It was so hard to deal with this problem because this has never happened to me in my whole life before. I would just drift off. I didn't realize how bad it was getting until one guy whom I met in jail said that he was calling me, and I wouldn't answer him. Then as he approached me and got my attention, I would wake up. It was real weird. I realized that I would drift off somewhere, but I don't know where. Sometimes it would happen for long periods of time, but what I was thinking of or about, I don't know. I was just gone. I don't remember anything that I was thinking about at that time. Even to this day where I went to I still don't remember. I wrote this in all my letters I sent home. I guess I would be lost just thinking of where I was, what I had to deal with. All I remember is that I thought I was going out of my mind. But there's one thing that I can tell you: the fog that I was in was a part of my soul that they stole from me while I was in jail. That was the part that made me happy in life. I told this to the shrink that I was seeing at this time, and she said that it would take a while to get over it. It was because I was incarcerated. What I went through when the cops raided my home. She said the loss of my wife and my daughter also contributed to it along with my way of living on the outside. The worst part of it all was me going over it over and over again. Trying to adjust to this place was very hard for me. I kept seeing this shrink because it was time again out of the unit, and I had to talk to someone about all the scum that I had to deal with. This wasn't just some of the inmates; it was also all the fuckin' COs (pieces of shit). I always thought that what you told the shrinks was confidential. What a joke. When I told what I thought of the COs, life began to get worse for me. She was most likely seeing or fucking one of the COs and told them what I was telling her. After that conversation I had with her, there were more room searches, a lot more strip-searches in front of women COs. I was so embarrassed. After a while, the shame just started to disappear to the point that I would just do what they told me and tried not to let it bother me.

When I went to the garage to work on their cars, I looked to the side of the garage and noticed that they got in a car analyzer. It was like the one they had at school I worked at when I was a teacher. I went over to it and started to look at it. It had all the information on every vehicle on disks you need to repair them. It was like in the vocational school again. I was tempted to take two of the disks that I needed for cars that I owned at home because they would never use them. They just had three types of vehicles in that garage. At this time I looked up the ones that I needed, and of course they had them. I just put them aside and said I better not take them, but it was killing me inside not to take them. Well, this went on for a couple of weeks. Then it happened. I took two of them, just the ones I needed, on the way back to the unit. I was able to get them past the Cos. I had to get them out of here and tried to mail them out in the mail wrapped up in cards that I made. I did this because I didn't want to get caught with them in my possession. I kept calling my daughter as the week went by to see if she got them or received any of my letters. She said no. I just said to myself, "Shit." After a week I asked her again, and again she kept saying no. I then said they probably found them because the envelope was pretty fat when I mailed it out, but I still mailed it out. As I was talking to her on the phone, I noticed that the IPPS were coming up the ramp into the building. They looked right at me as they entered the room that I was in, and I knew they were there for me. They came right up to me, threw me up against the wall, and said that I was mailing out contraband out of the unit. I was going to be lugged back to Concord High Security. I didn't think that I was doing anything wrong because they were all over the floor. They weren't going to use them. I thought they were going to get all scratched up. I tried to talk to the sergeant, but he said to me that I was in their house and had to do what they told me to do, that

I had no rights at all while I was in prison and to get used to it. Then he said, "You did the crime, so do the time." I just gave him the look like I want to rip off his head. I just couldn't help myself. I've been told this by so many people that the look on my face tells it all it's like I could kill them with the look I give whoever I look at. On many occasions, COs would tell me to wipe the look that I have on my face off. I told him that I couldn't because it was the only face I had. I couldn't change it. When I looked at the IPPS sergeant, I had that type of face that looks could kill. To them it was a way of saying "fuck you." This was to just about all of them more or less. I said, "Send me where you have to send me. Get it over with." Even though I really didn't want to go. Well, I was on my way back to Concord again. There goes all my visits, as little as they were. Kiss my wife goodbye, along with the hand jobs I would get once in a while on visits when she came up, but I never kissed her on the mouth anymore because it smelled like sex. Also the one good CO that worked in the visiting room named Chapman was the only CO that wasn't an asshole, the only one that was decent the whole time that I was in jail.

On my way back in the transport vehicles, I was thinking, There goes my revise and revoke down the drain. How was it going to look like when I went back to court. As I arrived at Concord State Prison, I was brought into a holding cell not like the first time, but there were a couple guards there. One CO that just came in from the outside said, "What's he in here for?" The CO started singing the song riding that train pile of cocaine over and over again. He laughed, and I just said, "Fuckin' asshole." I was there for at least three hours, real sick of hearing the cocaine song over and over again. I was then brought to the main building, where I was placed again on the third floor, what they called a tear, but right outside the cell door were the phones. That's one good thing about where I was placed. As soon as they opened the door, I stepped out the door, and I had a phone in my hand. Most guys that wanted the phones would give me free food if I got them a phone when the door opened. I hated to wait to use the phones, but now they were right outside the door, and I never had to wait in line for the phones anymore. This was January 5, 2000. My court date was the only thing that I could look forward to because it was my way back home to my wife and daughter so I could try to fix the problem we had between us. But now that I think about it and me not being in my right mind, if I was to get out, I probably would have hunted down my wife's boyfriend, busted him up real bad. This is because my wife gave him a blowjob before she came in to see me. This would be one of the first things that I would do, and this would be just payback along with making me feel better. I shouldn't have done what I did because I was thinking that I was going to get out, beat what I was convicted of. Then I would just go on with my life. Of course without the drugs in my life, there would be no more problem. What a joke on me. I quickly adjusted to where I was as usual, but I still hated the guy that was in the room with me, but he was white. It was a lot better than any of the black guys that I had to deal with in the Bridgewater Minimum. I just kept to myself, just wanted to do my time, get to my next stop, hope what I did wouldn't hurt my revise and revoke.

After a couple of weeks, I was able to get in touch with my wife and ask her if she had heard anything from the Boston lawyer. She said that he wouldn't take her calls. She was really mad at me for what I did, thought that my daughter put me up to it. I said she had nothing to do with it. It was just something that I did on my own. I was able to talk to my daughter, and she called the lawyer, and she said that the lawyer was trying to get in touch with my wife, but she never called him back. The secretary told my daughter that every time she called my wife's house, she was never home. Now when I talk to her, all I can say is that I wish I let her do the time too, as I said so many times before while thinking of her being free. I called and asked my daughter, "I know you hate my wife, but please tell me the truth." She said that what she was telling me was the truth. Then right there I knew that she was lying to me when she told me that she was in contact with the lawyer up the time that she was talking to me on the phone. My bitch wife was free, had nothing to worry about but to go out and clubbing, powder her fuckin' nose, fucking her newfound boyfriend. I was so lucky being her husband, and to her, I was the last thing that was on her mind. When she would talk to me on the phone, she would tell me not to worry that she was going to wait for me to get out. In one conversation, she told me that she would never cheat on me no matter what. I should never think that but had all the letters right in front of me that I constantly read over and over again.

I needed to talk to someone real bad seeing that I wasn't getting any visits, so again put in a slip to see the so-called doctor that they had at Concord. I figured that maybe a real doctor will tell me something different from the shrink was telling me. When again it was my turn to see the doctor, I told him about me being lightheaded, disorientated; it felt like I was high on drugs. He looked at me, and all he said to me was that I will get over it. It's because of me being incarcerated. I'm just so glad I wasn't having a heart attack; they would have given me two aspirins and called it a day. They were either very bad doctors or just didn't give a damn. I think that they just practice on ways of getting out of where they are and hate what they are doing, looking so confused. So there I am in my cell with now, nothing to do but wait for my phone to be turned on, hoping to find a book to keep my mind busy, but even when I had something to read, I still would just drift off, think of my whole life, all that I did when I was free to do what I wanted to do. Then I would say, how could I do something like I did. So damn stupid, just to make my coke whore wife happy. Now just to think about it, I was a schoolteacher, a night instructor, a damn good one at that. It's all gone now. I remember opening the door to the school, walking in. And when the students saw me, they would say, "Are you going to teach here?" Every section I would pass through I would hear the same thing from the students from section to section. To me I felt like I was some type of a super teacher. I was called Mr. D by all the students. It felt real good—no, great. I loved it so much that I could never put it into words. I miss it so much to this day. To me it was the best job that I ever had in my whole life. It was just the student that I was able to teach some things that I knew.

I was not proud of what I did. I feel ashamed of it. If I could have done it again, I would have done it differently, sent my so-called wife to a halfway house to get her off the drugs or divorce her. If they would have taken a drug test on me at the time, they would have found that my blood was clean of cocaine. They would have known who was doing the drugs. The narcs said that they were watching the house for three months at the time of the bust. Now though all that they came to the conclusion that I was taking care of the whole South Coast. All I can say is what good police work? The messed-up thing about it was I was home all the time. I just about never went out. I was selling drugs up the whole East Coast? I guess I'd love to know how I was transporting all the drugs they said I was transporting up the East Coast. To this day, I would love to know who fed them that bullshit story. But they ran with it maybe just to be able to get a search warrant signed by a crooked judge. When I talked to some of these guys that I was in jail with, all I heard from most of these guys was how they knew what they did to get busted and were going to do it differently the next time so they won't get caught. Every jail that I was in I heard the same thing, how they were going to do it differently so that they won't return to jail, but they all had different plans on how to do it. It was real crazy. All I wanted was to get home to my family, and a lot of these guys were just thinking of how not to get busted the next time they did a job. I was still waiting for my stuff to get shipped from Bridgewater to Concord, see what they took and what they let me have. The property officer at Bridgewater was the one who figured what was contraband and what wasn't. When I did get my things, this dickhead said that most of my things were contraband threw out a lot of my things I think he got his rocks off on it. I kind of knew it would take a long time because it would be when he got around to it. That could be up to a month sometimes. You're always waiting to be called to property to get your things. I was hoping that it would be soon because I had no razors. I had a large beard starting; I couldn't stand it. Maybe because I never had one before. I had no money in my canteen and had to wait for them to put it in the Concord computers so I could buy some things from the canteen. I wasn't eating much of the food they were serving because the food was crap, so I just went without eating. It didn't bother me too much if I kicked off because it was like no one cared anyways. What was going through my head is that I would be better off dead than living the way that I'm living in here because of what I had to deal with. The inmates didn't bother me much the whole time. I guess because I looked like I was nuts. I felt that I was, and I also thought this of myself. I was messed with. I don't know what I would have done to anyone who did. I was in lockdown for at least twenty-two hours a day in an eight-by-ten cell. I was sharing this with another guy who never showered, so he stank real bad. I just was lugged from a place where I had some privacy, but now I had none at all. Now I had to cut a bedsheet so I could hang another sheet across so I could use the toilet without being watched. We got our clothes washed once a week. The bad thing about it was if we sent it all out, we would have to go the whole night without bedsheets so we used the same piece of bed rope to wash our bedsheets in the sink, dry them by hanging them across the room. When we did send them out, it was all put in a bag, and when we got them back, everything we sent in all came back blue from the dye from all the jeans that were put in the bag together. We would have to wash all our stuff at night because during the day, COs would take all the stuff that was hanging up and confiscate them. We would have to wait all day for the night guys to come in. Then if the CO was in a fucked-up mood, we would have to use our coats to cover ourselves to keep warm at night or wait till they felt like giving it back to us. Real assholes.

This was my second time at Concord now, and I kind of knew what I was in for but was making the best of it. The guy that was in the room with me was a fucking pig. I knew a lot of heavy people would never call them what this guy was. That was a stinky, disgusting bastard. This guy that was in the room with me looked like he weighed at least six hundred pounds and had a farting problem. He told me that he had medication for it but liked to smell what he put out. This man never took a shower but sponge baths. What a sight. It was done right in the room. Seeing the things he did would get me sick to my stomach, and he had no shame at all in what he did. He was just moved in because the guy that was in the room with me was transferred to his next stop. I had an open room, and they put him in with me. Again of course, I had to move to the top bunk because of his weight. Well, time went on, and I just learned to put up with his shit. I just turned my back to the wall and learned to deal with discussing ways and started to yell at him to either take a shit or take his damn medication to stop his farting, stinking up the room that smelled like ass.

Then I found out that my money was cleared, so I was able to buy a decent canteen, and I ordered fluff, peanut butter, tuna and bread. When I had to go get it, I just followed everyone else. What a walk it was, but I was able to get all that I ordered. The canteen was in a big lot, and you had to wait for your name to be called and walk up to a barnlike window to get your stuff and hope no one took your stuff. When I got back to the room, the guy in the room with me said that they didn't give him everything he wanted because he didn't have enough money in his canteen. Well, as the night went on, he did ask me for some bread because he had peanut butter, marshmallow fluff but no bread, so I gave him four slices. After that, he asked for more, and I said no because I had tuna I need bread for, said that what I had had to last me a whole week. Then I told him that I didn't like a lot of the food that they served in here, so I fell back on what I got from the canteen. He looked at me, and he just said that it wasn't right not giving him any more bread. When the COs called rec time, I went out to use the phone to call my wife so she could go pick up some of my property at the property officer at Bridgewater. The property officer at Bridgewater said it was contraband and couldn't send it to Concord. I wasn't supposed to have it. I called my wife and asked her if she could pick up my property. She said that she would but never did go. I lost a lot of my clothes, a new pair of sneakers that I just bought, so it was like she was saying "Fuck you" to me. Just as I finished my phone call, one of the guys that was a friend of the guy in my room came up to me and said to me, "You didn't give my friend any of your bread."

I said, "That's not right. I paid for it. I did give him four slices. If he wanted more, then you should give it to him." He just walked away. Just as I said that, they called everyone in for count, and that was the end of the night. I will be in lockdown until the next day. The lights in the room were still on. They were so bright it hurt your eyes, but you had to deal with it till the COs decide to dim them. I was in my bunk, and my roommate was pissed off at me for not giving him any more bread. He was eating his fluff and peanut butter just out of the containers using his hands. Now as I was reading my book I found when I was out of the room, I heard a noise coming from my roommate. I looked up at the door that entered the room. There was a piece of glass that ran up the door. I was staring at the glass, and I could see my roommate on the bottom bunk, eating something and looked away. I just started to make out what he was doing, but it was just too hard to make out what he was doing at that time. Well as I was staring at him from the reflection from the window on the door, I noticed that he was picking the skin from the bottom of his feet, dipping it in the peanut butter container, and eating it. As I was staring at what he was doing, I saw big pieces of skin that he was taking off and eating.

    I asked him, "Are you eating the skin from your feet?"

    He said "Yes, I have no bread. It's from my body, so what's the problem?"

    I couldn't believe what I was hearing. This guy just gave himself a sponge baths. He still stank real badly, and he was eating skin from the bottom of his feet. I just couldn't believe what I was seeing. I just went back to my book because what could I do? I just said to myself, if he wanted to eat pieces of his body, so let him, let him be. He worked on the peanut butter container, broke it in half, and licked everything out of the jar. I mean cleaned it out along with the fluff container. He did it all in the same day we got our canteen. As I continued to read my book again, the bed started to shake. He started to jerk off in bed. The whole bed was shaking like crazy. I yelled down at him and said, "Why can't you wait till rec time, when I'm out of the room?" Then he said it just came over him at that time. He would be done in a minute. What could I do but put up with it. Then again I looked into the window of the door. When the bed was done shaking, I figured he was done. I saw him through the reflection on the door again, and I noticed he was licking his hands. I said, "What the fuck are you doing now?" All he said was "It's mine" and "Waste not, want not." Then I said, "What the hell are you talking about?" but I knew what he meant by that. I had no more to talk to him about after seeing that. Never in my life have I seen anything like that until I came to a place like this. Now I've seen just about everything. Well, we were in lockdown, so I slept very lightly through the night because I didn't trust my roommate not to go in my locker and eat my food. If he was doing what I saw him doing, I think he wouldn't hesitate to go in my locker for my food.

The whole time that he was in the room with me, I had a bar of soap in a sock just in case I had to bash him because he was a big motherfucker, so I stuffed it under my pillow. If he went into my locker in the middle of the night, what do you think they were going to make him do if he ate my food, pay me back? Right. He was in for forging checks, credit cards like he had money. He did tell me what he was in for, that he won't be in jail for long because they had no proof that he did what they said he did. They would drop the charges very soon. When I woke up the next day, the room smelled like ass and body odor. I knew it wasn't from me, so I had a good idea where it was coming from. My roommate was using the toilet at the time. It was just something that you would have nightmares after seeing. I'm real glad I didn't have to fight this guy because I think he definitely would have won. The COs would think when they did count that I found some way to escape because he probably would have eaten me. Guys like this give heavy people a bad name because he just didn't care and just did disgusting things. I was hoping that they would release him. I can only hope the next guy was a decent guy and again hoping that he was white. They started to let us go out of the room, so we were able to go to the gym to work out, or you could go to the sports room. I hated sports. It was just playing ball sports, so I just went to go to the gym and work out because I thought if I got real big like I was when I met my wife, I could win her back. When I was at the gym, I went over to pick up some bell bar and tried to put thirty pounds over my head. I just can't believe that I couldn't do it, but I kept trying, then realized that I was really out of shape. I think back and think of the things I was thinking of when I was in the places that I was at. It gets to the point that all you think is what you had before you went into jail. The messed-up thing about it was what I was going through in here now was going to be the same when I get out. You're just lost in time.

The other two guys I hung around with were decent guys. The black guy was normal, didn't act like all the others I was stuck with in Bridgewater Minimum. The date is January 13, 2001, and I'm in the gym. A young white guy came up to me and asked me to help him because there was a black guy picking on him and won't leave him alone, so I just said that I didn't get involved with anyone else's problems and said, "You can stay here, work out with us. Maybe he will leave you alone." He asked me what the black guy wanted because he wouldn't tell him anything at all. I said, "He probably wants you to be his boy." He said that he wasn't like that. I turned to the black guy and told him to leave the kid alone with my two friends beside me. Well, as I was telling this guy, two other white guys came up an asked what the problem was. The black just walked away. He was what the guys at Bridgewater called themselves, a nigger. What a thing to call each other, but you being white, you can't call them the same as they call each other. You're considered racist. I thought I was going to get into some shit, but it just worked out okay. The kid just stuck around when we worked out. He stuck like glue to us at least till I was moved. There is one thing about being in here. You can't back down no matter what comes your way. You have to follow through with it. Never make eye contact unless you intend to take care of a problem with that person. So rec time was over, and I returned to my room. The fat guy was gone, and the stink was gone. He took that with him. Great. I was just hoping they put a decent guy in now. I was only alone for one night, on the bottom bunk but on my own mattress. The mattress that they give you has to go back to property room when you leave the room or you are moved somewhere else in the compound or the COs will have one of their gophers do it because the COs are as lazy as they come.

As the morning went on, they moved in another guy. A little guy, real mousy-looking. I had to move back up because he was a junkie and needed the bottom bunk because of his problem. I really didn't care because they were interviewing a lot of the guys to move out of Concord. Just about everyone was thinking where they were going to be sent. I didn't want to go to Plymouth house. It's a real messed-up place. No weights to exercise so you fill up garbage bags with water to lift. No weights are allowed at all. It's just big dorms, as I was told. In the interview, they asked me where I wanted to go like it really mattered. I asked to go to Plymouth Forestry because of the weight rooms they had. He looked at me and said that that wasn't going to happen. He then said that they would call me in a few days to let me know what they decided. It must have been a couple of days. I saw the caseworker walking in the unit, so I asked if I could stay in Concord. He said only if I was willing to work in the kitchen. I said I'll wait to see what they are going to give me for a move because if you work in the kitchen at Concord, you start at 4:00 a.m. and worked till twelve noon washing pots and pans. That's a lot of pots and pans. I did take the afternoon shift just to make some money for canteen that I needed. My wife still wasn't sending me any of my money. I didn't want to ask for it in fear that she wouldn't help me with the attorney from Boston that she hired, even though I kind of knew in my heart she was going to let me rot in here. At least the food was there for me to eat while I was in the kitchen, as long as I wasn't caught doing so. I did drink a lot of milk, ate a lot of raisins when I was working. When I was working, there was a head sergeant who did all the cooking. Would watch him so I could learn to cook some foods that I wanted to make when I got out. As I watched him, I noticed that he still didn't wash his hands and would flick ashes from his cigars into the large kettles of food as he was cooking it. One thing about this CO the whole time that I was there, I never saw him spit on the floor, not even once. I will not say any more about that. Just think about what I just wrote. It was just a little extra flavor added to your food. As I came back from the kitchen one day, the young CO that was in charge called me to the desk and said that he did a shakedown of the room that I was in. He said that he found some razor blades out of the casing. I said yeah. Well, he then said that I was so lucky that he didn't put it in the hole for that, but I'm in Concord (what). I just thought about it, how can the hole be any worse than where I was at. I think when they put you in the hole, as they call it, like a single room where food was delivered to the cell, I'd read all day, do pushups all day, it's what I'm doing now. I wouldn't have to smell my dirty roommate's farting ass that they put in the room with me all day long that was as bad as the first, watch him go to the toilet and smell his shit. All I said to him was the razors that he found was used to make cards. I said that I wouldn't use them as a weapon. He just looked at me and said, "Don't let me find it again."

The torture that I was put through was really bad. You have no one to complain to. Plus the COs got off on fuckin' with just about everyone, so you just have to put up with it. But the razors can be put into the end of a pen and pushed up when you need it. When it's down, the plug hides the razor. Then I did think about the time I went to a pond to kill myself. The gun that I had didn't go off because it was rusted. I just figured that it was a sign not to do it. Now I think about it, I think what it would have done to my daughter, how it would have messed up the future. You've got to think about the future before you do something stupid like that. I then thought, there must be a reason why I'm here. I'm just not done doing what I'm put on earth for. I started to cry and then thought and called myself quite a few names. Now I realize that I was still expected to live to help my daughter, bringing up my grandson. All I can say if the gun would have gone off as my back was to the pond, there wouldn't be too much of a mess, and the fish would have gotten a good meal. I just didn't want to leave a mess for my daughter to clean up afterward. I know now when my daughter reads this part, she will be really pissed off at me knowing what I was going to do. As for the gun, I threw the rusted piece of shit or should I say the remains of the gun into the scrap yard next to my home. I wonder to this day if it's at the bottom of the pile. After all the time that I was in jail, I thought about it and what I did with the remaining parts of the gun. I think it's probably a part of a car by now or in Japan being formed into something else. Well, I returned to my room and was wondering how long it would be before I got some sort of an answer from the caseworker in reference to where they were going to send me. The Plymouth Correctional was still on my mind. I was hoping that they wouldn't send me there because it's like being in Concord. There is no weight room. If it came down to it, I would rather stay at Concord, be willing to work wherever they wanted me to just to have my daily exercise workout.

I was showing the new roommate what I did with a bedsheet, how I hung it from one side to another in the morning when I went to the toilet because I still wanted, needed some privacy when I went to the toilet. Again this guy had no money at all and wanted me to buy him some stuff. I said that he would be working in the kitchen real soon; he would be able to buy stuff with his own money. But of course, I ended buying him a few things, like jolly ranchers. In jail that's a big seller, just about everyone bought them, some tuna, mayo but that's all. Then he told me that he would pay me back; I said maybe he wouldn't have to because I was waiting for my move. I just wanted to go to a place where my wife could come see me; I wanted so much to see her face even though she was fuckin' around with other guys. It took a while, and I realized that I didn't marry a virgin; she was pregnant by another guy when I met her but never realized that she was a damn coke whore. If she would have had the baby, it probably would have been addicted to drugs because of her coke habit that I was too stupid to realize and pick up on. But that was something I should have picked up on because my friend was picking up weed so he could fuck her that night. I wasn't perfect either. I asked myself what I would do if it was the other way around. Then I remembered I did marry her for better or worse. As I remember, I never looked at what she did before. I met her after she grew on me. She just became my best friend. This was all before I found out all the stuff she had done with different guys in conversations we had after we were married.

Well, I got the news today. They are sending me to Bridgewater Maximum. It's still behind the wall but, I'm not going to Plymouth Correctional, a real messed-up place. I don't know if they have a weight room, but I hope so. When I was at the minimum, I would look across the street and say I wouldn't want to be there. Now this is where I'm going to end up. Now I'm looking forward to where I'm going, and most of the guys that I talked to said that where I'm going is a real dump. To me, I really don't care. I just want this nightmare to come to an end and get back to my wife and daughter. I didn't know when it was going to happen but now all I have to think about is adjusting to this new place but somewhat glad I'm going closer to where I used to live, and so my wife can visit. I can't wait to get a visit from her because it's been a long time. All I can do is wait till they say "Pack your stuff" and say "You're out of here." Maybe people will come to see me. No one will drive to Concord because it's too far to drive and I don't blame them. I'll tell you one thing, if it was my wife and I was on the out, I would be there every other day to see her no matter how far it was. I would make sure she had money whenever she needed it. At this time, I felt and looked real bad. If I were on the street, all I would need is a cup, stand outside any storefront, and they could mistake me as a homeless person. That's how bad I looked. I felt just as bad. This morning they called count, and I was dreaming of my old life. I mean before jail. I started to jump down at the last minute. The CO caught me in the process of jumping down, and he said the next time, he was going to write me up. I looked at my roommate and said, "Why didn't you wake me?"

He said, "I thought you were up."

I just looked at him and said, "Right," I will remember this. I don't want to get written up because they will take rec away from me. I didn't want this to happen because it was just about the only thing I looked forward to doing in this damn place. The CO came in and said "Pack up, you're out of here." I started to pack up and was at the door, waiting to go to property room, when the CO came to let me out, so I thought, then he said to me, "What the fuck are you doing?" Then said, "Not you, your roommate." I had to put all my stuff back. I had a bunch of stuff to give to my workout friends. I had to make my bed again then move down again to the bottom bunk because he was gone. The CO on duty was a real asshole, like most, and hated everyone. I think he even hates himself because he knows that he's an asshole. Well, it must be black day. All the black guys were all making phone calls. I'm just listening to them call each other niggers. Such disrespectful bastards. While I was listening to some of their conversation, I heard one saying how he was going home.

"I can't wait because I'm going to fuck my white bitch girlfriend right in the ass because it's been a long time, even though she doesn't like it, but she will do what I tell her to do. Then after that, I'll go over her girlfriend's house, do the same to her." Then he said that he treats all white girls as pigs. I just went back to my book and was disgusted with their messed-up conversation. I was waiting for the nighttime to come so I could go to the gym to work out. It makes me forget a lot of shit that I was carrying on my shoulders, to clear my mind because of what I heard all day long. The black guy I worked out with was a real decent guy. I told him what the black guys were saying outside the doors, and he told me that if he was going out with a white girl, he would never disrespect her in any way. Then he said that she would smash something over his head if he did. He just said that this was what gave black guys a bad name. He told me that he was in for burning down houses for landlords because they would pay him to do it but got caught because the landlord put gasoline all over the house before he got there, and he didn't know it. When he had got there, someone had already called the police. They were waiting for him, and he went into the house. He was caught and charged. Then he said that was what he was doing time for even though they couldn't prove it.

He told me how he did it. He takes some potatoes chips, a cigarette between a book of matches, then he puts it next to a receptacle next to curtain so they think it was a wiring fire. Also next to some rags sometimes, a little lighter fluid, he says that's all it takes. He said by doing this, it gives him enough time to leave the house because potatoes chips are real flammable. They go up real fast, and when they can't find any chemical at the scene, then they mark it as wiring problem. He would get ten thousand dollars for a job like that, another five when the insurance paid. He was doing a five-year bid but would be out way before me because of the good time he will get for doing programs. He had fifteen thousand dollars waiting for him when he gets out. What he told me was that he had done this quite a few times before; this was the first time he got in trouble for it, and that was because his girlfriend ratted him out. His wife had a lot of the money put aside. He was putting it toward an attorney to see if she can get him out earlier, but he's got to stop messing around with other women because his wife told him this will be the last time.

Well, they just called lunch, and they were serving tuna. I'll eat it if they don't put onions in it. Most of the time I won't eat it because they put larger pieces of onions in it, and it looks like there is no tuna in the sandwiches. It sucks. I ate it even though it smelled like cat food. As I was eating, there were three older guys across the table from me. I overheard what they were talking about. One was talking to the other, and he said that he needed glasses, some medical stuff done so he got himself busted, sent to jail so they could take care of the problems that he had. He was homeless and couldn't afford a doctor. What a damn shame when someone has to come to jail to get medical help, to eat, have a warm place to sleep for the winter. As I'm leaving the mess hall, I was stuffing some apples in the lining of my jacket. I was hoping that they wouldn't check me, because I get hungry during the night. That will hit the spot. Well, they are checking two different guys at the door good while I snuck back to the room again. I got the apples out of the mess hall. Now all I had to wait for was for them to call rec. I hope it comes fast. I hate being locked up in this room. It feels like the walls are closing in on me, the night gets worse. When the night comes, all the animal noises start. These noises the guys make when the lights go out, this is every night. You have no choice but to put up with it, what else can you do. To think, these are grown men doing this. I hate the way these cops look at me. They really think that they are better than me. If they only knew that I hung around with their fellow buddies before I came into this place. I watched them do coke and get really fucked up. They'd probably freak out.

The whole time that I was in Concord, if I fell asleep and woke up, I wouldn't know if it was day or night because you tend to lose track after a while between day, night, so you try not to fall asleep. I just wish that they would just move me out of this place and get me to my next stop so I can get my shit together. I'll be able to get adjusted to a maximum prison. At this time my so-called wife is really fucking me over because I'm starting to wake up. She doesn't realize she was involved with the product along with me. She's thinking that she had nothing to do with any of it.

This is January 14, 2001. The guy I have as a roommate just came in, and he stuck a pack of cigarettes up his ass. Before that, he stuck ten bundles of dope up his ass. Where he gets it, I don't know, don't care, but this brings in big money in here. As I said, I don't know where or how he got it, but it's none of my business. I don't want anything to do with it. As I'm writing this, he's on the toilet trying to shit out what he brought in. I told him I didn't want to know what he was bringing in, didn't want anything to do with it either. What a bunch of sick bastards. I'm in here doing time for drugs; I've had my share of the drug business for the rest of my life. Well, it's time to go to the gym; I look forward to this part of the day because we are locked up all day long except when we go to lunch, breakfast. It just gets to the point that I have to get away from the guy in my room, the shit he's involved with. I just don't want to get dragged down with him. When they opened the door, I just about run to the gym to get the bench we need to work out on. We just put our ID on the benches so we get first dibs on the weights. This is the best part of the day for me. As I entered the weight room, I met an older guy trying to keep in shape also. He said that he was sick, tired of being in Concord. He wanted out, that he was going to do something stupid to get a move out of Concord. I just stood away from him because I had no idea what he was going to do. I said he couldn't get a move out of Concord because it was a Maximum prison to begin with, that all he would get was a stay in the hole, and he said, "Watch me get a move." This older guy was serving a seven-year term. I couldn't believe they gave him such a long term to serve because of his age, but what he had, I don't know. I don't really care I just don't want to do anybody else's time. I have enough of my own time to do. That was the last time I saw him. It gets to the point you just want out. You don't give a damn where they send you because you adjust to wherever they send you. It scared me at first, but you get used to it real fast. The unit was getting empty. A lot of the guys were getting their moves. It was going to be anytime now for me. I felt that they would move me out to make room for the next batch of guys coming in. If they were going to send me to Bridgewater Maximum, I was hoping that it had a good visiting room where it wouldn't be too far for my wife to travel. Maybe she would come see me and I could get my hand jobs again. Even all the bad stuff my so-called wife was doing to me, I could always put it on the back burner, as they say.

I just kept telling myself it's not true even when I knew it was. This was after she came to visit me twice with cock breath. I just said to myself, for better or worse. What an ass I was. It will be any day now that the CO will tell me to pack it up, tell me that I'm out of here. As I'm writing this, another three guys are on their way out of the unit, are going to a different jail. I just can't wait to get the hell out of here now. They just moved in a new guy today. I thought he was going to tell me to pack up, but no, what a stupid asshole this one is. He started cracking his knuckles every hour on the hour, hummed, sang the same words to this song over and over again. Something by Guns 'n' Roses. He tried to carry on a conversation with me, but all he talked about was how high he got on the street, What he did to get his drugs. This last time he just walked up to a girl, took her bike, her pocketbook, then rode off with it, but he got caught with the bike but was able to spend the money that the girl had in her pocketbook. It went of course to buy the crack before he got caught. That was what he was doing when he was on the street, just robbing people. He told me that the girl was so scared that she just let him take it without a word or a struggle but was crying real loud. Piece of fuckin' shit. I didn't talk much to this scumbag unless I had to. I told a couple of other guys what he was in for.

Today I wrote the superintendent to see if I could get some of my money so I could buy some cosmetics, a new pair of sneakers, because you got to go through him before the property officer okays. It's so damn crazy. It's your money, it's going though the canteen, the purchase is going to you, so what's the problem. Every jail that I've been in the system is so messed up that it's so hard to put it into words. It's like I'm trying to talk to my parents. I'm just asking them for money to buy a pair of damn sneakers through the canteen. It's my damn money. They always give you a hard time about it when you ask to take money from your canteen. Now it will take a week before I get some sort of an answer from the superintendent. I'll probably be in the back of a transport van going down the highway to my next stop before I get an okay from him. It feels like I'm falling apart. I feel sick all the time. The conditions in here are real bad. I'm asking for sneakers because they sent my sneakers home. They gave me these slippers that they call BOBOs to wear, but my feet hurt real bad, and they are wet all the time because of the weather. I've never felt so helpless before in my whole life except when my daughter's mother kicked me out.

Well, this roommate of mine is driving me crazy. I want to smash him in the face but I won't because it might mess up my move closer to home. I realize I'm not on the street anymore, and they do what they want to do to you. I just found out today that this fuckin' kid ratted on his girlfriend. She was serving two years in jail. Most of the guys in here don't want anything to do with him. I just couldn't stand him, and this made it even worse. He was in the same room as I was in. I was waiting to go to the gym again. We were supposed to get out of our rooms first tonight, and the CO just forgot to let us out of our cells. It's been ten minutes, and all the exercise equipment will be taken up by the time we were out of our cells. Stupid bastard didn't realize that he didn't open up all the cell doors. He must have graduated first in his class, stupid bastard. He finally realized that he didn't open up all the cells because of all the yelling that was going on. Of course by the time I got to the gym, one of the other guys that I worked out with got all the equipment that we use. Just when I thought we weren't going to get to work out. This was just the only thing that I could look forward to in the course of the whole day. The other guy that I worked out with was a lawyer but wasn't a drug lawyer, but his wife was a firm believer in drugs and was also into doing coke. He did what I did, took the rap, but also was doing time for stealing social security checks from old people. When his name was put in the paper, his wife got drug tested at her job and lost her job as well because it came back positive for cocaine. They were making good money between the both of them. Now all she can get is working in a doughnut shop making just enough money to pay the mortgage payment with just a little left over. He was really upset because she sent him fifteen dollars to buy some stuff in the canteen; this was after she told him that she wasn't eating well. I wish I had a wife like that. My wife was out there doing all kinds of messed-up things that I don't want to believe. Before I left, I left her plenty of money, but she still didn't send me any of the money I left her. What

I would like to know is where the decent women disappeared to. I've been looking for one my whole damn life. When I think I've found one, she's out there fucking every guy in the city for coke. I always wanted to find a woman like the guy I work out with, a woman just like the wife he had, but a woman like his wife never came my way.

The ones I end up with, I always try to make life even better for them, and they end up fucking me over, running off with what I gave them or what they could take from me.

Of course he tried to send the check back to her, but it was already put into his canteen. They wouldn't take it out once it's put in. When he gets visits, he doesn't come back from a visit saying that his wife's breath smelled like she just gave a guy a blow job, as my wife did. As I was in his room, he showed me pictures of his wife. This woman is beautiful. Some guys are so damn lucky. He was an ugly fuck, how he did it I'll never know. When I was working out in the gym, I came across a couple of books to read when I'm in lockdown. That was great because it would put my mind at rest. I'll be able to stop thinking of how I got here. Anything in a form of a book is a great find in here. This is January 20, 2001. One of the kids that I talked to was sent out today. They sent him to Plymouth County. They said that he was going to Bridgewater Max, but all at once they changed their minds and sent him to Plymouth County. I hope they don't do that to me. What a fucked-up thing to do. If they do that to me, I'll just do something to get lugged again because it really doesn't matter to me where they send me now. You learn to adjust wherever they send you. I'll most likely come back here again. I'll just wait to get sent to another place. It doesn't matter to me. It's all time to me, but not to Plymouth County. It'd just like being here, so let me stay here. But if you have to send me to another jail, I really don't care as long as you send me to a jail that has a weight room or workout stuff. I'll be okay. This kid that I met in the gym was a young Spanish kid. He would call me OG. I didn't understand what this meant until I asked him. He said after some of the stories I told him, some of the things that I got away with, he just said, "To me you're an old-time gangster."

I just laughed and said, "That's what it meant? I'm far from that."

He said, "The best thing that you told me was never rat on anyone, never drag someone else down with you. Deal with what you got caught with." He said bye to me and gave me the shoulder thing and said, "Maybe we will see each other again in the system." He was a good kid and didn't deserve to be in this place. I look around to see if anyone saw this. You never know what guys in here start by seeing even a simple gesture like this. I look around and saw so many lives that were messed up by the court system on small-time drug convictions, how many lives that were destroyed by asshole prosecutors trying to make a name for themselves. I just can't understand how they mix all the decent guys with repeat offenders that teach us different ways to commit crimes. I'll never understand. Not only do you do the time that they give you, your life is messed up forever. I know you won't be able to get a job on the outside when you get out unless they don't do a query on you, or you know someone who gets a job for you. It took me five years before I was able to get a steady job that was through a guy that lived across the street from me. It got to the point that I started to say who will hire me again, to be a schoolteacher after what I was involved in was impossible, plus being a felon, I say zero to none. I have no chance in the world of that happening. But I was able to get a job working for a garbage company and became real good at it but hated the maggots that fell on me while I was working under the trucks. But the people that I had to deal with were as bad as the bugs that fell on me, but the good part was that it was a night job, so I didn't have to deal with any big bosses that would remind me of COs. I was glad I talked to the guy Tony that lived across the street from me. He ended up being a big boss at a garbage company. I didn't know this till I was there for a while. It was one of the worst jobs I ever had, but I was there every day, never took days off. To me it was a bad place to work, but it paid the bills. Of course, the whole time I was there, I was treated like shit. I worked at this place for at least five years, did what was asked of me, but I ran into night boss that was a real dickhead along with his son that didn't fall far from the tree. This boss was always threatening my job because I told him to stop telling me that I was good-looking, rubbing my back when he came by. I always turned, told him to stop, and gave him that look I wanted so much to bust him in the face, but I needed my job. As I came in on a Friday for my shift, the boss was passing out the checks. That was the boss who hired me. My check and his weren't there, so I was told to go to the office. As I got to the office, I saw one of the owners, and out of respect, I said hi with a return response. When I got into the office, I was told that there was a lack of work. They said that they didn't need my service anymore and for me to go down to collect unemployment. I was of course upset, left the office, and as I got back to the shop, I was told that they fired the boss that hired me also. I went in to talk to the so-called big boss owners and found out that he was a fuckin' asshole like the night boss. They must come from the same mold or giving each other hand jobs. I wouldn't put it past the boss that kept rubbing my back. I was told by him that I lost my job because there was a lack of work in a company DA. It was as they say, not who you know, it's who you blow. I kind of knew I got fired because they did a query on me. That was the real reason they let me go. They were informed by this guy Travis, a real piece of shit. After this I started to fall apart. It's all on the inside, where no one can see. I'm able to hide it real good like I always did. My heart is taking the hardest hit, and I tried not to face it, but I started to drift back, realized that if I didn't marry my wife, I would have been better off. The letters that I'm getting in the mail is killing me. I can't believe my wife fooled me for so many years, fooled me real good. January 20, 2001, I can't stand this lockup all the time. It's really messing with my head. Looking at four walls all the time really gets to you. When you're able to sleep, the dreams can get really bad. It depends on the person that you are. Some guys, it doesn't bother them, but to me being confined messes with my mind real bad. But you have to be able to put two and two together. Again no brains, no pain. The ones that have no brains run around all day playing games on one another because they have no fuckin' life on the outside. I look in the mirror, and I hate the person I see. I tell myself how stupid I was, feel, and look terrible. I look like a homeless person still.

As soon as I walked back from the chow hall, if you want to call it lunch, the CO said, "Pack up, you're out of here. Bring your mattress down to property." I just couldn't believe what I was hearing but wanted out of this place anyways. One of the guys I lifted with helped me bring all my stuff down to property. Before that, I put on double pairs of clothes on because it will be weeks before I get my stuff from here. Just can't believe it, why can't they just bring your property with them. We are going to the same place but that requires thinking. Again the shoulder thing, it must be a thing that guys just do, I hear, so I went along with it. I gave him all the stuff I had left to eat because it doesn't follow you. It goes to the rats or you give it to someone you know; that's what I did. I was handcuffed, shackled, and led to the van like an animal. Also treated like one, put in the back. I really hated the slamming of the doors of the van when they closed them. This CO drove like an asshole, like 99 percent of them do. When I say fast, I mean real fast. I was bounced all around from the time I got into the van till the time I was taken out. There were no seat belts to hold you in place. I was the only one going to Bridgewater Max; the black guy that was in the van with me was going somewhere else, at least I thought he was. I tried to talk to him but couldn't get a word out of him edgewise but got some sort of a response like a very dirty look from time to time. I at one time got a few syllables from him because he blurted out a few words like a mouthful of shit. Because when I asked him where he was going, I couldn't understand what he tried to say to me. I did tried to carry on a conversation with him, but he said that he "don't like white people." He said this straight out so I never said another word to him the whole time I was in the van. I just thought, Another Trooper. My body heated up, and I wanted to ask him what the fuck was wrong with him but decided not to say another word to him for the rest of the trip, even after he asked me a few questions and I gave him no reply, as he did to me. After a while I just said to myself another racist bastard just like all the rest I've ran into. Of course, most of them are at lease in jail. While I was in Concord, I saw at least four different COs that did cocaine with a guy I knew from the fish house named Danny. He used to go to different bars with COs to drink and would come over my house a couple of times a month. I saw them do cocaine right in front of me, but of course they did no wrong. But of course they didn't know me now because I'm in jail. They do drugs differently than I did, are better than I am.

What a long ride to Bridgewater. It took a while, and again I had to use the bathroom. I wish we could be there already before I pissed my pants. Finally, we arrived at Bridgewater, and I remembered what it looked like from what I saw before when I was here the first time, and it scared the shit out of me. When I saw the outside of Bridgewater Maximum Prison, it looked like a castle from medieval days like, I'd seen many times before in movies. As I was looking at the outside of Bridgewater, I was wondering if it looked the same on the outside, old and decrepit, then thought it must be real bad inside, but as I entered the prison, to my surprise, it wasn't as old looking but kept up, looked somewhat kept up with some modern improvements. As we approached, it looked like a drive-through at the bank we had to go through these doors. Of course, there were COs waiting for me to be strip-searched again before I entered. I swear these guys loved takin' guys cloths off guys. Again I was strip before I got into the van at Concord, now as I got out again. I had to see the nurse again was asked all the same questions as I was asked at all the others jails that I was at. It takes a long time before they get around to asking you the these questions. All the questions must be on a paper that the jail assign to them and are basically all the same from one jail to another. It's a no-brainer type of job except when a guy gets out of control. What a long wait. It must have arrived just when they were doing a shift change. The CO that was on at that time asked me what I was in for, and he just smiled at me and started singing the song "Riding That Train Pile of Cocaine." It went on for a long time over and over again; I had to put up with it as I did at the last stop. These COs must talk to each other before I got there, I think. As I was looking at the entrance, another CO walked in, asked what I was in for, and the other CO told him that I was in for cocaine. He just said, "He's not going to get the room service like he was getting on the outside." I tried so hard to ignore him, pay no attention to him but heard everything he was saying to the other CO. It just went up my ass. There was nothing I could say about it or do about it, so I had no choice but to put up with it. There was so much hate going through my body that I just couldn't explain it if I tried. It was almost like what the black guys put me through. I was wishing that I could see them after I get out, see if they felt the same or if they had the balls to say that when we were on equal grounds. I told them that I was hungry, and he said that I would have to wait till he got me signed in first. I needed to use the bathroom, and he just said that I would have to wait for that also. There was an inmate cleaning the floors that heard me saying that I was hungry and asked the CO on duty if he could give some of the sandwiches that they had brought in from the kitchen earlier. The CO just said that he could give the sandwiches to the guys that are in what they call cages. He just said, "As long as it shuts them up." Then he said to the inmate, "You better take care of your own because if they had to wait for me, they would be starving all night long." Then the CO said, "Fuck them, fuck them all. I hate them all. I wish that they could all be executed." Just hearing him say that killed me. It's bad enough that I'm in a damn cage like an animal, but to hear him also say "I don't care if they live or die" fueled more hate in me.

Now I can't have any animal that lives in a cage because I know what it feels like to be caged up. I tell my grandkids not to coop any living thing up because it affects me real bad. In the same conversation I also said that what's in the wild, let it stay in the wild. My daughter gave me a bird, and I would look at it in a cage, but I couldn't keep it because it looked like it was miserable. I just had to give it away because it's still with me being cooped up even after so many years of being out of jail. Getting back to where I was in Bridgewater cage waiting to be processed so I could be placed in a permanent cell, again I asked the CO in charge if I could use the toilet, and again he said that he was too busy and couldn't let me use it at that time. I did tell him that I had been holding it most of the day. He just said, "Hold it a little longer. When I get up to do my rounds, I'll let you use it." When I asked him this, all he was doing was sitting in a chair with his feet up reading the newspaper. If they put these guys in a real prison, they wouldn't last a day because someone would fuck them up in a seconds. All these COs were lazy motherfuckers. I mean most of them don't want to do their jobs. They just want to collect a paycheck. When they can they push their jobs on an inmates, it's all the better for them. The guy that was in the cage with me just started to piss into a cup that was in the cell because he also couldn't hold it any longer. He said that there was another cup in the cell if I wanted to use it, and I just couldn't believe what we were forced to do. Just when I thought I was going to be there for most of the night, a CO came up to me and said that I was all checked in. He was going to take me to my cell.

What a long walk to get to my cell, and when I got there, it looked like a dungeon or a cellar. The inside was just as bad, but I had to go stay where they put me because it was their house, as they say. As he opened the door, they were made of solid steel, very thick with large skeleton key holes. Anyways they were old locks in the doors, and it looked creepy. I would be surprised if the locks still worked. I was put in the cell, and I heard the CO just start to walk away, and I said to myself, He didn't lock it. I looked around; I had the cell all to myself. I never had a cell to myself. I was still up most of the night thinking that someone was going to come in while I was sleeping. But as I was looking around for a light but couldn't find one, I heard noises during the night and started to look for rats and was unsure if someone would come in while I was sleeping. During the night while I was as most of the time just lying in bed thinking as usual, of course, it was all about my family, how I missed them, I kept saying to myself how stupid I was for doing what I did. Then I said that I will never look at cocaine ever again as long as I live. Well, during the night, I really had to use the toilet, so I started to look for the CO on duty. He never made any rounds at all, so I just pressed against the door to the cell. It opened as I thought that he never locked when he left when he put me in here. I just walked out to the bathroom. All the time that I was in the bathroom, I was waiting for the COs to come running in like it happened in Concord because I wasn't in my cell, but it never happened. As I walked into the bathroom, I noticed that it was all modernized. It looked like it didn't belong in this place, and it didn't smell like shit and piss. I looked down the line of toilets and noticed that there was a roll of toilet paper on the floor next to a stall. I didn't go that far down. I used the toilet just before it. Now when I started to go to the toilet, I heard someone talking. I said, This guy is talking to himself while he was going to the bathroom, but it sounded like two difference voices. I just found it very strange but kept to myself but then realized that there were two different voices coming from the stall, but I paid no mind to it. In here you learn to mind your own business and just do your time, and you never see anything and you know nothing at all if asked unless you're a rat motherfucker. All that was on my mind at the time was saying I finally was able to use a toilet without someone watching me go. It was peaceful for once. As I finished and was walking out, the guy was coming out of the stall at the same time as I was, the one I was hearing voices from. All he had to say to me was, when I see a roll of toilet paper outside a toilet stall, you don't try to enter. The roll in front of the door is to let other guys know that someone is in there. Not long after that conversation, I noticed another guy walking out behind him. I didn't say a word. I didn't even look surprised. I said it had nothing to do with me. In a place like this, you see things you just ignore and you really won't understand, but you mind your own and just go on your way. I made this mistake once. I just opened the door to a toilet, and there was a guy rubbing one off. He just started yelling to close the door. This is how I found out about the toilet paper outside the door and never did it again. The guy came over to me and said that it was no problem, said that he couldn't get his girlfriend off his mind; he thought that was the best way, just to go rub one off. I really didn't give a damn what he was doing I just wanted to use the toilet and have peace of mind not having to put up a sheet so I could go to the toilet without being watched. I would hang up the sheet from our bunk to the door to have some privacy from my roommate when I was in Concord. There I was, hanging up a sheet not to be watched; this CO would look in and watch me through the window to go the bathroom, just stare at me. The whole time that I was at Concord, I never was alone in any of the cells that they put me for more than a couple of hours.

BUSTED

It took a long while, but I was getting real used to being in a cell all by myself even though it looked like a dungeon, but it was a single cell. Just not having to smell another guy's shit all night was a big plus. As I was sitting in my cell, I was wondering where the chow hall was. I didn't see it as I was being brought to my cell and just said I guess I'll find it when the CO calls count in the morning. Well, morning came, and when count was cleared, I just followed all the other guys, and they led me right to the chow hall. The COs don't tell you a thing. They put you in a cell and just about forget about you unless there's a problem. I wanted to use the shower but wanted to know where they were. I found that they were in the same room as the toilets right up against the walls. I didn't see them when I went to use the toilet. As I walked into where the toilets were, I noticed they were right up against the walls. They weren't flooded with water, among other things that 99 percent of the guys deposit in the showers. So you must take it upon yourself to wear shower shoes because you have no idea what you can pick up from what these guys leave behind in the showers. Even though it looks somewhat clean, it's not. I'm not talking about clothes. The bathrooms or shithouses or whatever you know them as, inmates are the only guys that clean the showers. With just about no chemicals, how clean can it really be. I leave this up to what is on your mind right now as you read this, but remember, this shit was not the worst. This was my first day in this place. I was taking one day at a time, and now I was wondering where the canteen was. I was hoping I didn't get lost like I did in Concord and be able to find my way back to my cell. This was my first time being incarcerated. This place was real big, so I tried to keep to myself because the attorney told me no to get into any trouble because it will mess with my revise and revoke when I was going into court again. I already was here for a week and already went through their count procedure, of course, I was always up before count. There was a young black guy in the next cell who was a sleeper. I had to make sure to wake him up most of the time, but he was a real good guy, very respectful guy. This guy must have had come from a good family just by the way he acted.

Now I'm waiting for them to clear count, then I will be able to go to breakfast to eat. I didn't hear them clear count, but they must have cleared it because everyone was leaving and walking out of their cells, so I figured they must have cleared it. I figured they were all going to the chow hall. I was still wondering where the chow hall was but just as I told myself just followed all the other guys, they just led me right to it. But as I was walking, I was counting all the building blocks so I could find my way back to my cell. I was in another big jail compound. Of course, they all looked alike. I didn't want to end up in another building again like I did in Concord, so I counted all the building as I was walking to the chow hall. What a long walk it was to the chow hall. When I finally got there, I noticed that the line was bent around in a large circle around the building. The line was so damn long that the wait was at least twenty minutes before I got to the doors, as I entered the building, there was another line circling, bent going up the stairs. The whole time as I was entering the building everyone was just pushing. All the guys were mooing like cows being lead into a slaughterhouse, but it was like the way most of the COs treated us, like animals. One of the guys was laughing when he heard what they were doing, so he started to moo like everyone else. I just couldn't believe that I was in a place like this. As I got to where they served the food, the smell was just unbearable. To this day I know it was the smell of some of the food that was being cooked, but it could be mistaken by some of the guys who don't believe in washing up because some of them would sleep for days on end and just came down when they were hungry or up for count. But most of the time the food never had a good smell to it. It would stink but you had to eat something to stay somewhat healthy. After I got my food and utensils, I walked to sit down and realized that it was as long as the walk to sit down and eat as it was to get to the chow hall. Today it was cereal like it was most of the time. I was real hungry because I didn't get any canteen as of yet, so I had to eat whatever they served. I looked at the cereal and said what can they do wrong to cereal but you can never know! I ate all of what they gave me. The guys that was across from me asked me if I wanted his cereal. He looked at me and said no strings attached. You never just take food or anything like that from anyone. As I looked around, I noticed that there was a mass of tables all over the place. I watched where I sat because there were places you just don't sit because they are reserved and one thing you respect. I ended up getting a job working in the kitchen. I knew what food to eat, the food not to eat because I loaded, unloaded food that came in to the prison. When I entered the freezers, a lot of the food was uncovered, exposed to the cold, sometimes it would be there for days uncovered, sometimes had mold on it. At the end of the week it would be made into soup. But working in the kitchen, I was able to eat the food that was made that day or the day before because I knew it was just cooked. I ate a lot of raisins, drank lots of milk without the COs seeing me because if you got caught, it would be the last day you worked in the kitchen. Sometimes I would take some of the food back to the cell to eat and would bring a plastic bag with me, but a lot of guys would just slip it down their pants and bring it back that way. Just think about it. Some of these guys would stink real bad. They would put the food that they took from the kitchen down their pants and eat it later.

Most of the time, the guys would bring back the chicken it was good to mix in with our rice that we got from canteen and recook it in our hotpots that we would wire to boil. But we had to remember to make sure to take the wire out of our hotpots when we were done cooking the meals we made. I made all my food myself or watched where it came from before I ate it. I just didn't like the extra flavor that some guys didn't mind. If I was to get it from someone else, I would make sure I watched where he took it from because I didn't want the taste of their balls along with my meal. One thing to remember is that you don't take anything from anyone unless you know them like candy bars that some of the guys would slid under the doors of the young guys among other things for favors. This was done for dirty deeds favors or what you want to call them that some of the guys wanted during they stay in jail. I'll just let you think what favors they wanted besides them wanting to get a young kid to be their bitch. This was told to me from a guy I hung around with and that was in the system many times before. He was at Concord with me. You only take the things from guys that you know and hang with. If anyone offers you something and you don't know them, you might have to give something up in return. I figured that seeing that I was behind the wall, I thought that I wouldn't get searched as much, but they still wanted to look up my ass. I'm sure there wouldn't be a weapon up there that may be a cigarette, but who really gives a damn. Let them smoke the fuckin' thing. But when they found something even in the form of food or maybe sometimes a cigarette, it would be like they found a gun or drugs. Again if the inmate wanted to smoke something that was up someone's ass, all the power to them, just maybe they liked that extra tastes. What fuckin' assholes a lot of COs can be when you get caught with fuckin' cigarettes. You would have to watch to see who would be on duty before you brought any food back with you. If they changed the COs to the door to the unit, guys knew he was a real dick. They would leave a load of food or whatever they had on the ground before we entered the unit because we didn't want to get caught with it.

The next day when I was eating breakfast, I ran into the same guy at breakfast, and he was with his friend. He asked me if I wanted his food again. He said the same as the day before. Of course I said okay. The conversation went on. He wanted to know where I came from. I said, "I came from New Bedford," and he said he was from Fall River. Then out of nowhere he said that he was gay. "As for you being gay," I said, "I don't care. It's your life, you live it as you want." He told me that he was a black belt and knew how to use it. Then he asked me what I did as a job on the outside. I told him that I was an instructor in a high school, and he was surprised to hear that and said, "You're in a place like this." This guy was the second-degree black belt that was giving me his breakfast; he was a real decent guy. He started the conversation from the start starting that he was in for attempt of murder; he didn't do what they said he did. The conversation went on for the length of our time we had for breakfast, and never once did he say that he was a so-called nigger. After the third day sitting in the same place, talking to the same guys, I started to get dirty looks. I didn't give a damn. I talk to who I want, didn't care what anyone had to say. No one ever said anything to me except one of the guys I hung around, and I told him I didn't care what people said. If they had any problem with it, they could bring it to me or the guy that I sit at the table with. I sit where I want to sit because no one was there in the beginning. As with him being gay, I don't give a damn what he was. Nothing was ever said to him as far as I know. If they did, I think they would have got fucked up. You don't want to get beat up by a gay guy in jail because you will never live it down. But from that day on whenever they came to the table, they would ask me if I wanted their food because they said it was garbage to them, but it was cereal. They told me that they cooked their own food in their cells, but I always asked them how much they wanted for it, and they said nothing.

Just in conversation he said to me, "What the fuck are you doing here?"

I said, "It's not a choice of my own. It was the court decision, not mine."

Then he said, "They fucked up, you should not be here. You should be in a drug program then. If you messed up again, then do the time."

I told him that my wife hired a Boston lawyer to see if he could get the charges dropped, get time served, and he looked at me and said "Good luck, hope you win."

I said, "Me too."

Well, it's canteen day again. I have to get my canteen bag, just hope my money cleared so I can get some stuff that I need so I have something to do while I'm up at night. Now I'm starting to sleep a little at night because I'm alone in a cell, don't have to watch guys at night do their fucked-up things to guys at night. But I'm still paranoid and put things in front of the door. It will wake me if someone comes in. Even though I'm in a cell alone, I still put things in front of the door because the door doesn't lock, and I trust no one in this place. Well, I'm on my way to pick up my canteen bag, and as I'm waiting in line, I'm looking around, and I'm seeing guys opening up their canteen bags, giving stuff away. On the way back I saw guys taking canteen bags away from guys. I just can't believe what I see. As I'm walking back to the unit, I'm holding on to my bag really tight, say no one is going to take it away from me no matter what, what I have to do. At this point I just don't give a damn, realize what type of guys these guys are, what this place makes you into. It gets to the point you will do just about anything to take care of you unless you enjoy getting fucked over. In here it's just like they say, it's a dog eat dog world. Everyone is for themselves. They will fuck you over any chance they get especially if you came in to a place like this as stupid as I was. I just want to get the fuck back to my cell, go through what I ordered to see what I got.

I'm really getting to think that I got another fucked-up lawyer, thinking I fucked up again letting my wife control something important. I had to do just about everything on the outside when it came to organizing bills, things that had to be done. She was always out there. Now my wife is the one talking to all the attorneys out there in my behalf. Now I'm thinking I'm really screwed. Now what's going through my mind now is that I'm going to do all the time the court gave me because I don't get any letters from him to this day. He never answered any of my phone calls. This so-called big time Boston lawyer was no better than the lawyer who got me five years. What a waste of money. To get a guy's hopes up is really wrong. My wife, what a damn joke she is, I'm starting to think, realizing that she also is no fuckin' good. She is all for herself and was too blind to see it. I'm still getting letters. And they say that she's out there partying, fuckin' different guys, the letters that I'm still getting. The letters are probably coming from one of the guys she's fucking; it's killing me inside just thinking of this all the time. What's killing me the most is that she's letting me rot in here; she's having a good time spending my money I left her to help me get things I need in here. By now it's up her nose, and she'd forgotten I gave it to her to give to me a little at a time. She tells me she went through it, and now it's coming out of her pocket. As I looked at it, as they say for better or worse as long as we shall live, what a fuckin' joke. The joke is on me. With her mentality, she must look at it, say to herself he left it to me, I'll spend it any way I want. That's what she is doing. For most of the women these days, it's just a one-way street. Being married don't mean a thing to most women today. It's so weird I just realized. It feels like still living in the past, with my daughter's mother. I thought, what a fuckup; I did it again. I got involved with a coldhearted woman in which love meant nothing to them because they were and probably still are coke whore. Some women will do anything for a line these days. Cocaine is everything to them, and this can be a guy's best friend. If you don't believe it, ask a girl if she wants to do some lines. As the night goes on, put a line on your dick, watch them go down on it, tell them that it's a cokesicles. They'll just laugh and do what you ask them to do.

Right now I've been in a single cell for three weeks now, and I finally got a notice from the property room to go and pick up my things from the property that came from Concord. I took my long walk to the property building. As I approached, there were at least six long lines for guys to stand in that have ordered things or are waiting for things from other jails. It was a long wait before I entered the property room. Of course when I got my things, there were a lot of things missing. When I asked where it was, they said it was taken out because it was contraband. I couldn't have it. Well, this meant I had to buy some more jeans, get some pocket T-shirts from guys that just came in because they don't sell them in the canteen. If you come in with no money, better have decent clothes on. You can sell them so you can get canteen. Just use state clothes that the prison give you. Well, as the week went on, I found a guy that wanted to sell some clothes. As I was checking them out, I then found most of my clothes that they said was contraband. I couldn't believe it. All my clothes that was missing was being sold. The guy that was selling them worked in the property room. This guy would steal inmates' stuff from the property room and resell to the inmates for canteen, fuckin' asshole. I told him that the stuff that he was selling was my stuff; he was surprised, and then I told him that my name was on the bottom of the shirt. He didn't know what to say. He looked at me, and I just gave him something for it, took my stuff back. I didn't rat him out to anyone. In time he will get his from someone else. It finally started to sinkin, and now I knew my so-called wife was no good and was cheating on me, because this kid I taught at the school told me that he seen her at a bar fuckin' around. This was the woman I put in charge to help me get out of here, and it hurt me real bad to be told this by my student. I really don't know what's wrong with me, but I still wanted to see her because when my wife wasn't high, she was great to be around, a real fun person. After thinking about it, I said that means that I really know that I'm still in love her, knew that love is blind. There is nothing that you can do about that either. It's what you have in your heart. I know it hurts now, and I know it will take years before I get over her as it did for my daughter's mother, but there will always be a place in my heart for them both but realize now it's over. Now I kind of knew it when she came up to see me because she didn't have to drive to far for a visit. I think she just felt obligated to do so. It wasn't because she loved me as I still did her. I also think she thought this wouldn't mess with her social life that she was leading, thinking I didn't know. She just went back to the life that she was leading before I met her. I know this to be true because she told me in one conversation on the phone that she had sex with more guys than I had fingers and toes. I was just lost for words. I made off like I didn't hear what she told me. I didn't know much about her, but when I met her, she was pregnant, dressed terrible, and had a piece of junk of a car that I rebuilt for her. Why I let her into my life was because I felt sorry for her. She just kept coming around every day. The girl that I was going out with at the time saw her, and that was when she broke up with me. After that I got so used to her coming around I started to go out, taking her with me every time I went somewhere. Then one thing led to another. Of course I started to help her with all the problems that she had. She just became part of my life.

 Being in a jail like this, it's so hard conversing with your attorney because the time limit is so short on the phone that you are able to use. They should have a place where you can have more time to talk to an attorney about your case. At this time I was still calling my so-called great Boston lawyer who was hanging up on me every time I called or even better having his secretary say that he was in court. This was all the time. But the weird thing about it, I still thought in my heart that he was going to get me out. I was really thinking that I was going to beat the case, get to go home to be with my family. This same day when I went to use the phone to call my lawyer, of course, he wasn't there again. His secretary told me at this time not to waste any more time with this lawyer. She said that he's been in the office most of the time I called. Then she told me that I shouldn't waste any more time calling him, to find someone else because he was doing this to other clients also. I told her that he had all the money I had and couldn't retain another lawyer because he had it tied up. I started to say there is no God in here because there is so much evil in here that he will never come into a godforsaken place like this.

After that I started looking around, saying over and over again "fuckin' scum" then saying "five fuckin' years." I had headaches most of the time after my Boston lawyer secretary told me this because I really thought that he was going to get me home to my family. I can't believe the stupid things I would think of like is there going to be dust on all my toolboxes in my body shop, will my cars start, will my wife come home when I get out. Will my daughter remember what I look like—just so many stupid things. When I'm thinking this, I have all the pictures of everyone in my hands. I kept looking at them for long period of time and realized what I lost with messing around with that shit. This stuff went on day after day to no end, cursing my Boston lawyer every day and the court system. It seems like this is all I do along with counting days every day. I've been down now close to three years. I hate all these motherfuckers, even more than the ones who can live this way and not have a care in the world. I just can't understand how grown men can just run around, joke around, act all of thirteen, not have a care in the world or even better think of their family, and still ask their families for money. I have so much hate in me I want to bust a lot of them in the fuckin' face, but I keep to myself, just stay in my own world. It's real good to have a single room. It's dark, but that's okay. I don't have to deal with all the pigs that were in the rooms with me prior to me getting here. I know now that when I get out of this place, I'm going to have to restrain myself because my way of thinking is so messed up. No doctor is going to be able to help me. I know I'm brainwashed. No one will be able to help me but me because they don't I know what I've gone through. I just received a letter from my so-called wife; I just can't wait to read it. I'm in the chow hall, and I'm going to finish eating first. Really I want to save it till I get back to the unit so I can take my time reading it over and over again, as I always do. To get a letter in here is so great that I'll read it till it falls apart. She is probably going to tell me that I'm not too far. She will be up to see me more often. Well, I started to read it, she did tell me that she is coming up to see me, but she has something very important to tell me. She doesn't want to tell me in a letter. The first thing I started to think about was that the lawyer went over my case, that there is nothing that he can do for me; she just didn't want to tell me this in a letter. She wrote in the letter that she will be up to see me this weekend to explain what it is she wanted to tell me. Of course, I just couldn't wait to see her even after she was fuckin' me over for the last three years. It's been at least a year since I've seen her because I commented on her breath, that it stank like sex. When I asked her what she had done before she came in to see me, she froze up and just looked at me. I'll give her credit; she gave a great blow job but was terrible in bed. After sex she would just lay there, say that when I had sex with her. She said that she never had sex with a guy like that before. This was probably because she was just used by guys for just a piece of ass, a place for guys to bust a nut, but they had to coke her up first.

Well, of course, I still couldn't wait for the weekend to come; it came very slowly maybe because I was counting the day's right down to the hours, minutes. To this day, I don't know how I could have feeling for this girl after all the bad stuff she had done to me, but still I did, my daughter hated me for it. Finally the weekend was here. I waited impatiently for the COs to call me for a visit. I was telling one guy that I was in for a long time, that I was getting a visit from my wife. It's been a very long time that I've felt this way and just can't explain it. I just felt real good inside. It was well after one o'clock, and I was wondering if she was going to come up or have an excuse why she was unable to come up as she had done many times before. They did call my name for a visit. I was almost running to the visiting room to see her and was told to walk, slow down. When I got there, I made eye contact with her. To me at that time she was the most beautiful girl in the world. Well, at least though my eyes. At that time I was so very happy to see her. I just wanted so much to kiss her, but again she had cock breath. Before I got close enough, she backed off because she probably knew that I would smell it. How a woman could do this I will never know, especially when they knew they were going to see another guy, or in this case her husband. She just sat down as I did. I began to tell her how much I missed her, but she cut me off to tell me so bluntly that she wanted a divorce because she wanted to go on with her life, wanted to marry another guy. This was the guy she was sucking off from the beginning when I first smelled it, probably the guy she was going to marry. I cursed him for it. I tried to change her mind, told her that I'd be getting out in thirty months and just about begged her to wait to file for divorce. She looked at me, said no, and wanted to go on with her life. I just stood up, told her that I was going to turn my back on her and walk away. I started to do so; that killed me so bad inside but I composed myself till I got to where I was going to be searched by a CO. He just told me, "You know what to do," I just looked at him, started to break down, had tears coming from my eyes. He looked at me and asked me what the problem was. I just said that my wife just asked me for a divorce. He looked at me and said that he was sorry for me. I paid him no mind because I thought he was messing with me as they always do. To have that kind of pain and being in a place where you couldn't do a thing about it is torture. Slowly as time went on, all friends and most family members drift away, then you realize you're all alone doing time. At this time I knew I wasn't going to get any more of my money I had left her, so I started to make cards. Sew clothes again even more than before just to eat decent. I met this guy, he asked me if I wanted to buy card material off him because he cleaned all the offices out when they needed it. He could get me some folder that I used to make cards. Of course I said yes. He came back the next day with a barrel full right from the offices. All he wanted was to be paid with cans of tuna, soups, or whatever he needed from the canteen. I made more than I gave out. All I gave him was from cards that I sold anyways. I was running out of the good thread. I met a guy that worked in a sewing shop, and he was able to get me some real good thread, and of course I paid him with canteen also. With what I got from him, I made fifteen times what I paid for it as I did for the card material. At this time I was thanking my daughter's mother for teaching me how to sew. It did come to good use as she told me when I was watching her. I started to make a lot of canteen and was starting to trade it for good clothes because you couldn't have too much canteen or the COs would take it, give it to their rats for snitching. I started to get rid of all my state clothes and replaced it with outside clothes. I started to feel like I wasn't a panhandler anymore. I still felt sick all the time, and my mind was still in a cloud. I just couldn't shake the thought of my wife that I was always thinking of, just couldn't believe she just left me, forgot about me so easy after all I had done for her. When she needed me, I was there, stuck by her in her time of need, and told the cops that she knew nothing about the drugs. I guess it must have been that easy because as soon as I went to jail, she started to go out with a guy who was selling coke. I was in jail, and she still didn't have to go far to power her nose even though she was being used. I just kissed the money I left her goodbye and did the best I could do with what I learned in here to buy canteen. Just knowing that she was fuckin' another guy out there from the beginning, it was taking a real toll on me, but my hands were tied. There was nothing I could do about it being in here. If I was on the outside, I would have busted him up, thought nothing of it, then I would go out to lunch and would feel good about it. I would make sure she saw me do it also.

 I was still sticking needles in my legs so I could feel pain, it would keep my mind off my wife for a while, but I still had a lot of feeling for her. I couldn't help myself. Still the long walks around the yard were a thing I did whenever I could. It would help me cope with all the bad that was going on in my life. It was so damn stupid of me to still have faith in the lawyer my wife hired for me even though his secretary told me he wasn't going to do anything for me, to seek counsel somewhere else. This fuckin' lawyer had the nerve to call my wife up and ask her for more money, but my wife refused to give it to him until he showed some results of helping me. I don't think the lawyer asked her for any more money because my daughter said that the attorney has been trying to get in touch with my wife for a long time. I was trying to get money off my wife for at least a couple of month with no luck. I think the problem was that all the money that I had given her went up her fuckin' nose along with her boyfriend's. It wasn't easy for me to leave my twenty-two-year-old daughter in charge of my home to live in with her boyfriend; the thought of them not paying the mortgage was driving me crazy. If she would have lost the house, I would have ended my life as soon as I got out. If that would have happened, I would have taken out a lot of garbage people out with me especially the rats that put me here.

I was still seeing the shrink to see if she could help me get over my wife and help me cope with this fuckin' place, but she was as helpful as tits on a bull. No experience at all in the field she had chosen. The doctors in here were all assholes, just like all the other places that I was at. They really didn't want anything to do with inmates. But one of the doctors got a hold of my medical records in here, found out that I had colitis. Every time I had to see her, she wanted to stick her fingers up my ass. I kept telling her no, but she insisted, and I told her what part of no she didn't understand. What a look I got. At one time she said that she could get a CO to make me do it. I again said no. I never seen her again in the remaining time I was there. In the cell next to me, the young black kid who also was convicted for cocaine. He bought a lot of cards from me to send home to his mom so his mother would forgive him for what he was in jail for. He was doing a five year, as I was for cocaine. What a good kid. He was wasting a good part of his young life for drugs. What a waste of life. He did tell me he had no idea that he could get so much time for what he was doing. He said he just wanted to get high with his friends, that's all. He told me that he wasn't doing for a long period of time; he was ratted on by a so-called good friend that was trying to rip him off. I told him I was also clueless about the drug, didn't realize how much time I could get either for the possession of the drug. Just a short time later after that talk, he returned to his cell. I heard him crying, then I realized that he was a really good kid. When I was growing up, everyone smoked weed. It was just the drug era, drugs were just part of life. I thought nothing of it. It was just something everyone I hung around with did. I soon found out how much time you could get for possession of cocaine. I just couldn't believe it, then reality hit me when I found out. Now that I think about it, I now realize that everyone these days people are just rating on each other. They don't care who you are as long as they don't do the time these people will probably rat on their own mothers. In my case my so-called cousin and a so-called friend named Bob that my cousin turned me on along with a couple of other rats. The guy I bought the drugs off ratted me out so they wouldn't do the time, but they didn't realize that they have to do it forever not just the time that they got caught. When I was in a store buying paint, I saw one of the guys that I bought the drugs off. He tried to talk to me, but I just ignored him. I turned my back on him and walked out the door. It was like he wasn't even there. I have no time in my life for fuckin' rats. If you get caught, do the fuckin' time as I did. There is one thing I can say. I can walk down the street, and I will never have to worry about getting stabbed in the back. I took all the names to jail with me. Just remember the friends you think are friends are not always the friends they appear to be. In this case my cousin, my wife, two others I thought were my friends, and they turned over on me. After I got convicted, even the guy I bought the drugs off turned, then he took his life piece of shit may he rot in hell. I found out a short time later that he killed himself by cutting his wrists in a hot tub. To me it's no loss. He should have done it the time he got caught with the drugs. If he would have done it at that time, he would have saved the other guy he ratted on from going to jail. I know this because I talked to the guy he ratted on when I was in Bridgewater. This guy bought some coke off Mr. Kill Myself. They got pulled over in his car, and the cops found some coke under the seat. He said it wasn't his and put on the other guy in the car with him because he had given him the money, so to him it wasn't his anymore. (Piece of shit.)

 I have realized that all black guys that I met in jail were not all bad, at least some of the ones I met, but I watched them very carefully. I always expected bad from them. But it wasn't just the black guys that were assholes; the white guys who wanted to be black were real dickheads also. There were a lot of different nationality, like some of the Spanish guys that I met or were housed with were real scumbags, but none of them were as bad as the blacks I had to deal with in Bridgewater Minimum. The COs that put the black guys in the room with me, they were pure scum, and this Sargent knew this. This was just payback for what I said about his wife even though I said it under my breath after the rude thing about my wife. The worst of the blacks were the guys who wanted to be addressed as a nigger. This asshole named Trooper that was in the same room as I was in. I'm still hoping in his travels he caught a bullet in the head and I'm able to hear about it along with the cop that raided my home. If I was to find this out that he had been killed, this would make me a real happy man to find this out. After all the trouble I had with this black guy Trooper, I was very careful with all the other black guys that I met in jail. I just had to remember where I was, that these guys were not my friends. You a lot of times didn't know what they're in for, as I made a lot of mistakes. I tried to get along with everyone I came in contact with. But a lot of times while I was inside, I was told to stay away from guys that I was talking to because they were skinners, women beaters. I didn't realize what they had done to put them in jail. I got along with guys who were accused of attempt of murder or robbery, drug dealing, but there were guys that were accused for different crimes. I never got a chance to converse with a lot of them or I didn't want to remember them. The ones that I did talk to did say that they knew what they did to get caught, what they did it was wrong. The next time they were going to do it, they will know how to do it, not get caught. Again as all the guys I talked to was they found why and how they got caught. The whole time I was in jail this was a constant thing I heard and how they won't get caught again. I was so damn baffled. I could not believe what I was hearing, couldn't believe they would even think of doing what they got caught for again. The time that I was doing was so hard for me that I wouldn't even think of messing with drugs ever again. They are taking five years of my life away from me the thought of not making love to a woman, not seeing my family was the hardest part for me to accept. They could have given me a year and I would have learned my lesson. Maybe my wife would have never done what she did to me, would have waited for me to get out.

Every morning that I get up in the jail that I was at, I prayed that the lawyer that I got to reopen my case will get me out. I can go on with my life, try to make a son to take over my body shop, while the daughter I have will be the brains to keep my paperwork in order, then I know it will run like clockwork. I just wrote my so-called lawyer again, offered him my Corvette that I owned for payment to get me out of here, but like all the other letters, I never got an answer. I realized that his secretary was right when she said to me to try to obtain another lawyer because he wasn't going to help me get out. Now I don't think Boston lawyers are not any better than any other lawyer. They all have to go the same schools, take the same bar exam, so what's the difference. The thing is how much effort they put into their cases to really help inmates in jail, or do they take on drug cases just to take inmates' money from them? As my first lawyer did, he called in another lawyer, and the first question out of his mouth was how much money I had. I told him that the police took all the money, and then he said, "Where did all the money you made on selling drugs go?" I said there wasn't any. He then looked me right in the eyes and said, "Do the time and start over again."

When you're in a jail like this, you realize how much your freedom means to you, what you lose when you're in a place like this. If I had a million dollars, I would gladly give it up for my freedom. I know in my heart I will always carry hate in my heart for the rest of my life to all the correctional officers that fucked with me while I was incarcerated in the places I was held at. You fuckin' COs know who the fuck you are, fuckin' scumbags. At this time I'm still writing letters to my wife, just about begging her to keep in touch with the lawyer to try to get me out but to no avail. I never received any response from her the whole time that I was in jail. The whole time that I was incarcerated, I must have gotten seven letters from my wife, and that was in five years of me being incarcerated along with about fifteen visits. She was very good at what she did. This was lying to me, stealing whatever she could, getting away with it. She was just like the lawyer that I got to try to help me, She figured I was in jail; she just fucked me over with a smile on her face. A lot of people say that God doesn't sleep. I really hope so; my ex-wife has the chance to enter hell as I'm in right now. I just can't believe what she was doing to me. To me this is hell that I'm in. All I can hope for is that she gets caught with her newfound boyfriend and gets to spend time as I did along with all the other rats that I talked about while writing this. What a cokehead my wife was. What I told the cops was that she didn't know anything about the drugs that day even though she was downstairs at the time, powdering her nose with all the drugs around her. I was upstairs watching a movie, drinking some beer before they raided my home. What an ass I was. Just some things men do so there wives don't get in trouble, go to jail, and I would have just about done anything for her.

Prior to the police coming, I was talking to my cousin Charlie rat, as I called him in the book that I'm writing at this time. We were was down in the cellar, smoking a joint. In conversation I was telling him that this has got to stop. My wife had to seek treatment because it was getting real bad. My wife just looked at me and said that she had it under control, that she would quit when she knew it was getting out of control. I then said, "It's out of control. You have to go to someplace to get treatment because you will never say it's out of control yourself." I told her that I was being watched. I had seen cars on the next block, and I was scared of getting busted. She said that it was just in my head. It was the booze talking. The weird thing about the bust was my cousin just called prior to coming over. My cousin mentioned coke bluntly over the phone, and I just told him to stop saying what he saying over the phone. I just told him just to come by. He should have known better than that, fuckin' jerk. When he was dealing coke, he always had a code he made up, and it was something everyone he dealt to had to follow. One knot was an eight ball, two knot was a sixteenth, so forth. There was a so-called code for everything we did. The whole time I had the coke, I never considered it to be dealing. It was just a way to pay for my wife's habit because she was doing so much along with my so-called friend John. There were just a couple of guys I was getting it for to help me with the price that I was paying. At this time my wife had a thousand-dollars-a-week habit, and the guys that I was getting it for helped a lot with the price. The guys that were helping me didn't know where to get it. Seeing that I was getting it for my wife, they asked if I they could also. Of course I said yes so the price of the coke wouldn't hurt me so much along with helping them with their problem also. I didn't think anything could help me with the price that I was paying for my wife until they asked me. The weird thing about it was it never came to mind that this shit could take someone's life. You don't look at it in that way either, but yes, you can kill some with this shit. When I was getting it, I was just thinking I would have enough to shut my wife up. Now that I look at it, I could have lost my wife at that time also because she was doing a real lot. I could never live with myself if anything had happened to her.

During the bust, the cops were questioning me. They kept telling me that I was selling drugs to the kids at the school that I was teaching at, and I kept saying that I wasn't. It was multiple questions being asked at the time. I was worried for my wife, whom they had in another room. They said that I said that kids from the school put it there. They were just putting words in my mouth. I said that anyone could have put it there. (Fucking assholes.) Then they informed the newspaper that I was dealing drugs and supplying drugs up the whole East Coast. Again they kept saying that I was selling drugs at the school that I was teaching at over and over again. I said no multiple times, but they just wanted put something real good in the paper, maybe get their pat on the back. Well, it did make the front page, and they probably gave each other blow jobs because they didn't do drugs, or did they. I would never sell any drugs to any kids no matter what. It was just my friends, who were adults and liked indulging in cocaine like most of the country was doing at the time of my bust along with their wives. The cops will say anything that will make them look good in the newspaper. This will include just about anything to get a bust no matter what it takes. They have ways to do things to hurt you without bruising you along with shooting your dog in the head in front of you and/or holding family members over your head during a bust. They do this to get you to say something that they can use to make their case solid.

After they pushed me around for a while, they just about rammed my hands up to the back of my head while being handcuffed, and they dumped me off at the Acushnet Police Station in the town where I lived. I was there for a long while, then they transported me to a jail in New Bedford called Ash Street then to Dartmouth Correctional. I was there for I think six days then was bailed out by my cousin Charlie Rat. This made him look like a real good guy, so I thought for a while until I was able to put two and two together and then realized why he did it. When I entered my home, I walked in and there was a mess. My home looked like a war zone. As I walked in and looked around, the house was turned upside down. The refrigerator was open, running it had defrosted, there was water all over the floor, everything in it was no good. This was like this for over a week while I was in jail. At least they could have closed the door. When I went up into my attic, it was the same, things thrown all over the place. A lot of things that I had up in my attic, like my baseball cards and ornamental scales, were gone. In my safe my jewelry, money, watches, my coin collection was gone. Of course they said they didn't take it. Of course they would say that. To them it was just fringe benefits. Now as for my cars, they were still at the local police station in plain sight. I was hoping that I wouldn't lose them, because my mom left me the money that I never told anyone about, even my cousin because he was a greedy bastard. The money that she left me is how I paid for my Corvette I owned. They said that I was dealing drugs up the whole East Coast; this was something that was still stuck in my head. I couldn't believe where they got that bullshit story from. The cars that were confiscated were two old cars at the time that were going to be junked; I repaired them for my use to get around the city. If I was such a big drug dealer, I'm sure I would have paid off my home, would have put everything in someone else's name, would have been driving a luxury car along with having a safe house to keep my drugs at, not have buried them in the backyard. They said that they were watching me for three months. they must have seen me driving all over the place and standing on street corners selling drugs. Of course dropping off all kinds of drugs to all my so-called customers. What they saw when they were supposedly watching me was me going to teach at the high school for change and picking up parts for my shop. This was how I paid for the mortgage on my home. There was no drug money used, and what I made in my garage paid for other bills I had to pay. Oh yes, as they said, I was a big drug dealer. What great investigators they were, and after all they said, the most they had to say was I was selling drugs to the students. This was after three months. One thing I would like to know, where the hell all the money I made dealing drugs up the East went. I haven't seen any of it to this day. They said I was selling to all these people, and I would like to know and meet all the people I sold drugs to. All the money I supposedly have made, I'm still looking for it, and I just can't find it. I could really use it now. I worked for the school because I loved doing it so much. To me it was the best job I ever had in my whole life. I was doing things I enjoyed doing the most in my life. Of course they got their bust. I was sold out by my so-called attorney that was also busted for drugs but never convicted. I was told by him to plea out to a five-year term or go to trial and get fifteen years to life for dealing drugs. At that time all I wanted was to get this over with, get back home to my wife and daughter, so I took the five-year sentence. As they said, may it go so fast.

Now getting back to jail, I met this guy when I was at the maximum prison who was in for attempt of murder of his girlfriend. In a letter she wrote him telling him why she had done it. He was more or less convicted of this even before he went to court. He told me that his girlfriend came at him with a knife, and he just punched her right in the face. She had to go to the hospital. She told them that her boyfriend tried to kill her, that's why he was in jail awaiting sentencing for attempted murder. Since then she has tried to drop the charges and get him released, but they will not do it because of the offense. She told him in so many letters how sorry she was, how much she loved him. It's so crazy how the guys are always to blame. The courts are always ready to throw the book at the guys, but this is what some guys do, they just stick up for their girlfriends or wife so they don't do any jail time, as I did. We used to talk a lot. I told him that at least his girlfriend told him that she was sorry, told him that she loved him. My so-called wife who took off even before a year was up came into prison on more than one occasion after she had given her new boyfriend or whoever she happened to be with a blowjob. What really gets me pissed off was she till went to kiss me with her cock breath, with the smell still present on her breath. It was so strong that it just turned my stomach, so I didn't kiss her on her mouth. When I just backed off, she just looked at me and said, "What?" This dirty bastard guy that she was with could have washed his dick before the blow job, or she could have brushed her fuckin' teeth. When this happened, she just looked at me and just said she hasn't been up to see me because she's been working a lot of hours. She said that there wasn't enough hours in a day for what she had to do. I was just thinking at that time, This fuckin' lying cunt. I said to myself, I didn't get mad. I just agreed, but I still could smell the smell coming from her breath from across the table. But true is true, it took a long time before I realized that she was what she was, that I could never change her way of living. She's just no damn good as a wife. I should have known this because I ran into same thing from my daughter's mother, but smoking so much weed at the time I was walking around with my eyes closed. It's not fair that an inmate can't have sex with our wife while in jail. We are in jail and incarcerated and I really wanted to have a son. I really wanted a son from my wife, but because of my incarceration, I never got a chance because of the time I had to serve. At least this would have found her to be useful in that way, even though I probably would have gotten the kid when I got out. Plus I would have loved to give back a little something to her boyfriend also as he did to me, fuckin' scumbag. He would have had to look at my kid. Before I got convicted for drugs, we were trying to have a baby. My wife at the time wanted one also, so she said, well, at least I think so. She could have been fooling me about that also. But because of the time that I received, maybe it was a godsend because of the drugs she was doing. Maybe the baby would have been born with drug addiction. Knowing my wife, she wouldn't have been able to take care of the baby. Most likely, she would have given it up for adoption until I hunted it down for me to raise. Now that I think about it, maybe it was better that she decided to leave me and tried to go on with the rest of her life with someone else. Not long after he died, he left her with nothing. But as I was told, she moved from one guy to another and went back to her old way of living, becoming a motorcycle mama. I should have figured this out when her father wiped his mouth off when she kissed him. When she got married to me and yelled at her, saying, "What do you think that I'm one of your boyfriends." After that I just never talked to her father and considered him to be a piece of shit also. After a while I realized why he just turned and wiped his mouth after my wife kissed her father. It was because he knew more than I did about her. Now the last thing that I heard is that she has been just passed around from one guy to another in some motorcycle club that she was hanging around with. Of course I found this out from letters I was getting from the street. (Stupid bitch.) Well, what really killed me inside was that someone was getting what my so-called wife could do so damn good—giving great blowjobs. Now as I said, she was real bad on her back. That's because in her whole life, she has just been used for meaningless sex. I never realized it because she was just too stupid to see it. When I got these letters, it just made my time go so much slower. I curse that unknown writer and hope it happens to him so he can know what it feels like.

Well, it was canteen day again. I had to go for that long walk to pick up the stuff I ordered and hope I had enough money for everything. On the way to the canteen, I met my so-called girlfriend better on the way and knew it was not true because I saw the court papers and what he was convicted of. It was just a label that the courts placed on him. When he saw me coming, he called out "Hey, druggie, what's up?" to me with not much of a response from me but a grin. As we were walking, we talked about each other's wives, and he sounded, I knew he had what I always wanted in a wife. As we got our stuff, I noticed there was a guy standing around with a large canteen bag. There were a bunch of guys standing around him. I pointed it out to my friend, and he just said that I should stay away from that guy. I then asked why, and he then said that he was a skinner. He raped a little boy and killed him, and all the guys that were around him were all the same kind of scum. He then said that they all think that they have done nothing wrong, but a lot of the guys in here know what they are in for. If you talk to any of them, the guys start to ask questions about you. Most of the guys who have skinned kids or raped women or so much as beat them are always hanging around with their own kind, staying away from general population. They were in their own world, hanging around with their own kind. They get large canteen bags so they can buy off guys who more or less know what they had done. How they know this is because the COs drop the word around. When they are found out, they are moved out real fast and are put into a special unit with their own kind where they won't get touched by anyone. He said, "Just stay away from these guys. Do your own time, and always remember they are all pieces of shit or scum or whatever you decide to call them. They won't be here long. They are moved around the system a lot or until they are released back onto the street. It will be before us." He then said to me that he would like to talk to me about my sentence and said to me not to get upset. I said okay, and he then said that I was putting too much into the lawyer that I had hired to get me out. He looked at me and said that the lawyer that was supposed to try to get me out was not going to do anything for me, that I was taking myself apart thinking that he was going to get me out of jail. Then he said that he was just taking my money like most lawyers do. He will put in for a Revise and Revoke, and when that doesn't work, he will say that there was nothing more he could do for me and walk away from my case.

As we were walking back to the unit after the talk my buddy had with me, he noticed that I was really upset and said that he was sorry for telling me what he told me. I then said it wasn't that. He said, "What then?"

I just said, "I think that my wife is really no good and wish she was more like yours."

He just looked at me and said, "Try not to think about it. Just do your time, go home, and don't fuck up again." I told him that I my wife hired a real good Boston lawyer. He said that maybe he could be wrong, that maybe he can do something for me again. He said not get my hopes up. I still was hoping that I had a good chance of beating it. Then he said, "Good luck. No matter what I tell you, you're still going to try." That was the last time that I talked to him about it. In my heart, I really kind of knew he was not going to do anything for me, but it was something for me to hope for just something. I didn't want to hear what he had to say. It was a long while. I said to him, "It's been a while since I talked about my attorney to you." I told him that I talked to his secretary, and she told me that I should find another lawyer. Then I looked at him and said, "You were right."

He looked at me and said that she noticed what he was doing to me. She figured that she would try to push me into another direction because she knew that I was expecting too much from the lawyer she was working for. Then he looked at me and said, "We both are going to do our time. Once you're in a place like this, it's just too hard to overturn a decision that the court has made, especially a drug crime."

At this time I was carrying a lot of baggage in my head along with cursing my so-called wife for what she did to me along with the time I have to do. I remember it like the day I bought the coke I needed it for two of my friends, of course my wife. As the night went on, my wife said, "Maybe you should get another eight ounces in case we run out." What made things a lot worse was that she had her face full and just walked away from me, keeping all the money I left her, not lifting a finger to help me. When you're in a place like this (I mean jail), you realize how long a day is, especially when you have nothing to do but count the days, months, years as they go by. I still make cards and sewing clothes to make canteen because of the messed up food they give you to eat in this place. I do get sick from it, but I got to eat. All the COs are always watching me. Everything I do they search me so damn much that I should just walk around naked from all the rats in here. They know that this is how I have a locker full of food most of the time. When they stop to search me, they throw a lot of the stuff that I'm carrying on the ground. A lot of times they just say leave it where it lies. They tell you that I just don't need it as they do when they shake down my room also. I just look at them, and under my breath I say "Fuckin' scumbags" and want to grab them right by the neck and squeeze the fuckin' life out of them. I know this place will be with me for the rest of my life with the ongoing thought of my con number burned into my brain. Even to this day I think about it. This is with me every minute of the day even as I'm writing this. Lots of these guys have no trouble coming back to these places because they have been in and out so many times before they already know what to expect. When a lot of them get caught up in another crime, they just walk in like they went on a trip, and they are coming home. They just blend right in, and in one day they are up to their old games running around like nothing has happened. I talk to a lot of them, and I write a lot of it down in my letters. Now I send it all home to my daughter, and she reads them, puts them all in a box and just can't believe what I write in my letters. I talk to my daughter a lot of times, tell her about the weird things that these guys do, get caught for. Most of the time it's the same things that they got in trouble for prior to this. I entered this place and still can't believe the fuckin' lowlife guys that I've met from time to time, how many times they get in trouble for the same things, just keep doing it over again. All I can say is I know I won't come back. I'd rather die first than have to put up with these fucking CO's shit, who of course do no wrong. I will have to live with what they did to me for the rest of my life. It's got to the point I don't look at the mail list anymore because I do not get any more letters. The letters I was getting from my unknown writer has stopped also. Maybe it's because he was able to brainwash my ex-wife into divorcing me. I guess he got what he wanted until she gets sick and tired of him or he gets thrown in jail for drugs as I did.

When I was teaching, I met a teacher named Leon Trip. I was writing him because he said it was all right to write to him and tell him what goes on in a place like this. After I sent him one letter, I received a letter from him with a check so I could buy a hot pot to cook in, and the letter said, "If you need more, just ask." I just couldn't believe that he would say that. The next week he sent me some stamps. I just couldn't thank him enough. It felt really good that a teacher could find it in his heart to put aside what I got in trouble for and still want to bother with me when everyone else turned their backs on me, including my family. He carries on with me as nothing had happened. He has never condemned me for what I was convicted for, and for the rest of my life I will never forget him. The stamps were like a gift to me. They came in at the right time I had just ran out of them. This is something I really needed to have so I could keep sending the letters I'm writing home. All the letters I sent out I was hoping to get someone to send me at least five dollars so I could get some things from the canteen or just a letter to read, just news from the outside, but I got very little in return. When I got letters from my brother, he would always say that I'm not missing a thing; everything is the same as when I left. I just can't believe what he put in a letter, stupid bastard. He just doesn't understand I'm fuckin' locked up, dealing with a bunch of fuckin' assholes. This includes these damn COs. When I was behind the wall, I had to eat most of the food they served but had to load it up with salt because there was no taste at all to the food. Everything was made out of turkey meat. Most of the guys would tell, "Don't drink the Kool-Aid, it has solt peter in it. If you do, say goodbye to the dick you knew." When I could get seasoning through the canteen, it made the food more tolerable, but the food was real bad. When I worked in the freezer, a lot of times I saw the food in the freezer for weeks uncovered, so I went without eating sometimes, but it didn't go to waste. It was made into soup.

I really didn't want to give up on my wife, so I sent a couple of letters to my wife, tried to change her mind about the divorce because no matter what she had done, I still loved her so much. At that same time I did ask her for some of the money I had sent her, but it must have gone in one ear, out the other. I never got a reply to any of them. When I could, I was in the law library trying to find a way to beat my case. It always lead to possession. It would say, "Did you have it in your possession?" Of course I did, so I was guilty of possession, but dealing was on the table. Possession still carried a long sentence, but I still kept reading the books anyways. I never was given my rights when they arrested me; it was their word against mine. Now just think about it who you think they were going to believe the person with the drugs or the cops in shining armor, the ones who stole a lot of the stuff in my home, beats me. It got to the point that my so-called big fish in a big pond Boston bigshot lawyer was not going to do anything for me; all he was good for was taking money from guys who were in jail or what guys owned. I would just sit down and think of what I'm going to do. This lawyer had all my money, and I was in jail, how was I going to get my money back? It just got to the point that no one was going to help me out of the situation that I was in, so what could I do but the time that I was given to do. Now I still was calling that fuckin' Boston lawyer of mine just to piss him off now that's the only way I could stick pins in him before I called the Bar Of Overseers on him. I really hope there is a hell because he will have a real hot seat waiting for him. As I was reading the law books on Revise and Revoke, I could get a reduction in time but again I could get more time added on. That scared the heck out of me. All I wanted to do was to get home very soon to see if I could save my marriage, the home which my daughter was struggling with to make payments. What killed me the most was watching guys in here get visits, watch them leave the unit. It killed me inside. I was always thinking that my so-called wife would come up and tell me that she had changed her mind, even after what she had done to me, but it never happened.

My appearance was real bad. My money hadn't come in from Bridgewater as of yet. In my whole life I've never had a beard, and it took coming to a place like this to grow one. When I was waiting for my money to come in, to clear, I had to deal with a beard. I hated it to the point in which I kept asking the CO in charge for a kit that they would give guys as they come into jail. The CO kept saying that my money would be coming in real soon; I will be able to get it through the canteen. I did have a lot of cosmetics in my locker, but they took it all away because they claimed that I exceeded what was allowed. They said that they would keep it in the property room until I had a chance to send it home or have it destroyed. At that time that they took most of my cosmetics, my razor blades, soap, just about everything else went with it. Seeing that they took my stuff, I asked them for soap, razor blades again in a kit that they ended up giving to inmates, and he just looked at me and said no! I told him that they took all my cosmetics. He looked at me and said, "Wait till you get money cleared as I told you beforehand." No way was I going to beg for it. (So fuck it.) This all came about because I gave him a dirty look after I told him to watch where he was grabbing when he was searching me, so because of that, he was making life hell for me when he was on, so I just let my beard grow. I got to look so bad I could stand outside a store holding a cup in my hand. Again I'll bet I could be mistaken for a homeless person. The way I looked at it, I was homeless. I was still getting over my wife leaving me, doing all the fucked stuff she had done to me from the time that I was put in this godforsaken place.

This guy named George I went on some buzz ride with along with working on some of his cars was the one who brought my so-called future wife over my house. This guy always could get real good weed, so I would get it off him. At this time he just brought this girl with him because he just couldn't shake her, so she just tagged along with him. He came over that day, and he asked me if I could get him some weed. He told me at the same time that it wasn't for him. He said it was the bimbo that he was with, who always wanted to fuck, and he just picked up in his travels. This one girl looked a lot like my daughter's mother; I just couldn't stop looking at her because of the likeness to my daughter's mother. A lot of people say if you break up with someone that you really love, you're always looking for someone who looks, acts just like them. Well, I guess the way that I was looking at her, of course she noticed it. Before I knew it she was coming over, talking about her problems as she told me that my friend had got her pregnant the first time he had sex with her. I just kind of looked at her. The real weird thing about it was she told me that she felt it forming in her right away. I talked to my friend George about it, and he told me that he had just gone out with her twice, and he said, "I got her pregnant?" She told me that she knew it was him; she started to chase him around, trying to find out what he was going to do about it.

I did talk to him again, and he said that she was crazy. She probably got knocked up by her old boyfriend. He was sure it wasn't him. I knew what he meant by that. I talked to her about it, and she said like the first time she knew it after she had sex with him. She felt it, the baby forming inside her right away. She said she knew it. I looked at her and said she's got a screw loose, like he said. I just thought she was slow. Even I knew that she wouldn't know this for a while, but she made it look like it was my friend that got her pregnant, and she was going to his house, hounding him about it. He just started to avoid her. When he saw her car pulling up, he told his parents to tell her that he wasn't at home. At this time her parents didn't want anything to do with her, so she just started to hang around my home. It was always when I was ready to go out to see the girl I was seeing at the time. It didn't take her along to find a sucker like me to listen to her with the problems that she had. Of course that was me. It got so bad that the girl that I was seeing broke off with me because every time she came up the street, she'd see her car. She just called, said that it wasn't going to work out because of the other girl that was coming over my house.

This was the start to me buying the cocaine that I always had on hand just to support her habit that she had. This was the start to my downfall. I couldn't see it happening, but my family members could see it, but I was blinded by old memory. I didn't see it, but my sister-in-law Carol saw right thought it but was amused by the thing she did naturally. My so-called wife was the one that you could watch short periods and just laugh at whatever she was doing at that time. I stuck by her when she had all these problems, right to the end, but when we both got in trouble for drugs, she just lasted about three months, and she was gone. After I got sentenced, I made it last much longer because of me trying to get her involved with getting me a lawyer to try to get me out of jail, but she took all my money, hired a lawyer, left me hanging, and expected me to do the rest in jail. This is about the time that I started to get letters from some guy that she started to see. She just pulled away from me, said that she wanted to leave, go on with her life with someone else. The worst thing of all was it was someone that my sister knew, and my sister never told me about it. Well, when the divorce papers came in for me to sign, I told her that we never had any children. For me to sign any papers, she had to go back to her maiden name because I wasn't going to let her fuck another guy with my last name because I knew he was just going to use her for her money, for a piece of ass, and she was too blind to see. So what I'm saying is that she just went back to her old ways, and that was spreading her legs for whoever, moving from one guy to another for drugs.

Even after all the bad things she did to me, I still loved her, and I thought that it wouldn't work out with this guy. He would dump her like all the rest did to her. In my whole life I always loved the bad, dopey girls and was hoping that she would come to her senses, that she would come back to me. As I was just sitting around the unit, just thinking of all the things that happened before my house got raided by the narcs, she was hanging around this place called the Dog House. I was told that everyone was talking about her because of the large rings of cocaine under her nose, she was also turning on old girlfriends of hers on to coke along with a couple of guys. At this time there were at least three people that ratted on me, and to this day I still wonder if she turned on me like all the rest to keep her from getting jail time, as my rat cousin did because two of his so-called friends told me so. As you know, all rats hang together. For the whole time that you are incarcerated, all you do is think of ways to get back at the ones that ratted you out. It all becomes like a videotape playing over and over again day after day on how your life was before you got busted, after you got busted. As time goes on, you just say how people can do that to you. You will never stop trying to figure it out. At least I will to the day I die. Now as time goes on, I have learned to live with what happened to me but hate the fuckin' narcs that busted me. They are worse than the worst guys that I had to deal with in jail. Pure scum. They are as crooked as they come. I hope they choke on what they stole from me, including the coke that I know that they cut.

It's been a while now that my wife has left me. I still read the few letters that she sent me over and over again, still look at pictures that I have of her, reminisce of how our life was. To me it was as great as my life was with my daughter's mother, but also really loved being married until she started to do the coke every day. In all my thoughts of how we lived our life, I never would think she would do what she did to me, leave me, get a dear John letter saying she's leaving me, how sorry she was. All I can say now is fuck her, what she did to me there will be a hot spot in hell waiting for her. But there is one thing about it. She won't be alone. She can go hand in hand with my lawyers and my rat so-called friends. The last letter she sent me was to tell me to have faith in God, he will help me through it all, and for me just to do the time that the court gave me, may it go fast. Yeah, it's okay if you're on the outside looking in. You're going out living your life like nothing happened. I'm on the inside doing five fuckin' years for her fuckin' coke habit which she displays to everyone. In my whole life I very rarely called a woman a cunt, but in this case, I realized that I married a fuckin cunt. The way her breath smelled, I knew where the dick went.

At this time I kind of knew that it wouldn't be long before they told me to pack up, tell me that I was out of here. Of course I was expecting it to be very soon. It got to the point that you don't give a damn where they move you. At this time I was used to it; it didn't bother me anymore. I would adjust to wherever they sent me. I was on my way back from the chow hall, and as I entered the unit, the CO said to me, "Pack up, you're out of here. Don't take too damn long doing it." Well, as the guys told me, I was going to the unit they called lower wreck. I said to myself, how bad can it really be? As I entered the building, looked around, it was all of what the guys had told me it was, a fuckin' wreck. That's what it should have been called. I could understand why a lot of the guys didn't want to go here, because it really was disgusting. This place was on the Concord grounds just a little further down from where I was at. When I walked in, the smell hit me. It stank so bad that I couldn't even put it into words. It was more a mixture of different smells. Right away I missed my single cell. I was surrounded by a bunch of assholes in one room, double bunks again throughout the whole room. As I entered the unit, the CO in charge assigned a bunk to me. The mattress was black, no fooling. I mean real bad looking. It looked like someone pissed and shit all over it. The first thing you do is put baby powder all over it to reduce the smell, wrap your sheets knotted on both ends on the mattress, and hope you don't stink like it did. As time goes by, you wait for someone to be transferred to another unit, then take their mattress and pillow if it's better than what you have. In my case, anything will be better than what I had. The smell was unbearable but I had to put up with it. I remember what one of the COs said to another about me was that I better not expect room service, because he thought I was a big coke dealer. I stood back a lot of times from chow just to see if someone was moved to another unit so I could raid their bed before someone else did. It was within a week the guy below was moved out, and I moved down, just kept what he had. It was a lot better than what I had, somewhat cleaner, and it didn't smell as bad. This made life a little better. I would get up very early to do my pushups, use the toilet, shower because at this time the showers were not so flooded with water, the toilets weren't full of shit. If you waited too long, the showers would be flooded, and all three toilets would be filled with shit. The smell would be real bad and make you want to throw up.

As the weekend came, I woke up to the smell of bacon, eggs. I hadn't smelled that smell in a long time. It smelled so damn good. I thought it was something we could eat, but I was very wrong. Well, I came to find out all the food that they were cooking was just made for the COs who worked in the morning shift and got the inmates to cook it for them. The COs watched them very closely to make sure the inmate didn't get any of it. Now the inmates that were cooking it kind of knew they couldn't have any of it even though they cooked it for them. I knew that some of the food would find a way into the unit because I knew one of the guys that was cooking it. I will never forget how good the unit smelled. It didn't smell like shit. It was covered up for once by the smell of bacon that was cooking. But all I could do was to think how good it would taste, but I had to go to the chow hall to eat cereal. After smelling that, it killed me. This was happening every weekend. You just get used to it and start to pay no attention to it. I would just say to myself, "I'll eat what they are eating again when I get out of this place." I just started to train myself to overcome all the things that I wanted to do, the things that I will have once again when I get out. The weekend COs would go out of their way to make life real miserable for us. Just walk around, stand in the doorway, eat what was cooked, look at the guys. Just looking at the COs do this killed the guys in the unit. As I was making my bed one weekend, one of the COs came up and said to me, "Do you want some of what I'm eating?"

I said, "No, I'll get all I want when I get out." I said this because one of the other COs asked me the week before the same question. He just said, "You wish," and just threw it in the garbage, spit on it, and walked away. One of the guys did dig it out. Just ran it under water and ate it anyways. It got me sick to see that but also mad. How can anyone do something like that to anyone. I think when I told the CO that I wait till I get out to eat what he was eating, it really bothered him, that's why he spit on it. This one CO would still walk around the unit, eat the food in front of everyone, say to some of the guys, "Wish you had this, don't you?" To me, this made him the biggest dickhead of all.

At this time I was still going through bad depression. The shrinks were not doing me any good as before. to this day I now know whatever they said to me wouldn't help in any way because the only way out for me was for me to get out of jail. It wasn't going to happen. It got to the point that I would stay back at the unit in many occasions just to look out the window, wish my time was at an end. I would be able to see my daughter, grandson but still had a good amount of time to do.

One day as I was looking out the window while cutting my nails, I noticed that the birds would be in the courtyard, I would said to myself, what stupid fuckin' birds they are, putting themselves behind the wall. Then I looked more closely and realized that they could leave anytime that they wanted. Just fly over the wall whenever they wanted. I said it's that easy for them to be free. Then I just said, how can I think of such stupid things? I just went back to cutting my nails, and I realized that I had real problems to think. What I was thinking. I went back to thinking about my lost wife and daughter. Then I looked down at the nails that I cut in the windowsill and started to think, I wonder if my nails will be here years to come. Then said, another stupid thing to be thinking about, but it was one stupid thing to another. Then some of the guys started to come back into the unit. The guys that cooked the food for the COs in the morning went through the garbage and was selling the leftover food that the COs didn't eat or throw out. This time the COs didn't see the inmates that cooked the food throw out the trash cans. They would take out the leftovers to sell the scraps to some of the guys in the unit. This was just one of the thing I saw go on in a correctional institution. I would see some of the guys that bought the scraps eat it. When I would stay back, I'd see this on more than one occasion. The worst thing about it, I saw the food come out of the garbage. I saw the COs spit in the barrels and walk away, fucking pigs they were, then watch the guys eat it. If that wasn't bad enough, we had to put up with this every weekend. To top it off, we had to put up with these COs doing childish things to grown men. Sometimes it got real bad, and we had no choice but to put up with it because they had us by the balls, and they knew it. Day after, I'd see the COs do things to piss off guys, from flipping their locker over to putting their things in other inmates' area, sometimes causing inmates to fight among each other, and of course ended up getting lugged out of the unit. It wasn't bad enough being in jail; we had to put up with these COs fuckin' with us day after day. A lot of times I saw them doing things to inmates, laughing about it as they were doing it. I just kept my mouth shut and just did my time, I had enough shit going on in my life, I didn't need any more added to it. As they say, do your own time, and it was their house, as I was told. I got sick and tired of being inside, so I decided to start to go out again, walk the track, try to get stuff off my mind. I ran into the guys I used to talk to that I met at Bridgewater Minimum. They said that it was about time that I started to come out again. They told me that I can't do anything about what happened to me, had to deal with what they handed down to me. I then just realized that I just had to do my time, block out anything I'd see and seen the COs do. Don't make life any harder than what it was already for me.

    A lot of people say that there is no drugs in jail. That's bullshit. As I walk the track, I see lots of drugs. I don't how they get them in, but there are lots of drugs in jail. Drug was the last thing on my mind, but I watched guys do them. Of course they watched me for knowing it. Just mind my own business. I guess they watched me because there are so many rats in jail they had to watch just about everyone that knew if someone was doing something that they were not supposed to be doing. So if you got caught, what can they do to you, you're already behind the wall. So what, they are going to put you in the hole? You're already in hell, so they'll just make life a little harder for you. You get your meals served to you, you don't have to put up with a roommate. I didn't give a damn if they did drugs as long as it didn't affect me in any way. I didn't get any more time for the things that there were doing, so fuck it. Let them kill each other. I didn't care. I just wanted to get out of this place and go home. You kind of knew who the rats were when you would see an inmate eating Dunkin Donuts. You can't believe what an inmate would do for a doughnut, a cup of coffee, of course, in their own cup, but you'd smell what they were drinking.

I was never incarcerated before in my life. All this was new to me, but I learned real fast and ran into a lot of scum while in jail, but I also met a lot of decent guys, as I said that were in the wrong place at the wrong time, as I was. To all you people out there, before you point the finger at anyone, think after you read this. If you could put up with the shit that I put up with in this story. Just place yourself in my place for a short period of time. Think if you could put up with the shit I put up with, not with just the inmates, the COs too. When I say scum, this is referring to the COs as well. They can mess up your life forever mentally, as I still carry all the things they did to me in my head to this day. I will for the rest of my life. If I was convicted for a major crime, I'd rather be put to death than spend a lifetime with the scum that I was dealing with. The five years I spent was way too long for the drugs that they convicted me for, even worse, a mandatory sentence. What makes me real happy is when a cop or someone in law enforcement gets convicted for a crime, and they have to spend time in a correctional institution and they get to know what it's like to spend time in a place like this, what it really feels like to meet some of the guys they put in here. This just happens when their cop buddies can't fix what they did. They are forced to do the time. All I have to say to those individuals is, "Fuck you and suffer."

When I was on the outside, I was a schoolteacher. I read all the time, but when you're behind the wall, you have a real hard time finding any books to read. They don't have any programs, but all shit programs that will not do you any good on the outside. The most common book is the Bible. Most of them read it because they want to make it look like they have changed their ways, want to teach the Lord's ways to a lot of the guys in jail, but most of them really want to make it look good when they go before the parole board, hope it gets them early release. It never fooled me. A lot of them would tell me in time how they will do what they have to do to get out early. One guy told me the crime that they got convicted for he will try it again because he had time to figure out how he got busted. The next time he will get away clean, as I heard from time to time. He must have learned it from reading the Bible.

Well, one of the guys I walked the track with gets the newspaper, and he gave it to me to read. I came across an article about two cops that who got busted for possession of drugs down the waterfront in New Bedford. It was a little time after I got busted for drugs. It was for cocaine. The whole time that I was reading it, I was hoping that it was for the drugs that they took from me, cut it, then was hoping that they would ream them a new asshole as they did me. Because the coke I had tested at 87 percent, but when I read the warrant that was given to me after the bust, it came back all different percentages. It all came from the same batch you figure New Bedford's finest. I was sitting down, started to think about it. At the time that I got raided, I was wallpapering a bedroom with my wife. There was a large amount of wallpaper paste in the room, which they held up, waved it in my wife's face, and she broke down, started to cry. What I found very strange is that everything that was white in my home was gone, from the wallpaper paste to all the baking soda that was in the refrigerator. Now all that I was hoping for was that the stuff that they took from my home was the stuff that they cut, got busted with, hoping that they got the same time as I got. But of course you know that won't happen because they are cops. Most likely they will brush it under the carpet, but in this instance, they didn't as they always do for their own. But these guys must have fucked up because it was in the papers. I knew they won't get any time. It will just disappear after a couple court visits, of course. Slap on their hands. But it goes to show you they have no respect for each other. They even rat on each other, have no loyalty to each other. When they got caught, the cops who busted them could have just thrown it in the river but didn't. I guess the cop that busted them must have wanted a promotion or wasn't liked by his fellow buddies. I did hear that the narc that headed the bust against me, the dick that short my dog, of course, ended up getting a promotion to Sargent. Now he's head of the narc unit. I read about the cop bust just one time, never heard about it again. They probably brushed it under the carpet, as I said. They just walked away from it. I knew with all my heart they wouldn't get any time for it because they were better than us, do no wrong.

While I was in jail, I clipped out so many articles about COs, police who have done no wrong as they would say what they did was printed in the newspaper a lot of times, nothing ever came out of it or you just read it once, never heard any more about it. I guess it's as they say: its' who you know that can get you out of trouble or get you in trouble. The other way is if you have large amounts of money to buy your way out before you are able to see the light of day again. But if you're like me, guys like me cops always need a fall guy to show that they are doing their jobs, someone they can throw under the bus. I mean throw someone in jail. From time to time, they need to expose someone, to put all the bad things they happen to do in the newspaper so that can ruin someone's life as they did to me. Now by doing this, they keep people like myself from getting jobs that we had before we took the wrong turn in life. Just fuck us over. They scared me into taking a plea deal because they said that I would receive fifteen to life in jail, so I just wanted to get home as soon as possible to be with my family, so I took it. Five fuckin' years. To me one year would have been plenty. One year with the scum I was in with would have been more than enough, then if I went back to it, then give me the five years or take me to trial, get me a fifteen-year term. The court system is so fucked up. The courts are just there for the rich and famous who can hire good lawyers so everyone is happy. Everyone makes large amounts of money unless the courts want it all, then you're fucked as I was.

These damn mandatory sentences are not justice. It messes up families, fucks up your life forever, but most of the time you end up losing everything you have worked your whole life for. I'm not saying all cops are bad, but a good amount of them are no damn good and have a license to do what they want. In my case when they went into my attic, a lot of my things were stolen from my home. I was told that they never took anything in regards to what I said was missing. In my case, I am a real good auto body mechanic. I'm able to carry on where I more or less left off but after fifty or more resumes. I'm left off doing a meaningless job just enough to pay my bills. All I can say to the courts is "Wake the fuck up, do what is right." Remember not all cops are good, and just because they wear a badge doesn't mean they do no wrong. Just take some time out, go out of your fuckin' way to change the damn laws. Do what's right, but you have to take your heads out of your asses. I guess if you were to do this, take us off the fuck you list. You wouldn't get as much money to line your pockets with if you're not convicting someone. Now look at it, cops can be crooks and drug dealers also in life and are protected by the law because the courts see no wrong because they are cops. Most of the guys I talked to tell me that what they do is what they are taught. It's the only way they know. I did it to save money because of the amount my wife was using. I couldn't afford it on what I was making in my shop. What the courts doing is putting a lot of people that are busted for drugs in jail, letting them rot there. It took me a long time to readjust myself back into society. Just about no one was there to help me. I was really messed up. Now I realize that only the cops are the only ones who can use their badges for capital gained, so now I will let the cops sell the drugs, do what the drug dealers do, with the courts to back them up. It's a no-win situation for everyone, so give it up. Wake up, people, do you really think they turn in all what they take from people? Stand back, see how they live on a police salary.

    Okay, back into the prison and walking the track as always at Bridgewater Maximum. Today I decided to go out, walk the track to try to clear my head. As I started to walk the track, I saw this big-ass fuckin' guy walking the track. The guy that I was walking with told me that he was a wrestler on TV. I looked at him and said, "Stop messing with me." He said, "No fooling." He was. His real name was Joe. He introduced him to me, and as I looked at him, I said to myself what a big motherfucker. He looked like he just jumped out of the TV set. Just the size of his hand could crush your skull. He was in a different part of the prison; we were waiting to be transferred to where he was. But before they transfer you to a new location, you have to go through all the places they have in Concord before to get transferred to a new location. So this meant I was moved from one section to another till I stood at every building they had in Concord Bridgewater. I guess they do this to squeeze whatever they can from the State.

At this time I was still in what they called the lower wreck. As I said, it was all of what the guys said it was, a real dump. This place was, is not fit for human habitation because of the stench, the filth. There was shit overflowing from the toilets, the showers. The women COs would just walk though at any time they wanted. Everything that was in this unit needed to be all thrown out. The pillows along with the mattress was black in color. I will never forget the smell endured the whole time I was in this place. I guess I was in the lower wreck for about two months to the best of my recognition. As I walked from my walk, the CO told me to pack up. I said to myself, "Oh fuck, again." I was transferred to the last of the last places that they had to offer in Bridgewater complexes. The next place was a big trailer. I don't know how many trailers they put together, but it must have been quite a few. I guess they don't want you to get too comfortable or used to where you are, so they keep moving you around, to make room for the next round of guys. It was much cleaner, but it was like an army barrack. All toilets in a row sinks in front of the toilets, the guys who were washing their faces, hands had their asses in the faces of the guys who were on the toilets. There wasn't any privacy at all. It was all open. All the guards were able to watch you on the toilet clearly. At least they could have put up some sort of a wall so that the women COs wouldn't stare at you when you're on the toilet. I would sit back as far as I could so that the women COs could just see my legs, my knees. When I was done, I was told not to sit back as far as I did because they wanted to see what I was doing. I just didn't pay any attention to them, said to myself I still have some morals in me. They couldn't take that away from me. But again when you took a shower, the stalls were always filled with water. They still jerked off in it, shit, piss in them. Just about every shower I went into there were pictures stuck to the walls of women, from the Kmart flyer to whatever that the guys would whack off to, what a smell enough to make you gag. So again I was up real early because I didn't want to have someone's ass in my face or someone wiping their ass beside me, so I put up with a woman guard watching me take a dump every morning before everyone got up. The bed that I was given was a lot better than I had in the lower wreck unit because it looked like no one had shit or pissed on it, but it still stank. I'll tell you this, the canteen must have made a killing on baby powder because this is what every guy used to kill the smell from coming from there mattresses.

As I looked around, I noticed there were a lot of the guys that I knew from all the units that I was in, even the guy Joe the wrestler. This was that big guy that I met earlier walking the track. I was glad that he was in the same unit. I got to talk to him to really see if he was a wrestler, he became my card-playing buddy just about every night. (Good guy to me.) When we were playing, he used to talk about the people that he knew in the wrestling world. It was like he knew everyone in the wrestling world. I just couldn't stop listening to him it was like I was in a hypnotic state. I couldn't get enough of it. I was so damn interested in everything he said. He told me about all the bad guys. He said that most of the bad guys were not bad guys. As a matter of fact, he said they all were great people. I was always home to watch all the great old wrestlers that started it all. He said they were all the ones he grew up with as a kid. I asked him about Fred Blasie, Lou Albano, and he said that Lou Albano was a great father, a good guy to Cindy Lauper. I never knew that until he told me that. He just told me it was just their job to be bad. They took it real seriously, really got into the sport. It was also their lives. I just had to ask him how he got his name. This is what he told me after a long wait because of what happened to one of his so-called brothers. He said that he was driving down the road one day, and they pulled up alongside of a car. On the side it said that it was a valiant. They decided to call their tag team the valiant brothers. I always wondered if that was how they got their name, because I worked for a Dodge dealership, and I always wondered if that was where they got their name from. We would play poker all the time unless it was on a weekend, when wrestling came on TV, in which case most of the guys would watch it. He would name just about every move they made, and just when we thought one of the guys was going to lose, he would say, "He's not going to go down yet." He was always right. He was a real decent guy, the most interesting person I had met the whole time that I was in jail. Most of the COs made fun of him every chance they got. As I said, throughout this whole story I really realized that those COs were fuckin' assholes like the rest. If he really wanted, he could pop their heads with one hand as he said, but he mostly liked joking around with everyone. There were all kinds of stories going around about him. I just took them all with a grain of salt as I did most stories. I just hope he got out, is doing well, thank him for all the stories he filled my head with. It did me good. If he ever reads this, I also want him to know I never believed any of the stories the guys said about him.

I lost a good part of my life being incarcerated that I will not be able to make up ever again. The time I spent in jail ruined my life to this day in every way along with taking my soul, my family away that it is burned into my brain; in place of a lot of it is bitterness along with hate for the cops, the courts who put me here. I would look around, say to myself I put up with so much shit with all these fuckin' assholes and was doing all the time by my-self with no help from the outside. I would curse my wife all the time. I had to still put up with the COs' shit every day. It was real hard to take the things they did to me, said to me I will never forget as long as I live. Everyone talks about prejudices of people. Ninety-nine percent don't come from the whites in jail, it all mostly came from the blacks or the wannabe black guys. But when the shit hit the fan it was always blamed on all the white guys. (Bullshit.) I'm not saying all the black guys, but most of them. To me, they were the racist bastards the whole time I was in jail. As I was walking around the track with an African American guy whom I worked out with in the gym, he told me that the blacks are for the blacks, the Puerto Ricans are for the Puerto Ricans, the white are all for themselves, I really believe this. Now I look at it and realize that the white guys do get blamed for a lot of things that go on in the unit. That's when the black guys call the white guys racist. Then he tells me just to stay out of it, said do your own time as I do mine, just say fuck them all. I see so many guys getting set up for a fall by the COs, putting things in inmates' lockers to get guys to fight or edging them on to attack a CO so they can get an early retirement or go out on leave. I know this because I overheard this in the minimum one day when I was upstairs getting parts for a car when I was working in the auto garage.

At this time I was still hoping that my so-called wife would start to send me at least some more of the money that I let her hold for me that she said she got back from the lawyer that she said she never got back. (Lying cunt.) The only things that I was getting from her was things pertaining to the divorce that she wanted so badly. I guess because she kind of knew that her so-called boyfriend was dying from prostate cancer. She wanted to marry him before that happened so she could put a claim on the house as she tried doing to me that he owned. But he kind of knew he was dying. He just maxed out the mortgage, so when he kicked off, there was nothing left, so she got fucked in a different way. Whatever was left went to his daughter. It came to the point that I didn't even have enough money for shoes, other things I needed. I started to open locks for guys to get canteen. This was on all the combo locks that were found around the unit so they wouldn't have to buy one through the canteen. When you're in a place like this, you have to find different ways of making canteen, not money because money is not allowed in this place that I'm at. The money that I left my wife probably found its way up her fuckin' nose along with her guitar playing wannabe asshole boyfriend fuckin' coke whore. I was just looking at the whole thing, just said to myself, it's just another obstacle placed in my way. It's put there for me to tackle it. I looked at it as a lesson in life. I kind of knew there would be lots more obstacles in my life as time went on.

When I was walking the track, I was looking at a good amount of guys while I was walking. Most of them looked like they didn't have a care in the world while they were involved in playing sports, different games. They just were getting into what they were doing, just like all the other jails that I was at. I just can't understand how they could be doing what they are doing even knowing that are in a place like this it baffled me to no end. I knew I couldn't do what they were doing knowing that I was losing a good part of my life being in this place. There was nothing I could do about it but watch it take away a good part of my life away. I guess this was payback for helping a fuckin' junkie that I happened to be married to. I have so much hate in my heart for these COs for what these bastards put me through, all the shit that I had to put up with in all the other places that I was at. From one place to another, they just did the same shit to guys just to piss guys off. Now when I see a CO when I'm out with a Correctional uniform on, a warm feeling goes through my body just waiting for whomever to say something to me in the wrong tone to me or say that they remember me. I really would tell whoever to go fuck themselves and deal with what came after that. I'm on my way back from lunch, I see this fat piece of shit CO that checks me every time I walk by him. He has a habit of rubbing me between my legs, caressing my balls. I jump every time just looking at him. I tell him all the time when he pats me down, I keep telling him to knock it off. This is something I just can't get used to, some guy touching my balls. This CO was at Bridgewater Minimum when I was there. Before I was lugged out of there, I would give him dirty looks when I'd see him. He always fucked with the guys as they walked by. I was new where I'm at now. I didn't really know what to expect when I first entered the prison system, just stared at the guards when they pulled a guy out of a crowd just to search him. I did see the same CO at Walmart, made eye contact with him, and then I think he recognized me, and he grabbed the little boy that was with him. It could have been his son or a family member, but to me he looked like a skinner. I guess he put it together, realized who I was, and just turned around while keeping his eyes on me and walked back out of the store. This time I gave him the same dirty look as I did when I would see him in jail, but this time he couldn't feel me up. I would like to know where his big mouth was at that time. He looked like he was going to shit himself. I did see some of the other COs that a friend of mine brought by my home before I was sent to jail. At one time they just walked by me like they'd never seen me before. These were the same guys that a good friend of mine named Al brought by my home a couple of times. He was one of my best friends that I had at that time. I didn't sell it to him. I just did some with him because he helped me with the cars I worked on. I gave my friend Al what he asked for in the other room, told him not to bring anyone else with him when he came by, and he said not to worry, that they were okay. I just said no more. He said okay. Now that he has died, I realize that he was the best friend that I ever had in life. When I made eye contact with them, they just looked at me like they never saw or met me before. I never saw them again but briefly from a distance.

I was now at the last place before they transferred me out of this compound to another prison; I was thinking how long I would be here before I got my next move. I think that they watch you very closely. When you start to get too comfortable, they move you out. I was getting just that, too comfortable. To this day I still can't believe the things I did to pass time. I watched this guy try to catch some small rats or they could have been mice in a box with bread. He said if he did catch one, he would boil it and eat it. That was something I would like to see. He tried; he just couldn't catch any of them, so I tried my way to catch them. I was right against the wall, and at night I heard noises coming from under my bed, so I started to feed them to see if I could catch one, so I put some bread on a large amount of tape on a piece of paper, put it under my bed, and waited. One of the guys I walked the track with said that I was hearing things, said that I was going nuts, so I had to prove to him that I wasn't hearing things.

I kept putting large amount of tape with food on it and stuff it under my bed. When I heard them under my bed at night, I pulled on the string. I had one stuck to the tape and saw that it was either a mouse or a small rat stuck on the tape. I put a cup over it, saved it for the next day to show it to my friend to prove that I wasn't hearing things. When he woke up, I showed it to him, and he screamed out just like a woman. He jumped back. He was really scared shit of something. He said he would eat it if he caught one. I just couldn't believe it. He backed down, when he said that he would eat a damn rat if I caught one. I told him it's just meat. (No answer.) This was a rat, but there was a lot of human rats in this place along with what I caught. Most of us kind of knew who the rats were. On one occasion, this snitch informed the COs about a guy that was selling cigarettes in the unit. They had every guy in the unit stand in a large circle, strip down naked, bend over so they could check up everyone's asses. At that time while this was going on, there was a lot of women COs present. They were laughing out loud when this was going on. I was so embarrassed. I did what I was told to do but just placed my mind somewhere else, just put up with it. This was just another way that the COs fucked with you. Most of the time they didn't find anything but put all the guys through it anyways. I just couldn't understand why an inmate would stick cigarettes up their asses when they were in the unit. When they would smoke them, all the guys that smoked would make a small circle, smoke them, and think none of the smoke would escape. I think it was their way to show you to what extent guys will go to hide cigarettes. Guys would smoke them even knowing where they were kept.

Every time you left the unit and entered, you would have to sign in and out. What I can't understand was where the hell do you think the guys were going to go when you're behind the wall? There was no way around it. I just can't believe a guy would chance it and climbed over the fence, get more time or take the chance, get wrapped up in barb wire that was above the fence, and there were two fences to go over. The best part is that there is a CO right outside the door, another CO walking along the outer part of the fence, which is doubled fenced with barb wire. If you get through one, you still have another one to get through. The whole time that I was there I just was thinking most of the time of where they were going to send me next. When I would walk the yard, I would look across the street and remember the dickheads sergeant COs who put all those black guys in the same room with me just to make life miserable for me because of what the Sargent said to me about my so-called wife. The worst part of being at the minimum was that the next day, the COs would always ask me how I slept through the night knowing that the guys they put in the room with me played rap shit music all through the night. This CO would walk by me singing, "How do you sleep at night." It would piss me off; there was nothing I could do about it. I just had to live with it. Now that I had time to think about what the CO said to me about my wife, she probably did go home with him, and he fucked her or did whatever. This was his way of rubbing my face in it. This is something I will never know. Now knowing what type of woman she was, the breath she came in with when she came in for a visit, she probably might have got it from some guy she came up with or the CO that she could have sucked off before she came in to see me. Again I will never know. What really bothered me was that I stuck up for her, stood by her when she had problems. I never thought she would hurt me so bad, leave me when I was down. At that time I would have done just about anything for her. I never would think that she would go back on her word after she told me not to worry. She said that she would be there when I got out, that I could trust her. When the CO said that she looked like a whore, it really bothered me. That's what got me real mad. Under my breath I said the same about his wife. That's when the shit hit the fan, as they say. But now I think about it, maybe he already took her for a spin around the block. The cock breath she came in with on those days was from the Sargent that put all those black guys in the same room with me. Not bad enough that I had to live the way I was living but had to put up with the garbage guys that the Sargent put in the room with me. I mean real garbage.

I was still calling my so-called lawyer, of course still being hung up on all the time, just wondering how many times a lawyer couldn't be in his office or him being in court with never a callback or a letter. I must have called him at least twenty times in a month, still no answer, so I started to write him to pass time, seeing that he was never available. Still I never got any answers from him, but he knew how to take my money, but I refused to let it rest. I wanted to go home real bad. The whole time that I was incarcerated, I was writing letters home about all the things that I would see, experience. I wrote most of it down in letters. That was just some of the things I saw. I still remember the stories that guys would tell me about things that they got busted for, what they got put in jail for, and I found them very interesting.

Well, the winter started to come in, and it was getting very cold in the unit. There were cracks in the floors, the doors were open 75 percent of the time, and you would have to wrap yourself in whatever you had to keep warm. Even the CO at the door would say that he couldn't wait to go home just to warm up. At night I would see the mice or baby rats run around the unit throughout the night. I didn't try to catch any of them anymore in case I got bit by one and didn't want to catch anything from them because the medical doctors were real bad in jail. The whole time that I was incarcerated, every doctor I saw were fuckups and as bad as the COs along with having their heads up their asses.

The COs started to come around just about every day just to check out what you had in your locker and dump it out right in front of you just to see if you would say something about it. I don't know if they got their rocks off on it, but they were always trying to get guys to flare up so they could have you lugged out of the unit. If you had pictures of naked women, they would say that it was contraband. Look at them in the COs office where you could see them reading it just to piss you off. As time goes by, you learn not to buy large canteen. Buy just what you need for the week. If not, watch what you get; everyone will be asking you for something. This is how fights start. You most likely will get lugged to high security because guys have ways to get you in deep shit. What you have in canteen doesn't follow you because they consider contraband. Then everything you own in your locker goes to the rats or to the guys who clean out your locker or the ones that ratted you out. In most units, there are the people rats. There are quite a few of them and will do just about anything for Dunkin Donuts or their coffee. You've got to watch everything you say to everyone. This means all the guys in the unit. Yes, I've seen COs eating inmates' stuff after a guy has gotten lugged. Again they called this a Correctional institution. What a joke. While you're in jail, you don't learn a damn thing but how to commit different crimes from talking to other inmates. They still think they are learning a better way to commit the crime that they got busted for.

The really fucked-up thing about it is they really think they will get away with it the next time they do it. I still try to nap during the day so I could stay awake at night so I could see what goes on during the night because the COs would either leave the unit or fall asleep after dark. Dealing with these assholes was a full-time job, watching guys steal things out of lockers, also to see if something was going to come your way while you were sleeping. You had to be on guard all the time. I sometimes wasn't the only one who stood awake at night. Some of the guys I knew did the same. I don't really know how many others did what I did but in here you don't trust anyone in this place. Whatever you had in your locker might look like junk if you were on the outside, but in jail after a while it's all you own. To you, you needed it badly, but the COs wouldn't think twice to throw it in the garbage again. Anything to get a rise out of you.

I watched the months, the days go by along with the seasons, just hoping for my time to come to an end so I could go home again, go on with the rest of what I had left of my life. The counting of how many days that there were left in a month still went on, if not on a calendar, it went on in my head. That's if you were normal. But the guys that didn't do this are the guys that make jail their life, like a lot of guys do. I was still doing the same stuff as I was when I entered this space. I just couldn't wait for the month to end or the year so I was able to cross it off. I just want out of this godforsaken place, try to put this all behind me, and be able to go home to the rest of my family I had left. I look at the time I got for the drugs that I got caught with, and it wasn't worth it. I would think about my so-called wife on the outside with another guy, carrying on like nothing ever happened. I stuck my neck out for my fuckin' junkie wife. It goes right through me knowing that she just forgot about me, then say how could I have done such a stupid thing, but maybe because she was my wife I would have done just about anything for her. At that time I would have done just about anything for my wife if she asked me to do. I was thinking that she was so small, that she wouldn't last a week in jail. The one night that she was in jail, a black girl took her jacket from her; she just gave it up without a fight then asked me where it went afterward. Now I just think about what I did and ask myself, would I ever do what I did again knowing what I know, what I've been though? I say hell no! No way would I do that again. This girl turned her back on me, walked away, just let me rot in jail without a care in the world, so I hope what goes around comes around. What I went through will someday happen to her so she knows what I went though. I think about what I did, and maybe she wouldn't have been such a cunt if she did time right alongside of me but in a different jail. They would have probably sent her to Framingham Correctional, where her best friend in jail would have been a piece of pepperoni or maybe she would have given it up to a CO for a cheeseburger. The word *cunt* is one word that I haven't used too much in my whole life, but in her case, she fits the word.

Now I was waiting for my divorce papers to come in. It was hurting me real bad inside. I kept saying to myself I shouldn't let it bother me so much, but it just did because my love for her was so deep. Even after all the bad stuff she had done to me while I was incarcerated, I just couldn't shake the feeling I had for her. My daughter was really mad at me because of the way I still felt toward her. What she couldn't understand was I just couldn't help myself. I felt the same way about her mother. Because of all the shit that I was going through every time a CO would mess with me, I looked at all of them in the same way. The hate that ran through my body was so bad for them that I could never be able to put it into words. I hated them so much for what they put me through.

I remember this so clearly like it was yesterday. A CO came over to me and said, "You got your move." I asked him where I was going, and he just said, "Pack your stuff, bring it down to property office, get out of my face." I guess they don't tell you in case you refuse to go to your next stop because you don't like where they are going to send you. If you refuse, they lugged you back to Concord, and you start all over again. It doesn't bother them one bit. It didn't take them long to get me into the van for transport to my next stop. It didn't bother me one bit where they were going to send me. I was used to being treated real bad. When I was in the back of the van, they told me that they were going to transport me to Norfolk. I said to myself, What the hell did I do to get put behind the wall again? I had no idea that they had a minimum. It was a long ride, and I had to put up with the smell of fresh coffee and what they were eating. The smell went right through the entire truck. Again all the stops they made, me asking them that I had to use the restroom, all I got from them was they will be there very soon. All the stops they made, I know they did it knowing that I had use the restroom. Well, I finally got to Norfolk, and I knew I had to make the best of it. I noticed that it wasn't covered in any barb wire and realized that they had a minimum. I thought I was going to the maximum. I walked in, and the place was real clean, I mean real clean. The best-looking place that I've been in since I've been in jail. It smelled good also. I had to wait for a long period of time to get checked in as usual. I asked them if I could use the restroom, and they said when I got checked in, after they showed me the room that I was to stay in. The room was upstairs. I couldn't believe my eyes. It had bedcovers that looked like a bedspread, and it was the best cell or room I'd ever seen the whole time that I was incarcerated, but when I looked at the so-called bedspread, the color was more like a pink color, my wife's favorite color. Again she was on my mind. I did notice that there was a lot of scum walking around, but it was a hundred times better than any of the other places that I spent time at. It was a double-bunk bedroom. The first thing that I was thinking was watch, there will be a black guy in the room with me. While getting over the shock of the room being livable, a guy walked in, and I couldn't believe it; he was white. I just said, maybe it won't be so bad after all. He carried on a decent conversation with me, and I knew that he was a couple of quarts low, but he was white. I finally had someone I could talk to; I kept saying to myself. something has to be wrong here. Still had to use the restroom. I was told that the restroom was down the hall. As I walked in, I noticed that it had doors on the stalls, and the toilets had toilet seats. I just couldn't believe my eyes. Now I was thinking that now I could take a dump without someone hitting elbows with me or watching me while I was taking a dump. As I walked out, I noticed that there was a white guy cleaning the rooms. It was happening all over the unit. This place was the cleanest place that I was ever at, even the outside was clean. I asked if I could go outside, look around, and she said yes, in a decent way, not like she had a stick up her ass. The COs that drove me up there had something to say about her when were in the van. It wasn't good. As I walked out the back door, not the front, there were no fences around the unit. I was expecting there to be one. I felt pretty good about this place even though I was still in jail.

I looked around the yard, and I noticed that there was a gym and a weight room; I just rubbed my hands together and said, "Now I can work out again." I was able to walk around the part that they called the track. I was able to see some of the visits coming in to see inmates, the cars, and the people were just a few feet away. I haven't had this much freedom in a long time, and I was wondering what I did to deserve this. I was feeling pretty good and said, "Something's got to ruin it, this can't be real." If I wanted, I could have taken off. It would have been a while before they found that I was gone. I could have been far away because I know how to hotwire a car, and there were quite a few cars to choose from.

One of the guys came up to me and said, "Thinking about taking off?" I just said no, then he said, "You wouldn't get far because they have seven counts a day. You will never see a minimum ever again."

Then I said again, "I have no intentions of taking off. I just want to do my time, go home."

Then he said, "I know what you mean." As soon as I finished the conversation, they called count, then he said, "See what I mean, didn't I tell you they are doing this because there were new guys that just came in. Two guys just took off a couple days ago, but they caught them in a couple of hours."

Then I realized I was going to have to get used to this place, feel out my new roommate to see what he was like. As I looked at him, he was short, was real dumb. I mean dumb as a stump. When I say dumb, he's at least three quarts low, as I noticed from the start. The way I looked at it, it couldn't be as bad as being in a room that was filled with racist black guys, listening to them playing rap all day and night long. I'm used to listening to Led Zeppelin, Pink Floyd, along with Eric Clapton, just some of the greats. Well, this is my first count. Like all the other places, the CO that was yelling out count. I will find out real soon that he will be the biggest asshole in the whole place. You have to be standing up and the doors have to be open as he looked into the room. He starts to stare at me like he knows me. It' a long, nasty look, like I just fucked his wife but paid no attention to it.

    This place looks like a real good place, but it's just a housing shell where they store people. They treat you real bad in every place that I was at. You get to realize no matter where you are placed, the COs always turn out to be fuckin' assholes. The whole time that I was incarcerated, I just met two decent COs. That was the woman CO, real good-looking woman at Pond Ville that had a chip on her shoulder probably because the men COs talked dirty about her, and she knew this. But she wasn't there long. She moved on to become a State Trooper. I wish her luck just because she never treated me bad. The other CO that was at Bridgewater in the visiting room was a decent guy also. I won't give out her real name, but I'll call her Tracy. You know who you are. She was behind the desk most of the time reading inmates' files on the computer, but she just doesn't fit the category of being an asshole but was very good to look at as long as no one saw you staring.

    I was on the second floor, I was right next to the phones, and I was hoping that they cleared my telephone numbers so I could bother the useless lawyer that my wife got for me and be able to call my daughter, the only one who stuck through it all with me. It took a week before I got my chance to call my daughter and sister. I told them where I was, the address they could write so I could get mail from them, and to pass it on to others in the family, hoping to just get some mail from them also. I was always hoping to get some type of letters from my family to read but got very little. They ended up all being all like my wife. Just for the hell of it all, I decided to call my big-time Boston lawyer who swam in a big legal ponds in Boston. He once told me that the lawyers where I was from could never do the cases that he did. That's why there were swimming in a small ponds in New Bedford; they could never make it in Boston courtrooms. Well, as I left the room to use the phone, I backed up a little. There were a couple of COs looking over the railing. They were talking, and the fat one said that he would like to fuck the woman CO Tracy right in the ass. Then he turned, looked right at me, and gave me a dirty look. As I was walking to the phones, I looked down and saw that it was who I thought it would be, the woman CO named Tracy of course. I used the phones as I was going to call my lawyer. I talked to his secretary, as usual, like I always did, and she said that he was in court still. This was late evening. I said to myself, court my ass, but at one time she did tell me to find another lawyer. I just shut my mouth and went on with my day and tried real hard to get it out of my mind. All I thought for the rest of the day was all the fuckin' scumbags I had to deal with all day long. I was surrounded by them all, including the COs.

As the day came to an end, every time I saw that CO that was commenting about that woman CO, the CO that was giving me dirty looks every time he saw me, I just blew it off and was hoping nothing would come out of it. But the time I saw him upstairs, he was with another CO. I was told that it was his brother, and to this day I really don't know if it was or if they just call each other brother like everyone calls each other in jail. If you were to look at them side by side, they would look like fat and skinny, the old-time comics, but in time they both made life a living hell for me. I really have to change the names when I'm writing about them because sometimes the truth can make people lose there jobs. Like they say, the truth hurts. If I use their real names, they will say it's not true to keep from losing their jobs. If the right person reads this, they might want part of the book that I'm writing. Maybe they can act human, have morals, even get to the point that they can be human but still fuckin' assholes. One of the COs was called Hinny Wrecker. Boy, did he say all bad things about this woman CO even when we were coming back from the jobs that we did for them. I once said that she was a good-looking woman, and he said, "She's a fuckin' cunt." Maybe because she turned him down one time or another. I think he forgot I was an inmate for a brief second when he was knocking her down and was really pissed off when saying what he was saying, then he realized he was talking to an inmate. When he was in the unit, all the guys would just stay far away from him. They would say "Wrecker is coming," and the guys would turn and walk the other way. He was a real piece of shit. We would hear his voice yelling over the intercom 98 percent of the time and would say, "Someone's getting lugged by Wrecker again." Maybe he wasn't getting fucked, but he led a miserable life, and he took it out on the inmates. By being in this place, you just learn to stay away from certain COs. Hinny Wrecker and his brother are the ones you stay away from all the time. I would love to run into him now at this time and would be able to talk to him the way I'm writing this. If he got out of line, I would tell him to shut the fuck up. If it led to something else, so be it. I would love to smash him and his brother in the face. This would make my life a hell of a lot better, make me feel that I got him back for the way he treated me. Then maybe I would be able to somewhat clear my head of him, make him feel the pain I felt. It also would be pay back for all the misery he put me through. The both of them were pure garbage. It got to the point that I wanted to go by the jail, confront him on the way he treated me, but my daughter talked me out of it. Fuckin' scumbag.

When this CO came on duty, he would be fuckin with all the guys right down to taking their bottles out of the freezer, throwing them in the garbage, right in front of them. This unit put a refrigerator in the unit for the inmates to use to keep things cold; he was told it was for the inmates, but he still he threw the guys' stuff out just to mess with the guys. All the things that he threw in the garbage or the Dumpster were the stuff from the inmates that he fucked with on a regular basis. He said, "Even if you're on your way home I will see you again because you all come back." But a lot of the guys had bowls with snap on covers. This was something all the guys wanted to store their food in, but when he saw them, he would throw it in the Dumpster. The inmates would try to get them back if they could. These bowls would keep their food fresh longer, and if it was cold, we would put them on the outside of our windows. But this asshole would walk around the outside of the building and look for them and again throw them out. When they did a shakedown, he would take all the clothes that were not state clothes and throw them out also. They would go through the property room first. If they were street clothes, who ever worked with the property officer was able to go into the Dumpster and take things out. We would exchange the ripped up state clothes for good street clothes they made you feel better wearing good stuff from the street. Some of the guys that worked for the property officer would take the stuff from the Dumpster and sell them for things we could get from the canteen in exchange. To get the CO in property to give you something from the property room, it was like pulling teeth. He even said he didn't care if someone could use it. We were here to pay for the crimes that we did. Then he said when we were out on the street, he told me it wasn't supposed to be easy stealing, selling drugs is no way out. That's why they made jails for guys like you.

There was so much clothes that could have been used, but it all got thrown out. I'm talking about brand-new jeans, TV sets, radios, hotpots, this stuff you couldn't take because it wasn't on your property sheet. Sometimes we would trade a good TV out of the garbage for a broken one if it looked more or less the same. That's how some guys made out. But if you got caught, the ISPS would be called in to fuck with you like you just robbed a bank or killed someone. After the interrogation, you would end up being lugged to high security anyways. I would cut a razor out of a shaver with a nail clippers, run it under the sticker that was stuck on all items that was owned by whoever, removed it very slowly. Most of the time we could trade our sticker onto the one we were trading for that was taken out of the trash and get away with it. I did show this to others guys so that they could do the same, but you have to watch who you show because of all the rats in jail. Like I said before, the inmates would do just about anything for a doughnut, a cup of coffee, like I said, that the COs got for free. The way the Cos looked at it, it was a way to pass some of their jobs that they didn't want to do onto the inmates so that they could just fuck off.

Every CO in this place was a piece of shit except the woman Tracy. She never did anything to me but offer me a muffin. I refused it because you never know who was looking. I was always careful not to be caught taking anything from any CO. The eyes were all over the place. It could be easily mistaken for kissing up to a CO for ratting. In this place, you have to work, hold a job. If they did find you a job, you had to be downstairs early in the morning because the transport guy was the one who kept you busy around the unit. When I say early, I mean early, as soon as they called count; that was about six in the morning. That's first count. This CO's name was Rocket. That's what he wanted to be called. If you missed three days in a row, you were on your way to being lugged to high security. He would never put up with any excuses in so many words. (You're gone.) He kind of knew you had to be downstairs to see him for a job because he kind of held it over your head. You being in a minimum was better than being in the maximum. He had no problem putting you back behind the wall again. When it came to lugging someone, he would get the Wrecker to do his dirty work for him because he knew he loved doing that to inmates.

Rocket just loved inmates kissing his ass. I think the best part to Rocket was left on the mattress, like Hinny Wrecker, but who really knows. Maybe they had the same mother. Whatever was left ran down there mother's leg. But rocket was just a different type of an asshole because the way he was able to belittle guys whenever he could, he did this with a smile on his face. Then maybe he would go jerk off afterward. This CO would yell at the guys all the time, always ask them if they were stupid, if they needed things drawn out so they would understand what they had to do. At one time he said to a guy, "You know how to sell drugs on the street, now you have to learn to work for a living. This is the best way, that's Rocket's way." Then he said, "You got to do what I tell you at the time I tell you or you won't be working for me for very long. So if you can't do what I tell you, there will always be a place behind the wall so you can do that nothing that you're so used to doing, but behind the wall."

The guys that he was talking to replied, "I didn't sell any drugs on the street."

Rocket then said, "Whatever, just do the job I gave you to do or you be gone." This means out of here, placed behind the wall. I listened and kept quiet. Rocket knew that I fixed cars I think on the outside. He made me the official car wash boy to clean the inside of all the transport vehicles, said that I better show him that I was able to do the job he had given me or he will turn me over to Wrecker to work for him. He brought it to my attention that he was watching me at all times. It was like he owned me. I was his slave. On more than a few occasions, he would put things in the cars to see if I would take them. I played along with it, see it, would work around it. When I would get into the car, I would notice what they called contraband in plain sight, like cigarettes, lighters, money, so on. I would clean it, place the things right back where I found them, but made sure that I cleaned where he put the things that he planted right back where I found them. This went on for a couple of months. Then they placed me in with the property officer from time to time. I was able to get some of the guys' things that was taken from them in a raid back to the guys that lost them that, of course, were considered contraband. So damn stupid. The stuff that was taken was extra clothes, pens, markers, a lot of electronics. I was told to throw it all in the Dumpster. Why! Still can't understand it was just to mess with the guys when he could just put it on their property list because they already had the things. What harm would it do.

When Rocket was on the road, Wrecker would fill in for him, when he would see me coming, he must have said to himself, "Time to fuck with this guy." He did this as much as he possibly could because I felt my buttons being pushed every time he sees me. I think every time he sees me walking by, it was pure hate at first sight. He just wanted any excuse to have me lugged for what he was saying to his brother about Tracy. Again I hope she made out well as a state trooper. After the fuck-me-over process, they ended up placing me in the auto mechanic garage because they found out that I worked at the other garage at Bridgewater. I guess I must have worked there for a couple of months. But of course I was somewhat interviewed by their mechanic CO. I was asked if he had to watch me at all times. I said, "No, I've been working on cars most of my life." He just started to put me to work on the COs' cars again. It was a pretty large garage, but of course what got me mad was all the kiss-ass motherfuckin' inmates, thinking they were part of the staff who would do just about anything for a doughnut. When I got in the garage, I was doing a lot of brake jobs, some motor work. From time to time, the auto body CO would come in, kept asking me if I wanted a job change, that he could really use me at his garage. He said that they got good food over at his shop all the time. If I wanted to eat good that it comes with the job. It took about a week. Wanted or not, I was taken out of the mechanic shop, and I got the job change. It was no decision of mine, but I was moved to the auto body shop to do body work. I was told to replace all the numbers on the roofs of all the institution cars, doing body work. I more or less figured that the numbers that they had me change on the roofs of the cars was so they could see them from the air if they needed to. It took at least a month to change all of them, and I was showing another Spanish guy how to do it as well. He was a real piece of shit. the guys called him Toyota. This piece of shit, I almost got into fights with him every time we made eye contact. He would go running to his uncle every time for protection. It was, as I said, a family affair.

It took me at least two months to find out, to realize that the body shop manager was a fuckin' asshole like all the rest and stuck up for his wannabe slaves. To me at first he didn't come across like that, but I soon found out that he always wanted the upper hand and wanted everyone to kiss his ass. This was because of the food we were getting from the delivery trucks. These Spanish guys would do anything for the food we were getting. I had no choice but to stay there unless they decided to move me somewhere else or give me another job change. I did ask them, and they said no, as I kind of knew they would. The body shop CO would give me the keys to the patrol cars, thinking in his mind that maybe I would drive off with one of them, but he was so wrong. This would have been so easy, but I never would do that because it would get me the rest of my time behind the wall. I didn't want that. This place was one big setup in so many ways, I guess to see if inmates would try to drive off with a car with a big number on the roof, but of course there were a lot of stupid guys in the unit, but as long as I was there, it never happened.

All the jobs that you do in this place are just given to you because the COs are just lazy motherfuckers. All they want is to fuck off all the time, give the most of the work to inmates to do. I'm real surprised that they didn't let the inmates do their guard job as well. For a cup of coffee, they probably would have done it because most of them were backstabbers. This job lasted about three months. The sight of me watching inmates work like dogs got me real mad. I was the one who was teaching them how to do bodywork. I hated it because they would suck up to the boss like all the rest, work for food that came on the food trucks that supplied food for the prison. All the drivers were real decent guys. All of them would leave us food if we would help them unload the trucks. Of course the Spanish guys that called Toyota was the first there, thinking he was a boss. I did eat real well for the three months I worked for the body shop, but I was always bumping heads with the body shop manager. He was just another dickhead like all the rest. This guy was always trying to teach me how to do body work. I was a teacher in a trade school before I came into prisons, and he didn't know this. This so-called auto body CO didn't know his ass from his elbow like most of the COs, and I wondered how he even got the job. This guy was always asking how to repair certain vehicles. When I told him how I did it, he would get mad at me, especially when it came to the epoxy used to glue body panels on vehicles. I said that I would just use that stuff if it was to put patches on or over rotted holes, not for major panels in case it got into an accident. I would think the panel wouldn't hold up to a major crash, and the vehicle would fold up. He told me to glue a panel on a Ford Bronco and I did it as he told me too, it looked real good all in primed, I told him to press on it, it held out then I said bang on it then press along the seam. Of course, it cracked, and he gave me a dirty look and said, "It's got to be good. They use stuff like this on the space shuttle."

I looked at him and said, "I'm glad I'm not going into space with this shit holding it together." What a look I got from him. He then tried it himself and said that I did it wrong. It did the same to him when he did it. I said, which I should not have said to him, "I told you so." After that he didn't want to be around me and didn't want to talk to me as much. I could feel it when he came to pick me up in the morning.

I was in this trade for many years. I knew what to do when it came to body work. I repaired total wrecks. I mean, cut-in-half cars. I didn't need this half-ass CO telling me how to do body work. After that I kind of knew that my time in in this shop was coming to an end. It wouldn't be long before they gave me a job change because of this. Of course it happened sooner than I thought. Well, I was at the unit, and I was ready to go to the body shop. The CO came to pick up all the guys. He left me behind, said that he no longer wanted me at the body shop, said that I wanted to do things my way, wouldn't listen to him. This is because he had his head up his ass, and I kind of told him this. I also was getting mad at the guys that were at the shop because they took the job in the shop as a real job, as you would do it on the outside. I would tell them work but remember where you're at. I told these kiss-ass Spanish guys, "Don't kill yourself. Remember where you are. You're in jail. It's not a real job," and of course they ratted me out. There reply was if they got the jobs done fast, the manager would get us coffee and doughnuts for a job well done, and then they said to me, "Don't you want any doughnuts?" I said I'd get all the coffee and doughnuts that I want when I get out of this fuckin' place. The guy that I was talking to was the guy they called Toyota. Whenever the COs brought in any doughnuts from Dunkin Donuts, he would be the first to put his hands all over the doughnuts. He would be licking his fingers while doing it. When even you would get close to him, he always smelled like he had shit himself. I was going to eat those doughnuts after he was licking his fingers, no fuckin' way, he was a fuckin' pig. If I was to see him now, I would spit in his face, bust him up just to see how bad I could make him bleed.

At that time, he just hung around with a couple of his big boy friends who protected him. He was most likely sucking them off for protection. This Spanish guy would rat out guys on a drop of a dime just to get a doughnut; I would see him get handouts from the COs when guys got lugged to behind the wall. They sucked up to this CO, did what he told them to, but I just worked at a slow pace. I told them that I won't rush for anyone. I'm in jail. I won't refuse to work, but I won't kill myself for any CO. Of course they told the CO this, and this was why I was removed from the body shop. These Spanish guys should have been glad that I was showing them how to do body work, teaching them body work so they could get their free Dunkin Donuts coffee from the COs.

These COs were all the same. When they brought us into the shop, all the CO would just sit in his office, fuck off all day long. One of the other COs was from my neck of the woods, and I got to talk to him once in a while. I would always make sure he talked to me while being watched by the other inmates. I would talk about what was going on in New Bedford, where I was from. It got to the point that he was more or less rubbing it in my face what I was missing being in jail. This CO would walk around with a limp. I wanted to comment on it but didn't. I made the mistake of thinking that he was different from the rest. It felt good talking to someone from where I was from. I had found some money in the cars that I worked on and asked him if he could get some coffee, stuff for some of the guys in the shop with the cash that I found. He stopped, looked at me, and said, "Don't get confused. You're a convict, I'm a CO. I do nothing for convicts. You guys are here for a reason and are no good in my eyes."

I just stared at him and said to myself, "Scumbag." I never said another word to him; he kept the money also that they had given him. In my whole life I was never good when it came to taking orders; I wasn't going to start now. Just because I'm in jail I had to keep telling myself over and over again where I was to keep from going out of my mind, which I thought was already happening. The whole time that I was incarcerated, I really thought I was nuts, but it was just where I was at. I could never adjust to this place or any other jail that I was at. It must have been the way that they treated me. My way of rebelling against it was real bad because they had a real good time trying to drive me crazy or, even better, train me. I knew that could never happen. No matter what they did or tried to do to me, I wouldn't let them break me no matter what they did to me. I just went into my own world and refused to let them in and looked at them. In my mind, I was saying fuck you to them.

Working at the shops were just a way of getting away from being in the unit. It was to me time out. I wouldn't have to stand for count all damn day. That was seven counts a day. Of course the Spanish guy Toyota told the shop manager what I told them. That's why I got the boot. This is why I wasn't picked up that day to go to the shop.

While you're at any minimum jail, you have to work as all the other places or you get transferred to or stay at a maximum prison. Again this place was a decent stop. It also had toilet seats on the toilets. You had an enclosed toilet; that was a big plus. So I went to work for the CO that they called Rocket again. After a while I asked him if I could get a grounds job. He just looked at me, put me to work doing grounds work, like picking up all the trash, taking care of all the flowers by dead heading all the plants, weeding around all the plants and trees around the unit. He said, "Leave the cigarettes alone." This must have been killing the Wrecker. When he saw me doing the job that I was given, he watched me very closely. I knew it. I made sure I didn't step out of line so as not to give him the satisfaction of having me lugged. I asked the CO that was behind the desk if it was possible for me to speak to the superintendent someday. By the next day I was asked to go to his office. I told him what was going on with the CO they called Hennie Wrecker, and he told me not to worry about a thing, said that's just his ways. He will take care of the problem. I then told him that I just wanted to do my time and go home. He then asked what I did to get him so mad at me. I said, "Not a thing." then he said that he would look into it. Then I said, "If you speak to him about me, then I know I will be lugged right out of here." He said we have our way of dealing with this sort of things. I saw the Wrecker the next day, and again it was hate at first sight. Along with a real dirty look, his head just followed me right to the door that I was walking out of because I glanced back as I was walking out, I saw that his eyes just followed me.

    I would hate to leave this place because it had a decent gym. I was able to walk around the track benches, where I would make cards, carve the days, months that I had left into the wooden tables that I made cards on. The cards I was making was making me a good canteen, I sold a lot of cards to guy's in the unit. I noticed one day as I was working outside the unit that the CO Hinny Wrecker was parked across the street in his van. He just was staring at me while I was walking around the outside; I was picking up all the cigarettes butts and made sure they all went in the trash. I was wondering if he had planted all the cigarettes butts that were outside the unit to see if

BUSTED

I was going to smoke them or was trying to set me up. Maybe that's why he was there watching me. I did this so-called job every day, and this day there were a lot of butts around. This was just another way of him trying real hard to get me lugged (prick).

After that day he left me alone for a while, but I kept my eyes open for him. Shit, he was trying to do something to me. Just me knowing all the stuff he was doing to me, I kind of knew he had something on his mind. I didn't know what. All I knew was that he was trying to set me up for a fall. It was late in the summer, and I saw a lot of loom being dropped off. When I said a large amount, it covered a good part of the side parking lot where the visitors parked. It was at least two large dump trucks full of loom. He came up to me with four other guys; I said that he wanted the entire amount of loom moved from the parking lot, put from one side of the jail to the other side of the jail. He said, "You have the grounds job, so it's up to you to move it around with the four guys that are here to help you." After that it has to be put, I mean the entire load of loom, around all the flower beds, around the whole unit. He came back with two wheelbarrows. I started to say where he wanted the loom brought to. These guys are here to help you get the job done so there is enough room for the visitors to park. Then he said, "Don't take a week to do it either. I want it done fast." He then said it was up to me to get the job done. I looked at him, and to myself I said, he wanted me to tell the guys what to do, but no way was I going to tell these guys what to do. I was no fuckin' CO. Well, the guys he left to help me lasted about a day. Between the smoking that they were doing, it didn't really add up to much work being done, and it was left up to me to do it. He came up to the guys that were helping me and said that he needed them to do other things around the unit, told me to finish the job. So I kept doing what I was told to do. I started to bring the loom from one side of the jail to the other side. It was a good distance to move the entire loom to. Doing what I had to do was kicking the heck out of me but a stubborn part of me was saying that he wasn't going to break me. He wasn't smart enough to do so. I just did what I was told to do day after day without it showing that it was killing me inside. I was working on my mind as well but refuse to show it.

Every day when he would see me, he would say what was taking me so long. He would say at the pace that I was moving, the job will never get done. When I sat down, he would say, "That's why the job is not done yet." Another time he said that there was no time to rest, said that he didn't tell me it was okay to take a break, and that he wanted the parking lot cleared of the loom. Then another time that he walked by, he said that I was not to take a break until the parking lot was cleared of the entire load of loom. That day I must have moved at least a hundred fifty loads of loom in a wheelbarrow across the prison compound to where he wanted it. I never said a word to him at all. I saw the guys that were helping me in the beginning. they were sitting at a bench, so I asked them what Hinny Wrecker made them do after he took them off the job they were helping me with, and they said, "Nothing at all." I said to myself, "That fuckin' bastard is fuckin' with me again. He had me working all day long, kept saying I want that parking lot cleared by the end of the day. That prick had me work the whole day long. Everyone else was just working half days like they always did." I just walked away, shaking my head, but again I didn't give up. It was cleared by the end of that day.

After talking to those guys he had helping me at the start then took them off, I said that must have been his way of paying me back for talking to the superintendent about what he was doing to me. I wasn't going to the superintendent again because when I did, Hinny Wrecker made life even worse for me. The superintendent never went outside to see what was going on ever. I think if he did, I think it would shock to him. That was because he was white as a ghost. He would probably fry when the sun hit him. He looked like a vampire. Now it goes to show that all he does is hold a seat in a high position and doesn't give a damn what goes on outside his door, really don't give a damn, just collects a paycheck like most and once in a while signs a few papers.

Now that the moving of the loom was completed, the parking lot was cleared. I went back to my regular job of cleaning around the outside of the unit, deadheading all the flowers. As I looked over where the loom was, I saw Hinny Wrecker moving it all around the unit with a backhoe. He was putting it all around the unit. A lot of it was going to where I took it from the parking lot. I said to myself as I looked at him, "You fuckin' asshole." He looked at me and just smiled as he broke the pile of loom down like it was nothing. It took him a few minutes. It took me a day and a half. He brought it pretty close to where I took it from the parking lot. (Asshole.) After that, he more or less left me alone. I guess he just got bored with me seeing that I wasn't showing any emotion to what he was doing to me. I went back to what I was doing before he made me his grounds plaything again. For two straight days, he worked me like a damn dog or his personal slave, whatever you want to call it. He made me pay real good for going to the Superintendent.

I called my so-called bigshot Boston lawyer again; I'll change his name to Lawyer Mr. Big Fish, the big fish. I should have called him Mr. Fuck U Over; that would fit him better. I had to get out of my room because my roommate was being a dick; he wanted the room in complete darkness just like the black guys that were in my room at Bridgewater. I just couldn't stand it. I needed light all the time. So I was in what they called a day room, and I decided to call my so-called lawyer again like I did every day. Of course he wasn't there, as I expected. I called him when I got bored because I kind of knew he wouldn't answer the phone. The person that I was talking to said to me, "I know you call a lot. Why don't you just get your money back. He's not going to help you. This was the second time I was told this, once by his secretary, now by this person also." Then he or she with a heavy voice said, "I see, hear it every day as I answer the phone. Just know he's not doing anything for you. He won't ever take any of your calls, just like all the others." So after that I started to write to the Bar Of Overseers, telling them what's going on, telling them that he won't take any of my calls, and he already took a large amount of money from me to represent me, but he has not done anything for me in years. I wrote Mr Big Fish quite a lot of letters. I kind of knew that he wasn't going to respond to any of them, but I was glad that I already sent out all I did. So I started to write letters to the bar of overseers to see if they could help me with my problems that I had with this attorney. In the letter I sent them, I was asking them if they could help me get my money back. I wrote in the letter that he hasn't helped me out in any way whatsoever. The last letter I sent Mr. Big Fish I told him that he hasn't done anything for me. it's been years. Then I informed him that I wrote to the bar, gave him a week for an answer, but he never responded to it. I did get a letter from Mr. Big Fish after a while, maybe because the Bar Of Overseers contacted him about my case. In his letter he said that he will contact me for a date in April of 2003. He could reduce my sentence down to three years. I just couldn't believe what I was reading. I never responded to his letter and sent it to the bar of overseers along with the other letter I sent Mr. Big Fish. The messed-up thing about it was that I was already in for four years that April. I only had nine months to go. He had no idea what was going on in my case. So I wrote to the bar again to follow up with the letters they were sending me. There was a lot of paperwork, but they got back to me right away with no bullshit. They said that they would assign someone to my case. That happened like I was right in their office, filing the complaint in person. I had to call my wife to find out how much she gave the Boston lawyer Mr. Big Fish. She said the full seventy-five hundred dollars. As we were talking, my wife just added to the conversation, said, "Why you don't just do the time they gave you. It will teach you to be a better person again, to believe in Jesus. he will never let you do it again." She added, "He will make life easier for you in the time you have left to do." She must have had this on paper right by the phone because it was like she said this to me in every conversation we had. There is this coke whore telling me that it will make me a better person. She is a fuckin' coke dealer, so she wouldn't have to pay for the coke she was probably still stuffing up her fucking nose. I said to myself, I'm doing the time, but this bitch is running around with coke rings around her nose most of the day, telling me how to become a better person. She was doing whatever she had to do to keep her nose powdered. What really got me was when she said that I should forget about the money that she gave the lawyer, to just do my time, then go home. Go on with the rest of my life. If it wasn't for her telling me to run out to get more, I wouldn't be in here now. Of course her telling the police that she knew nothing at all about the drugs I had, I still have the tire marks running down my body where she threw me under the bus to save her ass. Within a couple of weeks, I did end up getting some paperwork from my ex-wife that she sent to me. I sent all the paperwork that was related to my case to the bar. All the lawyers that were handling my case at the time were all great. The lawyer who helped me, I wish him the best because he didn't mess around. He did what had to be done. It took a while, but I received a letter. It said that I needed to sign a few papers. I would receive my money back very soon. I believe it came within a month. They added that they were going to take his right to practice away for a year. Big deal. I really don't care anymore if he wasn't going to help me with what I hired him for. He just should have said no from the start. Now if he does it to anyone else, then they should take his license away for good. Bigshot Boston lawyer my ass. Then I hope he drowns in his so-called big pond he told me about all the time.

The whole time that I was incarcerated, I never had a decent roommate. We were all dickheads maybe from being brainwashed by the COs. Most of the inmates that I had for roommates always had the damn shades pulled down in the rooms that I was in so that the room was always in complete darkness. I hated that, but what could I do besides nothing. At this time, the CO came into the room and told me that I would have to move back up to the top again because I was getting in a roommate that needed the bottom bunk. So again, I said here we go again, back to the top bunk again. I was thinking it was some overweight person or some damn junkie, but I was wrong. Well, as the new guy walked in, it was a guy I knew from the last stop that I was at. He would tell stories of his so-called gangster days, how he worked for the Mafia, what he did to guys on the street. This guy's name was Ron, and he was pretty old. A short white-haired man with a booze-looking face. He was in jail for driving drunk again. This was on more than one occasion. He swore that he tortured guys in his basement to get money that was owed to him. One time he told me about one guy that stole jewelry, watches from a jewelry store. He owed him a part of the robbery. He had to go hunt him down for what the guy owed him. He told me that he waited outside his house till he came home. It took a while and had spent all the money from the heist but had no way of giving him his share, so he tied him up, killed him, threw him in the river. To this day it sounded good in jail. That was because I was very gullible at the time and really believed him. For a while we got along real good, but it didn't last long.

After a while, the stories that he was telling me started to sound like bullshit stories. It was getting real old as he was. I just started to see right through the bullshit stories that he was telling me. I kind of knew it must have been all lies or to many late-night movies that he had seen. Then I just realized that he just wanted to be a big man in jail, didn't want to get fucked up. But all the stories that he would spread around the unit got a lot of guys to believe them because they were as gullible as I was. It got to the point that the guys started to call him OG too. He ate this up, and this meant Old Gangster in jail. It came to a point that he was trying to run the room, wanted me to do his running around for him. He started to fall asleep with my TV on. I told him that I didn't mind if he used my TV, but when he was going to sleep, which was all the time if he could shut the TV off. This was because I wanted to last till I got out of jail. This went on for months. It got to the point that I just took my TV, put it on the top of the foot of my bed where I was, told him to leave it alone because he was leaving it on all the time. Now this was the beginning of us hating each other. He told me that he was going to have me beat up when I returned home and dumped in the river. I just said, "Yeah right." After that, we didn't speak to each other at all. I would kick the end of his bed to wake him up for count, and of course he would give me a dirty look. After a while he tried to make life miserable for me by leaving the lights on all night, playing music through the night, just like the black guys that were in my room in Bridgewater. It got to the point that I got a room change. I moved into a room with a young kid that was across the hall. It sounded good, but this kid was controlled by my old roommate because he was scared of him. It even got to the point that I had to defend myself against a few guys because of him calling them on me, but I took on all comers. After a while it stopped. I did what I had to do. I said next time, I told him, I was going to bring it to him. I told him not to worry. It would be real fast and he wouldn't know what hit him until he woke up. He left me alone after that. After that, I just went with it. I just wanted my time to end and go home, so I either would stay in the weight room to work out or walk the track or make cards to pass time and tried not to make waves. When I was down to a year, I would scrap months, weeks, and days into the table that I made cards on even larger than I did previously. This was done every day just to help me cope with the shit I was going through. Staying away from the old man was the best thing to do at the time, so I wouldn't bust him in the face like I almost did with the young kid that I was in the room with. I started to realize that my time was really coming to an end. I would be going home, kept telling myself it wasn't that far-off. Believe me, doing close to five years in this fuckin' nuthouse was a real long time. The good part of it all was that I could see the end of my stay in this fuckin' place. Well, what I mean was I was under a year. To most guys in here, they would consider that to be short time. This means I was going home very soon. To stay away from Mr. Mafia and his sidekick was easy because for me to stay away from pieces of shit like them would be like turning off the radio. All this so-called Mafia wannabe that wanted to be what he claimed he was, but all he could do was dream about him being in the Mafia, but all he could ever be was a Mafia wannabe. He was too stupid to be in the Mafia. Being as stupid as he was, he probably would have been used, and then he would disappear because of his stupidity. This was because he probably would have shot himself on a hit and would never have made it to be as old as he was. He wanted to drive me nuts like the ones I had in Bridgewater. He would have to try much harder after the black guys I had to deal with. But as I looked around, I realized that I was outnumbered, was surrounded by scum, that was including the COs, not just inmates. At this time, I was still carrying so much hate in me that I felt that I was about to snap at any time, but I would just go outside, think about where I was, and I would calm down. I would just look around and realize that I was surrounded by so much scum. I hurt so bad inside that I want to break down, but I only did this when I'm in the shower, where no one can see me. I miss my daughter so much because she was the only one I had left now after my wife left me to go on with life that she had left. Those were the exact words that she used. As I was thinking about my life, I realized how much I had lost being in jail. I didn't want to see the shrink because, as I said, she didn't do me any good. She really couldn't help me. The only one that can help me is me. It took me a long time to figure this out. It just got to the point that I had to tell myself what to do to ease the pain, and that was to block everything out all around me, taking it one day at a time, as the alcoholics do with the twelve-step programs. This is what I needed to do for the rest of the time I had left to do. I still looked like a bum in here. I just can't believe that I have done so much time in a place like this, put up with so much shit more than I ever put up with on the street. I would have never put up with what I was dealing with if I was out on the street, never ever. I just looked over at the calendar.

As I'm writing this, it's March 3, 2003, and I have ten months left to do. I still see my wife's face as clear as the day I last saw her, hoping that she will come back. This was torture to me the whole time that I was incarcerated. I was still thinking that as soon as my wife sees me when I get out, she's going to come back to me, but really I know this will never happen. It just helps me. Things like what I was thinking makes you do your time better. It doesn't hurt that much, at least you kept telling yourself this. Even after all the shit that I went through, I keep telling myself all I really wanted was to get my life and my wife back and hope that I adjust to the outside again. Sounds crazy doesn't it. Then after that, I have my daughter and grandson waiting for me. I couldn't wait to see how big he had grown. I guess the first thing I can try to do is to see what I have lost in the five years that I was gone from my grandson and daughter. He now was getting to be a big boy. The letters and cards I sent them are just things that are coming from my heart. To them it must look stupid, but I do these things to keep my mind active, my mind straight. Before this all happened, my best friends were my wife, my sister-in-law, of course my friend John Mello, but they all drifted away, left me to rot in this place. What a surprise, a wake-up call that was to me. I was like in a dream state. The biggest hurt to me was my sister-in-law. We were really close, but she just turned her back on me. I was there when she needed me, but that's the way things are when you go to jail. I just could have gotten more letters from her, but what I did get they made me very happy. She was so much fun to be around; I had a great time with her as I did with my daughter's mother, until she just wanted to hang around with her so-called friends she made who fucked her over also. At this time it wasn't long before she kicked me to the curb and was just going out with her friends now nightclubbing. That wasn't for me, like my wife, I was getting phone calls telling me that she was messing around with different guys. I never wanted to believe it because I was taking too many stupid pills. All the things you take for granted you tend to think about when you're in a place like this. All you can do is reminisce about the past because there is no future when you're doing time. You just think about what you did all the time when you were on the outside if you're somewhat normal. What I find hard to understand is why my wife, my daughter's mother said that no matter what, we will always be friends, but as the time we had together came to an end, we became like we never knew each other. But no matter what, I will always remember all the great times I had with them, how much I loved them both. Why couldn't my wife be like my sister-in-law and drive around, just do things, but no, whenever we went out, we had to have a destination or she didn't want to go. When we got home, all she wanted to do was get all fucked up on coke. What a fuckin' life. I sometimes wonder if she realized what she lost.

In here I get along with what they call the real bad guys, the ones who attempt to kill their girlfriends or family members, of course for no good reasons or reasons that no one wants to hear about, but I have an ear for it. But there are always good reasons, but like I have said, no wants to hear the whole story. As in my case, they just say put them in jail. He was caught with drugs. The real good story was that I was selling drugs up the whole East Coast, at the school that I was teaching at (assholes). Now we can't forget the bank robbers who rob from the banks who rob from you when you go back on a payment. They don't hesitate to steal what you have worked your whole life for. I've talked to a lot of the guys who ripped off banks one time or another; they do it out of desperation most of the time. Who are the crooks in this case. I know this because I've almost lost my home a couple of times with no help whatsoever from the bank to help me to refinance. This jail that I'm at now is Norfolk Minimum, a decent place. I'll never forget where I'm at, but what makes it bad is the scum, the no-brainers, dumb motherfuckers who need to be told when to dress, when to wash, so on.

Again the whole time that I've been incarcerated, I've been surrounded by pure scum. Let me rephrase this. Lots of guys, most of the COs that I'm in here with are pure scum, will be scum as long as they live. These places, or let me say these jails, will never change them, but look at it this way, guys and COs will always have a home to come to. The stockholders want it this way. Let's say eight out of ten are just pure scum. They just stay with their own, but I still get along with the rest but watch myself very closely because I'm just careful, don't want to get caught up in the mix. It takes all I have to keep my head together in this place. I think most of the time that I'm losing my mind because I'm still in a real bad fog, but I now think it's because of where I'm at, like the shrink had said to me. Right now I'm still at Norfolk Minimum. It's been the best place that I've been at, as I've said, still can't believe how clean it is for a jail. The COs make sure of that. At this time I was still wasn't getting any money from the street. I was still making cards in the unit to be able to eat different food than what they gave to us to eat in the mess hall. It was all that, a mess hall. The Muslims make things even worse because they won't eat meat. Like really, a lot of them did because a lot of them ate a lot of the food I made in the unit lots of times; they knew what I put in it. Because of the Muslims, just about everything in the prison kitchen is made out of turkey meat. Of course, again, its meat.

One of the guys I worked out with was an artist that drew from photographs of people. After the workout that we were doing, we went back to his room, and he showed me a lot of his drawings that he had drawn of people. As we got back to his room, we had to wait till his roommate left because he was a real dickhead as the one I had in my room. He started to show me some of the things that he had drawn; I was shocked. It was some of the best drawings that I'd ever seen. As I was going through his drawing that he had done, I was looking at real people. Sometimes it looked like they were looking at me. I just had to touch them. The guy wasn't good. No, he was great.

BUSTED

It was so good that I couldn't put it into words. It was all done in colored pencils that we got from the canteen and, of course, some magic markers. His name was Antonio Rodriquez. I just couldn't take my eyes off some of the work that he had done, right in front of me. I watched him do it right in front of me. He did it so damn fast that I just couldn't believe my eyes. He took a picture of my grandson, drew a picture of him in about eight minutes just for the heck of it, and it looked exactly like picture I gave him to draw from. Another good thing about it, this guy wasn't a rip-off. He was just damn good, no, great. He really enjoyed what he did. He was doing his work for food, as I was. He just enjoyed to hear how people got off on what he did. As we started to talk, I realized that we both had roommates that in one way or another had trouble getting along with. But when it came to his roommate, all he had to do was to feed him with the food that he was getting from a drawing that he made and things would be tolerable. When it came to my roommate, he thought he was a main man in the Mafia. He was just a crusty, fucked-up-in-the-head old guy who told pretty good stories, but that was all he could, dream up stories. I really think he had done them. But after a while, it started to sound like reruns of movies that he had seen one time or another because if it was true, you never talk about stuff like he was. Telling me you take things like that with you when it's your time to die.

When I told my artist buddy about my roommate, he just started to laugh and told me that he had heard some of his stories also. He wasn't as gullible as I was. It was just some of the stories he told me about a guy he tied up in his cellar and killed him because he ripped him off for some watches he had stolen from a jewelry store and didn't get a cut from it. It got to the point that he didn't wash up and was stinking up the room real bad. There was white hair all over the place. He started to order me around, and I just told him to fuck off. Then in one conversation, he told me that I was going to get bumped off when I got out of jail. I just paid no attention to what he said and just laughed at what he said. The guy Tony, the artist I was writing about, laughed about the things I told my roommate and what my roommate said back to me. With the money that we both made from his drawing, my cards, we started to buy food together to cook. At the same time, he taught me another way of cooking the food that we were getting through the canteen. The food that we were stealing from the kitchen he showed me how to cook the food that we got. It came out even better than the way all the other Spanish guys showed me how to do it. We cooked all the food we made in a hot pot that we rigged to heat up and boil. It's so weird, but I still cook the food that I made in jail. A lot of people ask me where I learned to cook the food I cook to this day. I just think about it, just say it's a family thing, and laugh to myself and say, if they only knew.

This guy would just pull out work that he had done as we were eating. This was work that he had done over the years. I just wanted to send it all home no matter what it was because it was that good. I guess it's because my father was an artist also, but not too much with portraits, more ocean, land pictures, but he was also good. Being with this guy from time to time made life a lot better because the work he was doing helped put my mind at ease. But when I left his room, I still would look around, look at what I had to deal with, the scum inmates, the fucked up COs that were still causing problems. I did my best to block them all out. Hinny Wrecker still busted my balls every chance he got, but I just took it all in, kept saying to myself this will not be forever. I will be out very soon, so I just have to put up with his shit a little longer. At one time as he was drawing a picture, and he asked me why I wrote so many letters. I told him that someday I was planning to write a book about this place, say in it how fucked the COs are, what I went through from day to day. Then he turned, looked at me, and said, "Really. Don't forget to put me in it."

"Of course." I laughed.

Then he said, "You will forget about me when you leave this place, like most people do."

I said to him, "This will be burned into my brain until I die."

I hope he reads this knowing I didn't forget him. Now that he said something like that to me, I will copy and put the drawing in at the end of the book that he had done for me. This other guy that I met while cleaning the rooms was named George Sylvia. He was also in jail doing time for drugs but was straight in the head and helped me more than once with a good conversation and better than the shrinks did. Real good guy. He was also skeptical when I told that I was going to take all my letters and follow up with a book. He was able to get a job making decent money in a rehab center. I wish him the best.

Now getting back to this hellhole, I remember lots of times the COs would do shakedowns, and we would have to leave the rooms. Along with getting strip-searched, all our things in our rooms would just get thrown in one big pile after they threw out what they thought we shouldn't have, considered contraband to the COs. These COs would just take things from the guy who drew, take a lot of my stuff, just say these were things we didn't need, and just throw it in the garbage or just say that we couldn't have it just to be assholes, so we thought. But a lot of times I would be put in the property room to help the property officer who just about never worked as all the rest. I was told to throw lots of things out, but one way or another, I would get it back to the decent guys again. Fuck the asshole guys. I never saw any of the artwork that my friend had done in the trash.

I was still calling my daughter and asking her if my big Boston lawyer called. Of course, he hadn't; that was the answer I was expecting. I started to pay inmates to write the letters I needed to my first lawyer on the computer that was in the unit, but you could just go so far with it. I was hoping that I would get back to me on getting me all my transcripts from the trial so I could have the entire thing that the narcs wrote about me in court. The lawyer from the Overseers that worked to get my money back didn't fuck around. These guys were great. They had an attorney named Mr. Geller assigned to my case to help me with the money that was taken from me. This guy didn't mess around. As I wrote, he got most of my money back. The money that I didn't get back was the money that my wife kept and said she never got it, that she had given it to the lawyer. Well, she should have worked for my so-called great Boston lawyer because she was a crook as well as he was. I guess this was money she used to help powder her nose. It was money that she didn't have to suck cock for. So messed up.

I was going to come out of jail no job, and there my wife is taking money I could have used to start anew. When I would ask her about it she still insisted that she gave it all to the lawyer until I sent her the letters from the bar, then she never said another word about it, never responded to my letters either. In all the time after that, I would say I hope my wife fuckin' choked on the money that she stole from me, but it never happened. I was still counting the months and days on the calendar, scribbling it on the outside tables that I drew on as I was drawing my cards that I made from office folders. This helped me cope with all the shit I had to put up with, but it just lasted for the short periods in which I was drawing, but it also kind of took me out of there. I started to go to bed even earlier just so the next day would come so I could cross it off the calendar because I wanted to go home so bad. To me I paid my dues to society after the first year. I think I knew in my heart that they gave me too much time for what I was accused of doing. The court gave me five years on a first offense for keeping my wife supplied because I couldn't take my hard-earned cash to pay for her cocaine habit. I didn't know what else to do because of my love for my wife. But I never took into consideration that I could be killing her and had no thoughts that it could do so. I think about it now, wonder what other guys would have done if they were in the same situation that I was in. Would they do the same for their spouses? Of course, the narcs informed the courts that I supplied the whole East Coast; if this was true, I know some big-timer would for sure have taken me out for doing something like that. If I was doing something like that, I would like to know where all the fuckin' money is that I would have made.

I look at it now. It was a long time before I was able to get a move to Pond Ville, but to me it still was the best stop that I was ever at. I think about it now, and it reminds me now of a retirement home for insane people, but it was better kept than all the other places that I was at. There was no shit in the showers. But like all the others places that I was at, all the COs were and probably still are fuckin' assholes and were always fucking things up for everyone. But as long as you stood away from the COs as they were coming around, you were okay, especially Hinny Wrecker, his fucked-up brother, who always kept his eye on me. When his brother Hinny Wrecker went home, his fucked up brother took over and worked upstairs in the office next to my room. I called them fat and skinny. They looked alike, and in my heart they must have come from the same fucked-up mother and father because they acted the same ways. Of course they were both pure garbage. When I was working at the garage, Hinny Wrecker worked days most of the times. He was gone when I got back from the garage unless he worked overtime. That was somewhat good, but I had to keep an eye out for his fucked-up brother who was always on the prowl. But when morning came, I had to put up with him because he was the one who dropped us off at our workstations. He would make it a priority to drop me off last, always made the fucked-up eye contact with me but I would just turn away because I was living in his house, as they say to me all the time. Now if I see him on the street, I know the hate would still be in my heart just for all the dirty looks, the hard labor he put me through. Then I'd give him the stare that he gave me every time he saw me to see if he had the balls to give the look he gave me. This was all because I heard him say that he wanted to fuck the woman CO named Tracy in the ass. That's all it took, that's when the hate for each other started from just a glance from him because of what I heard him say. When I went to the superintendent told this CO that I called Hinny Wrecker to lay off me so I was told, but this superintendent was just a figurehead. What he said didn't amount to much because this CO did things to me on a low level. The Superintendent never followed up with my complaint. I was too close to going home to be lugged behind the wall. I just wanted as easy as it could be till it was time to go home. I kept my eye on him whenever it was possible. I saw him go home one night and thought it would be a good time to make a phone call, as I always did on a Tuesday. I thought I could make it in peace. I sat on the floor and started to talk to my daughter when his brother came out of the office. He looked at me sitting on the floor and said, "This is no vacation spot. Get the fuck up." I looked at him, said that I knew that it wasn't a vacation spot. I did ask him if I was bothering anyone, and he then said that I bothered him all the time. I was told that I was in his house. Then he said, "You do what I say, do what I tell you to do when I say it. Get the fuck up, stand when you're talking on the phone." I looked at him and started to mumble to myself under my breath. He then said, "Do you want to get out of here?" I turned and stated that I didn't say anything. He then he said any noise coming from me wouldn't be coming from inside Pond Ville, it would coming from behind the wall in a maximum prison. Now again I just wanted to finish my time where I was then just go home, but it seem more and more difficult to do. As every day went by, it seemed like everyone just wanted to mess with me. But it could have been or maybe because they knew my time was coming to an end, but I really don't know and don't really give a damn. So after he said this to me, I just hung up the phone, then I went back to my room. I didn't see him again for the rest of the night. At that moment, I had so much hate inside of me that I couldn't even now explain how mad I was at that time.

Even now knowing that I've been out of that place for a time, it still gets me so mad that I had to walk away from writing this and continue later in the day. If he was going to have me lugged, it didn't bother me too much anymore because I've been in the worst of the worst, but having to wait to talk to someone on the phone for two weeks would be the hardest because it takes at least that long to get your calls cleared. Plus getting lugged now to me would be going backward. I didn't want to go back to Concord; also I feel I've lived in hell long enough. Now at this time I was making a good amount of canteen by just making cards, sewing some clothes in here, thanks to my daughter's mother who taught me how to sew. Right now I'm making the big bucks working for grounds, making a whole five dollars a week. Yes, five dollars a week, but it just taught me how to live cheap. I worked so hard for the five dollars a week because everyone wanted my job that I was doing because of the cigarettes that you could pick up on the job, which I stopped doing because of Hinny Wrecker watching me all the time. I hated this fuckin' asshole CO with all my heart. The only thing that was on my mind was that I was on my way home. I didn't want to risk it, so I stood away from just about everyone. The only reason for this was that I just didn't want to get caught up in the mix. Otherwords I didn't want to get into any shit. I couldn't believe that I was so close to going home, just had my daughter and grandson on my mind.

At this time he was just turning five years old, and I was just hoping that he wouldn't be scared of me when I came home, after he's seen me. My artist friend was just about the only one I could say what was on my mind to and not worry about it getting around the prison. This was how much I trusted my artist friend. The only thing that I didn't tell him was that I was getting scared to go home in a way because of the way I was cooped up in jail. He was working on a picture for me. It was a drawing of me and of my grandson being held in the arms of a dragon along with my two Dobermans. Alongside of them was my daughter running beside me dressed in the medieval clothes. He didn't let me see it till the end of the day. When I saw it, I was just lost for words. Well, it must have taken him about two days to do it. It was fantastic—No, Great. He drew it on a bedsheet, and believe me, it looked just like me and my daughter. I think he charged me ten dry soups, a couple of sodas. This guy would get bedsheets and pillowcases and just draw on them, but when the COs would raid his room, which was all the time, they would tell him not to do it because it was State Property that he was drawing on, but he still did it anyways because it was his way of doing his time. These COs go home at night and they don't have to think about time as we do, so we do what we have to to pass time. Whenever they do a raid on his room, they would take all his drawings away. They did this on a regular basis. I've seen them throw all his drawings in the garbage, or so it looked like. I think about it now when I was still working with the property officer from time to time, and I never saw any of the drawings that the COs took from him in the Dumpster. I really think the COs who took his drawings kept them for themselves because they were that good. I would look around and never saw any of the stuff that was taken from his room in the Dumpster. When they raided both of our rooms, they took a lot of the stuff from our rooms. The drawing he did for me that the COs never got was now framed is now is hanging in one of my rooms. I show it off every chance I get. I'm glad I had a chance to own one of his pictures that he did. He did call me once, and he told me that he was working in a tattoo parlor. I can just imagine some of the work he must have put out. I never heard from him ever again but wish him well. Who knows, maybe he will read this book, and he will contact me. We can get together, talk about the shit we went through in the fucked-up prison system that we were at. They lock you away and try real hard to erase your past life away, along with all your memories. To this day I know there is something wrong with me, like there is something missing inside of me. I really think I will never get it back because I think what they took from me was part of my soul.

My time was coming to an end real fast, and I just couldn't wait. I would listen to different songs that were related to me leaving this place, going home, especially the one by Queen. Being locked up in these four walls, hate just went through my body. I really hated the court system, all the COs that treated all of us like animals. I hope the worst on the prosecutor that put me in here. The CO Hinny Wrecker, the property officer would say to me, "See you on your next trip in." I would say, "You will never see me again in a place like this." I was really thinking how I would love to see any one of them again on the outside, fuckin' scumbags, see if they wanted to speak to me the way they did in jail.

Not long after, the CO that they called Rocket called me in again for a job change because the guy went home who cleaned the showers or maybe he got lugged, one or the other. He asked me if I wanted his job cleaning the showers, mopping the floors along with throwing out the garbage late night after count. He would tell me to be downstairs as soon as they cleared count. Every time I did as he asked me, I went there directly. Sometimes I would be there like he told me to be to do what was expected of me. He would say, "Go back to your room," tell me that he wasn't ready for me yet. He was always fucking with me every chance he got, just like his buddy Hinny Wrecker. Most of the time when they called count cleared, the Spanish guys would be there and start to push the guys aside to get all the easy jobs, because there were so damn many of them, just like the blacks. I wasn't going to fight over some fucked-up job just for five dollars a week, so I would just stay back and wait so that those kiss-ass motherfuckers got what they wanted. I don't really know this for sure, but one day the CO Rocket was outside walking around, and he saw me drawing. He came up to me and asked me if I knew how to scrape paint. I said yes, ad he said that he wanted it done right, not like the other guys did for him. I asked him what he wanted done, and he said that he wanted some building painted around the unit, asked if I could do it. I said that I did a lot of painting on my home. He looked at me and said, "You have a home." I said yes and just ended it there before he said something stupid to me. Well, the next day waiting for the painting job that Rocket wanted me to do, he told me to report to his office after count cleared. So the next day I went down to his office, and when I got there, that fuckin' dickhead Hinny Wrecker was in the office and said that Rocket had to leave. He said, "You're here to paint, right?" I said yes. He glanced up at me from the book he was writing in and said in a cocky way, "You know how to paint?' I said yes, then he said, "You're a drug dealer, aren't you?" I just blew it off and didn't answer him, as I did to all the other COs who asked the same question. As I was standing there, he then looked at me and said, "Don't you see the paint on the floor?" I said yes, then he said, "Start painting." I looked at him then said, "Where?" He said "I'll show you" in his pissed off way. It looked like it was going to kill him to get up (Scumbag). I started to follow him, and he turned to me and said, "Well, pick up the paint. You don't think I'm going to pick it up. You're the convict, not me." So I picked up the paint, and he showed me a large building and said, "You do know how to scrape paint off a building before you paint."

I said, "I painted houses on the outside."

He looked at me and said, "We will see. After that I want the gym done also. If you do it right, I give you different jobs around here to last you until you go home. I want it done right."

I thought he was setting me up for a fall and was very careful of what he had me do all the time. I would look around to make sure he wasn't going to put in a place that I would be out of bounds. All I was saying to myself was I hope Rocket gets back. Hinny Wrecker went back to his other asshole detail of fuckin' around with all the other guys, leaving me the hell alone. Well, Rocket did come back the next day, and he checked out what I had done. He was pleased I think for what I had got done the day before. He then looked at me and told me to ignore the count, when they called it, to keep painting; he would tell the CO in charge that I was outside painting. I just said okay. The count came, and to me it was real weird not to be standing for count. It was taking a real long time for count to clear. All of a sudden, the CO came out and started to yell at me and said that I was out of place. I said that Rocket told me to ignore the count, keep working, he will tell whoever is in charge that I was working outside. He looked at me and said, "I don't care who told you to ignore the count. I want you to be there for count no matter what. No one told me anything."

Well, Rocket came back and told me that he wanted me to paint the inside of the gym next. He never said anything of what happened the day before. I didn't tell him either. I was all for painting the gym. This kept all the Spanish guys out, and I was able to work out for most of the week. I was all by myself, and it was great until the Spanish guys started to complain and ratted me out. The CO in charge came out to talk to me, and I just said that I was just waiting for the paint to dry but never told him that I was using the weights in between painting. I had good workouts before the CO caught me himself. When I finished painting the gym, Rocket gave me the job I was doing before I started to paint the building, and that was cleaning the unit again, taking the garbage out, washing the toilets and showers again. This was after night count, and this took a while. No one could use the toilets till I was done. I loved to make them wait, pieces of shit. To me it was just payback. This job was just at night after count, and then in the morning till noontime, that was enough for me. After late-night count, at night the inmates would be pissed off because they were not allowed to use the restrooms till I was done, and I took my time. They got so mad over this the guys were wiping shit all over the place on the walls, on the floors. A lot of times they would jerk off on the inside of the stalls, all over the toilets. Good thing they had gloves or I wouldn't want to do it. Again this kept me out of my room that because of my wannabe mobster roommate was across the hall now, would be telling my new roommate, which was another asshole, his bed time bullshit stories that he was still telling me at one time. He was as gullible as I was. But if I look at it, most of the guys in here knew guys that were in the Mafia and had stories to tell, of course all the dirty deeds they had to do for the so-called Mafia, and a lot of them were in for stupid crimes. Of course they were doing hits for them (bullshit).

The stories that I heard coming from my old roommate's mouth I couldn't even count how many he told me he had done or even believe any of them if I tried. The best were killing stories; there were a lot of them. Of course most of the guys that were telling these stories were in jail. Of course they all ended up to be bullshit stories or figments of their imaginations but loved to hear themselves talk. I knew it was lies right from the start, as soon as the story started with the Mafia. But what beat them all was still my old roommate, how he cut up a guy, took all the stuff this guy got from a jewelry store robbery, which was gold watches, bracelets, etc. But the whole time he was in jail, all he wore was a cheap Casio watch, no TV, and asked all the churches for money to help him while he was in jail. The only thing that he had that was good was the Casio watch, which was the best watch to have while in jail because they really last. It's a great-built watch. To this day as I think about it, and I think he watched too many late-night gangster movies. He was just was reenacting stuff he saw on TV, but the best one was when he said that he knew guys like Whitie Bugler and all his right-hand men. I just couldn't believe it. I just busted out and laughed at him. He was really too stupid to have known these guys. The thing I noticed was when he was telling the story he would be talking from the corner of his mouth. That was his giveaway. This so-called big-time mobster was in jail for the third time for drunk driving, so I really believed his stories. (Not.) To believe him was just like believing all the guys in here that told me similar stories unless they showed me the proof of what they were telling me.

Yes, the whole time in jail I had just nothing but assholes for roommates, but at least this one was white. The worst thing about the stories that pissed me off was most of them were the same stories over and over again. A lot of times I would pray for him to fall asleep, shut his damn mouth, and let me watch my TV programs that mostly never happened. I started to let things go in one ear, out the other. I really started to stay to myself, as I usually did, just walked the track, weight lifted. I was glad I moved out of the room that he was in. Still on my days after I was done with my so-called job, I still worked on my cards outside on the tables just to pass the long days, making cards mostly for this guy Bobby who was in a wheelchair. A really good guy who had great stories about what he did on the outside, what he got caught for, how much jail time he had gotten. This guy always wanted me to make cards for him because it was his way of keeping in touch with the outside, as it did for me. The cards that he bought from me made a decent canteen for me, and I needed it at that time to buy stamps to send home. You will know why I did the stamp thing as the story goes on. I helped this guy Bobby out a lot of times, cutting his toenails and fingernails because the doctors never wanted to do it for him. He showed me it, and I almost got sick when I saw his toenails. They were all curled up and yellow. I did it because my father would tell me how much it would bother him when he had the same problem. The doctors, as I said before, were real bad in jail. They would put you off all the time, just never wanted to do what was expected of them. To me, most of them were unexperienced anyways or had their heads up their asses. What I did for him in cards, clipping his nails, amounted to very large canteens. My friend the artist would cook, and I would supply the food, of course give some to my wheelchair friend also. The showers in this place were real dirty. It was real hard for the handicapped guys to wash. After I clipped his toenails, I wouldn't touch anything at all. I had to leave right away just to wash my hands, just couldn't help myself. In this place that I was at, it was just like all the other places. The COs, they didn't give a damn if we were found dead during the night. They probably leave whomever there till the next shift came in. These COs were and are in here just for the money, to do as little as possible. If they had to get up, it would be just to go to the room to shine the flashlight in everyone's faces till they were to wake up just to do something because they were bored. The only time they were to get up was if someone was coming in, and they needed the room for another inmate. When they called this guy Bobby, who was in the wheelchair, for the appointment that he had made, he would say, "Forget it. It was already done, say no more." Then the CO would ask him who cut his nails, and he would say that he did it, because if he said me, I would get lugged and sent behind the wall. I really think the COs knew that I was the one who had cut his nails because Bobby would bullshit for hours sometimes. He would tell me he would rather me doing his nails because the medical people in were real bad. If you were to see them for a cold, we would have to wait for our canteen to come in for the medication that we needed to treat the colds that we had. If we didn't have any money in our canteen, we were screwed and would have to deal with it. That meant we had to suffer or trade off something we had for something we needed. Today I was called up to Rocket's office, and he told me to see if I could find out who is still shitting in the waste barrels, tell him who it was. I just told him that I would keep my eyes open. (Like hell I would.)

Well, I picked all the cleaning supplies that I needed while I was there, what they would let me use, and when I got to the bathroom that Rocket said that guys were shitting in, I saw a guy standing outside the door, and he asked me if I could come back in a little while. I just looked at him and said, "I told the guy at the door that Rocket wanted the cleaning supplies back." I said I wanted to get it over with so I could fuck off for the rest of the day. So as I walked into the bathroom, there was a guy sitting over a trash barrel. I said, "What the fuck are you doing? Are you shitting in the barrels." He looked at me and said that he was trying to pass out some cigarettes, a lighter that he stuffed up his ass.

I said, "Are you kidding me?"

He said, "No, it might take a while." He said that he thought that I was a CO coming in.

I then said that he just had to make sure he wrapped up the bag after. I'll take it out after. I walked out and just couldn't understand how he could do such a thing to stick stuff up your ass. I then asked him afterward, "Are you the one that's wiping shit all over the walls?"

He looked at me and just said, "I'm just trying to get this stuff out of my ass, not wiping shit on the walls. I'm not shitting, just trying to get this out of my ass."

I guess this was just his way of making money. Everyone has their way in this fucked-up place to make money. Cigarettes were going for three to five dollars a cigarettes. It depended on the person, so I was told. I guess this was a good score for him. I came back later in the day, and there was no sign of what he was doing; he got rid of the bag somehow. I did see him later in the week, and he brought me over some canteen and said this was for not saying anything to the COs. I just said, "Keep your stuff." I didn't want anything. I said, "So long as you clean up after, I didn't have to."

The whole time that I was in jail, on the street, I never ratted on anyone. When I get out back on the street, I will never have to watch my back when I'm walking down the street. When I get out of this place either. Today CO Rocket called me down to his office; he asked me if I had seen anyone shitting in the barrels, and I said that I haven't seen anyone doing that as yet. I never told him that I did see a guy trying to remove cigarettes from his ass over a barrel, but again he wasn't shitting. To me I was just doing what he gave me for a job and that's it. If he wanted a rat, he would have to look somewhere else. But as the day went on, I was hoping that it wasn't a setup when he asked me if I had seen anyone shitting in the barrels because there are so many rats in jail. You don't know who to trust. It was real weird. He looked at me for the longest time after I said what I said, but I paid no attention to his staring at me, just waited for him to tell me what to do for that day. The shitting thing was happening more and more often. I knew that it wasn't the guy that I saw because he was using a different bathroom. I really didn't care because I was going home real soon. To me it wasn't my problem. He had plenty of guys that would turn in their mothers for a coffee. I guess because I wasn't giving Rocket any information, he just gave me more and more to do. Now seeing that he put me back on grounds work, again he gave me to Hinny Wrecker for snow removal. He sent me out cleaning snow in front of Norfolk where the COs would enter, said that he wanted me out every hour on the hour. He wanted it down to pavement. These COs were so lazy that no matter how much snow there was, they would call the inmates to clean it up. It was like they were allergic to work no matter what kind of work it was. The whole time that I was in prison, I never had any good clothes until I traded for good stuff. But when it came to most of the guys, they were all messed up unless you had the money to buy it through the canteen. Now when it came to the way most of the inmates looked and dressed, let me put it this way. If we were standing outside on a street corner with a cup, they would consider us as to be homeless people. Now think about it. This is how bad we were treated by the property officer. He kept the clothes in the property room. It was like they belonged to him, not the State. I remember putting plastic bags over my socks to keep my feet somewhat dry. When I went out to shovel the snow in front of the prison, most of us had just sneakers, no boots. If we bitched, they would say that they could find a place behind the wall where we didn't need any boots or worry about working. Sometimes when my shift was over, the lazy motherfuckers who would sleep instead of shoveling early in the morning or wait till the COs called them would cry because there would be a lot of snow to be shoveled. Of course Hinny Wrecker would say I did a bad job, tell me to go back out, help the Spanish guys that were crying about the amount of snow that there was to be shoveled. The reason why Hinny Wrecker treated me so bad was because of what I heard him tell his brother about the woman CO that was in Pond Ville, the one who left to be a State Trooper, Tracy.

Now I was down to months, was trying to find ways to get home when I was released from this place. I didn't even know where I was. I knew it was in Norfolk, but where the fuck is Norfolk. I wrote a letter to my divorced wife asking her if she could send me a train schedule so I could find out where I was and study it to be able to find my way home, but I never got an answer from her, but that's what I expected from her. But what I was really hoping for was for her to pick me up and bring me back home, seeing that she didn't do a damn thing for me the whole time I was in prison. She could have sent some sort of reply, but then I realized that she had a new fuck partner now and had no use for me now. But at this time, I was writing to this guy named Allen Pearl that I was incarcerated with at SECC. I told him what I was going through, and he said not to let it bother me, that he would come up to get me, bring me back home.

Now whenever I saw Hinny Wrecker, I didn't let him bother me anymore. I just went on with my daily chores and just didn't make any eye contact with him. I just stood away from him when I could, just walked the other way when I would see him coming.

When I ran into him with no choice of my own, he would give me that "fuck you" look. Just followed me with his eyes as I passed because he knew I was ready to go home. It was probably tearing him apart knowing he didn't get a chance to lug me. Seeing that I was on the way out, if any of the COs gave me a hard time, I would have put in a request to speak to the superintendent again. This was to get this fat piece-of-shit Wrecker off my back because he would send his puppets after me because of the earlier complaint I made about him. Hinny Wrecker was a waste of oxygen to me. If I was able to see him now, I would bring to him and tell him to kill himself (Scumbag). It was on a Sunday. I was in the rec room, and I needed to use the bathroom. When I looked into the urinal to take a piss, I saw Hinny Wrecker's son's picture stuck to the back of most of the urinals. Guys were taking a piss on them because the urinal was full of piss. It wasn't being flushed. It looked like no one had flushed any of them in a long while. I thought I was the only one who hated him, but it looked like he was well hated by everyone. I know now that there were other guys who hated this German piece of shit. By the looks of it, they hated him as much as I did. They brought this right to his family. That's real bad. He must have seen it because he was in a fucked-up mood all week, didn't see him fucking around with too many guys. As I thought about it, I just laugh about it, said what goes around comes around. He deserved everything he got.

During the last week as he walked by me, he paid no attention to me. That was real good. I think he was in his own world because of what went on with the picture of his son being in the pisser. So now he must know what it feels like to be fucked with. but this was just one thing that happened to him. Just imagine if something like that was happening to you every day. I really didn't have anything to do with it but would have felt better if it was his picture instead of his son's, but I still did piss on it and said, "Fuck you, slimy bastard, what you brought into this world."

BUSTED

This is now December seventh just before Christmas. I was now down to a month. I was getting excited to go home but was scared also because I didn't know what to expect. All I had on my mind when I got home was to hug my daughter and grandson but was also scared to see them. What I wanted so bad was to show my daughter Lisa the picture the guy Tony drew of us together side by side. The weird thing about it was that I was just scared, and the only thing that was on my mind was to show my daughter the picture that I had got from the guy in jail. Now that I'm reading what I wrote in my letters I sent home to people and to my daughter, I really realize I lost my thought of what it was on the outside. When it came down to weeks I started to give a lot of what I had to the guy Tony who drew the picture for me but held on to some things. Why I did this I really don't know. Prison life really messed up my way of thinking. I started to realize it, and it really scared me even more. I kind of knew it would take a while for me to get back to my old self, at least that's what I was hoping for, but it never happened. I'm still lost in the prison system. It was really hard holding on to my sanity. I just kept saying it will be over very soon, don't let them take control of me. I kept telling myself not to let them get into my head. This was an everyday thing that took up a lot of space in my head. But lots of times I would slip away from their brainwashing technique and just think of my old life, how happy I was being married but not looking at what drugs was doing to both my wife and myself. You're just blinded to the fact. When guys knew that I was going home, they would tell me that it was bad luck to take anything home with me because it means that I'm saying to myself I'm going to return but this was their way of getting what I had but I was giving away to my friend Tony. What I can say to those guys is fuck them all. Those are the assholes who never did anything for me but wanted what I had. All of a sudden they knew me. This was just another jail thing that guys pump into your head when it's your time comes to an end. It just was one of the stupidest thing I ever heard. Even where my head was at that time, I still found it to be stupid. Now all I had to wait for was for Dartmouth to send Norfolk the time I spent there. They would deduct it from the time I had left; they were taking their sweet time doing so. I asked if I could stop doing my so-called job there, but Mr. Dickhead Hinny Wrecker said, "Not till the day you leave." They told me. "We might give you a half a day off." I looked at him with so much hate in me that if he had been there when I left, I would have told him to eat shit and die. I didn't give a damn what he said. I let it go. I just said fuck it. It was a mess till the day I left. What were they going to do, lug me for a couple of days?

This place like all the other places that I was at was one large nest of assholes. All the COs were. Not one of them was a decent CO in the whole fuckin' place. I guess this is part of their training that they go through. What really toped it off was their fucked-up programs, which amounted to nothing. It was twelve steps. The program was run by an ex-drug addict. The prosecutor, she was on my case all the time, said that I would go right back on drugs when I got out. Her name was Pane. I changed her name as I did to others in this story, but I asked her if I could stop going to the program because I was going home. She said that I needed it more than anyone that was in the program now. This was because I was on my way out. She then said the reason for this is because I'm going to be around drugs. I'm going to start hanging around with my old friends, so most likely I'll go back on drugs. I looked at her and said that I wasn't going to hunt down any of my old friends. I never hung around any street corners before this. My only friend was my wife, and she went on with her life with someone else. She just said no, told me to start reading the twelve-step book because she has dealt with guys like me before. We all thought we were better than everyone else; we just couldn't see it. I told her that my junkie wife was gone; she's going out with another guy that could take care of her cocaine needs and won't need me anymore. She told me no, so I had no choice but to stay for the meeting, and I told her at the end of the meeting that she had no right to judge me. At the end of the meeting, I talked to her and said that she didn't know me, had no idea what I was going to do when I got out of this place. I then told her that I would send her a card after a couple of months to let her know if I went back on drugs. I did send her a card, more or less told her that she was wrong, said I didn't go back on drugs. To this day I've only had three beers, and that was with a court officer.

It was getting close to Christmas, and I was daydreaming most of the time, said this will be the last Christmas I have to spend in this godforsaken place. Four Christmases I spent behind bars. I was so mad about it I cursed the courts, the fuckin' prosecutor. The reason for this is that I was guilty even before I entered the courthouse; they never looked into my case. My wife was right there and never told them about the problem that she had. The time that I spent in jail, the worst thing that could happen to me was when someone else had shorter time. They were ready to go home, and it killed me inside to see them leave, watched them leave from the front window. Of course I would speak to them before they left to wish them well, if they weren't an ass. They would say to me, "Your time will come." You will be saying this to someone else who has some time to serve, that their time will come also. I was thinking at last it's my time. It was finally here. I wished it came faster than it did. I couldn't believe that it was my turn to go home, still, I couldn't believe it. Now I'm thinking about the time that I had to do when I just came into the prison and was torn apart by it. I remember looking at a calendar that was on the wall of the prison and seeing on the calendar what five years looked like on one sheet. I just can't believe that I've done all that time. As I was thinking about my release time, I was so damn scared that I wish that I could die right then. There was more. I can't tell you about the thoughts that were going though my head and how terrified I felt knowing I was going to be released. Then I was remembering what the COs would say to me. They would say to me, "Don't worry you will be back." My response was "You will never see me again in a place like this again." After hearing shit like that, it got me to start thinking of my daughter, wife, somewhere in my head I was still stuck around the time I got busted and thought my wife would be there for me when I got out. My good thoughts were always interrupted by my thoughts of my so-called good friends my rat cousin and hate rang throughout my body. Then I would think, how could they rat me out, put me in a place like this, not let it bother them, just go on with their lives. Believe me, I cursed them every day that

I spent in this place and said I hope God didn't sleep through this. I hope they all pay for my time I spent in this place.

How can someone just go to the police, bring them right to my house with no other thought in their head, show them where I buried the drugs I had. What was in their head? Before my cousin, this guy Bob did this to me, but my cousin just about drew a map to show them where to find the drugs I had buried in my yard. If I was such a big drug dealer, don't you think that I would want to sell it to get my money back as soon as possible, so why would I bury it? Just before the bust and after I showed my cousin where I buried the drugs that I just got that week. So after that we went down in my cellar to smoke a joint with me and just talked about him getting into the coke business again. What really hurts was that I just smoked a joint with my rat cousin; he had a good time partying with me before he turned me in. (Fuckin' Judas.) This was on the first day of spring March 21, 1997, and I just got though going out with my wife to eat, and that was the last good meal I had for the next five years. At the time of the bust, I was still stuck in the seventies. I never thought that a family member would do such a thing to me after he was the one who dumped stuff off over my house because he was being followed by the cops. What he dumped off with me were things that had cocaine all over it. I had to wash it all in case the cops followed him when he came over my house. I guess it's the cops' way to find people who get in trouble for drugs, scare those with jail time if they don't give someone up because they need rats to do their jobs. Looking at the city's finest, a lot of them are no better than the people they bust. I know this firsthand. I've heard stories from guys in jail how a lot of them get paid with drugs from busts the cops make. If they don't keep supplying cops with information, they go to jail. After they do this to whomever, they become a lifetime rat; it's not just once, it's forever.

The guy that I bought my drugs from was a friend from when I was a kid. We just about grew up together, and he was another one of the rat motherfuckers named Tom who turned on me, brought the cops right to where I lived and what house I was living in. My cousin was the one who set the hook. Well, I saw this guy named Bob again when I got out of jail. He tried to talk to me, and I was in a store at the time. I made eye contact with him and called him a cock-sucking rat motherfucker. My daughter just looked at me, and she took my granddaughter off my shoulders right away. The girl that was with him turned her back on him and started to walk ahead of him like she didn't know him. As he walked away, I yelled out in a crowded store, "You rat!" Everyone just looked at him as he took the fast track to get out of the store. As he was walking out of the store, I wanted to follow him out and fuck him up, but my daughter stopped me. Well, now the biggest rat of them all, the so-called main guy I grew up with and the one I bought most of my drugs from, I found out that week prior to me seeing him in a paint store he went up to New Hampshire, sat in a hot tub, cut his wrists, and bled out. At least this was what I was told by an old friend of mine named Ronny. As he looked at me, he thought I would be sad about it. He noticed that there was no response or reaction from me. Then I looked up at him and said, "Fuck him, one less rat in the world."

He said, "That's messed up to say that."

Then I said, "Fuck that rat motherfucker, may he rot in hell."

He was shocked to hear me say that. But what he doesn't understand is I lost five years of my life because of that rat motherfucker along with my cousin. Now for the rest of my life, I will be remembering the five years I lost, thinking what I could have accomplished in that lost time. That piece of shit was a big drug dealer; he would somewhat look down on me because of all the money he had made, and a lot of the money he made came off me just to supply my wife with her cocaine habit. When the cops informed the newspapers, the news stations of the bust, they made me out to be a big dealer, a supplier in New Bedford. After the bullshit story, they must have polished their badges and gave each other a blowjob, lying motherfuckers. What a bitch when one of the guy I bought my drugs off killed himself. The fuckin' narcs lost one of their snitches for life. Now they will have to do some work for themselves or find another rat. What a bitch. But now I think about it, they can just turn to my rat cousin and his friend Bob. Between both of them, they can put someone else in jail for five fuckin' years.

Don't let these cops fool you. They are all not so good either; I really hate people that say how good cops are; they don't look at the whole picture. Now for the ones that do their jobs, do it right, God bless them. The country needs guys like you. You make the world go round in the right direction. Now for the cops whom people think that they are doing the job right, listen to the guys who do the crimes as I did while being incarcerated, then come back home, finds a lot of their personal property missing. A lot of cops are no better than the ones who do the crimes.

When the guys get out of jail after doing their time, they find most of their valuables are gone, as I did. What people forget is that cops are somewhat human too. They have a license to confiscate people's goods. When you ask them about it, they'd say it was destroyed or they never took the stuff in question. They can hide a lot of the things real good, seeing that they are cops. Just look for the ones who drive the nice cars, have the nice paid-off homes, you will find the bad apples. This is what they do to find drug dealers, and they just want what they have, so they find a way to have them checked out and then bust them. I never had any of the riches that a real drug dealer had or have. I was just a guy that worked real hard and had a druggie for a wife. These are the cops who point the fingers at all the bad guys, as they call them. You know who you are. These are the ones who doctors up the cocaine that they take from your homes, that's including every box of baking powder, along with wallpaper paste that was in the corner of the room that they were questioning my wife in. When cops get caught, it's real funny how things get swept under the carpet. I have a lot of clippings of a lot of them who have done fucked-up things and got away with it. I had a real good job at the time. I did it very well but got involved helping a junkie wife who couldn't afford drugs unless I did what I did for her. Now that I look at it, I'm a felon, can't get a decent job because of the jail time I've done. Believe me, it follows you. It's real strange. They say pay your debt to society, try to go on with your life. Believe me, I tried that, and it doesn't work. I've even had my record sealed, but even doing that, I've had no luck. It's still online for whoever wants to view my history. It tells you everything. If you have friends in high places to help you with this, you may be able to get work again, but it's this crazy. You still can serve on a jury to help convict another but can't get a job. Probably when I die they will give my daughter a hard time to bury me. As for me, they can flush me down the toilet. It wouldn't bother me at all because I'll be dead, so who gives a damn. I won't.

As I look at life, it can have some humor to it even after all the bad times that I had in prison with the COs. When I got out, I was introduced to a couple of court officers. I started to hang around with them, and they knew that I was incarcerated. They never treated me any different; they knew what I went through. Even though I was in jail, these jail officers never treated me like I was scum. I got along real good with all of them so far. I was never incarcerated or in this type of trouble before. It felt good that they never reminded me of it or treated me any different. The way I look at it, they were not the ones that were at all the jails that I was at. They treated me like I've known them for years, act like we were friends for years also. The best part, these guys do not do drugs like the other COs that came over my house years before. That's real good. The best part is that these guys just drink a couple of beers from time to time. They don't get fall-down drunk like most of my so-called friends did. They all see how I make my money. It's the same way as I did before I got busted. No change in what I do but no damn drugs allowed. We do talk about drugs from time to time, but that's all. They tell me that it's all in the past, tell me to try to forget about it. But what most of the court guys don't realize is that I just can't forget about it. It's with me all the time, every minute of the day. All these guys bring all their cars to me to be repaired, but the cruelty I encountered when I was in jail will be with me till the day I die. I hold none of this against these guys. As far as I'm concerned, they are my new friends in life. Now I hang around with the chief of the courthouse. We go out for breakfast, and he never brings up the past. If I try to, he tells me not to think about it. I did tell him before we started to hang around that I was in trouble in the past. He looked at me and said "I know," said that he knew a couple of other guys that were in trouble in the past. I then said that I didn't want any of his friends treating him any different because of me. He said to me, "That happened a long time ago, you paid your debt to society." He never brings up what went on in the past, tells me to stop thinking about it. He then tells me that his friends will not treat him any different. They all know that we hang around as friends. He tells me that I'm just one of the guys he knows. If I need help around the house, he comes over and gives me a hand, as I do for him. He introduced me to his family, invites me to most of his family functions. To me he was never a cop, just a good friend. I won't give out any names as I never gave out any name in what I wrote but changed them around but the scum will know who they are.

I've realized that there are a lot of decent cops out there, but finding them is real hard, but they are out there. On the day I was to leave Norfolk, a CO that was a prick the whole time that I was at Pond Ville called me down to his office to write me out a check that I received back from my do-nothing Boston lawyer sent to me. He told me that he will hold it to the end of the day, told me where the bank was to cash my check when I'm released. But as I was about to leave, he said that I had good time for all the programs that I did while I was in jail, but I couldn't use it because I was doing a mandatory sentence but gave me the time off that I spent at Dartmouth Correctional. Then he got up, he put his hand out, wanted to shake my hand. I turned around to see if he was messing around with me, setting me up for a joke, but there was no one behind me. I just couldn't believe it. I looked at him, told him I thought he was fooling around with the others COs, and he said no, he wished me good luck, wished me well. I was so surprised that he would do something like that to me I was just lost for words; I shook his hand but didn't know what to say but thanks. I think they call that a loss for words. I just couldn't believe it. He was a fuckin' prick the whole time I was there.

Well, finally the night before I was to go home came, and I was scared, was up all night. I just couldn't sleep wondering what to expect when I got out. I just couldn't believe that my time had come for me to leave this place. It was like this place was my life now, though I belong here. Well, my ex-wife never got back to me about the train schedule. Good thing I knew a guy that I was in jail with in Bridgewater named Allen Pearl. He told me not to worry, that he would be up to drive me home. When the day came, he was there. Not only did he give me a ride home, he went to the bank, cashed my check for me, and he didn't even ask me for gas money. I always said when I was ready to leave, I was going to fling a roller at that fuckin' asshole Hinny Wrecker and his fucked-up brother as I walked out the door, but I guess he wasn't on when I left or he couldn't bear to see me leave, upset that he couldn't fuck with me anymore. Well, if he is ever able to get one of these books that I'm writing now, this is what I wanted to say to you, Hinny, "Fuck you!" But when I was walking out the door, I just forgot all about it. I just turned around, seen that a lot of guys that were still doing time were just looking out the windows, staring at me as I was leaving, as I did when someone I knew was leaving, wishing that it was me. Well, it ended up my friend Allen Pearl who came up to take me home. I was really worried on how I was going to get home because I had no idea where I was. I was sent there by prison transport. When it came to me getting back to where I lived, they just about said, "Find a way." This place was way the heck out there. The ride home took a long time to get to where I lived; now I realized how far away it was from my home. Now I think about it and realized why my daughter and family couldn't come to see me because of how far it was.

Well, as I approached my home, I told the guy Allen, who took me home, to knock at my door while I hid beside the side of the house. My daughter opened the door, thought that he was me, and she started to cry. Then I walked out from around the corner of the house, and she was so happy that he wasn't me. She said to me that she thought that the guy Allen was me. This guy Allen was very thin from the time I met him till the time I was released. I had lost a lot of weight at the time because of the bad food that I ate while in jail. After I hugged her, she said to me, "Didn't they feed you?" She was really upset because she didn't send me money for food. I just told her not to worry.

"I'll be okay. I'm home now, I'll get back to normal very soon," but she continued to cry, but what really upset me was that my grandson hid behind my daughter. He wouldn't come out to see me. I wanted so much to hug him, hold him because it's been five years since I last held him. But that didn't last long. Within a week, he was taking walks with me, watching television, helping me trim my apple trees in my yard. To this day my daughter has two boys and a girl now. It's like the sons I always wanted and have two girls to go with them. This just about makes my life. This was something that I always wanted from my daughter's mother, my wife, but never got. After I was home for a while, I had the experience of watching my daughter have two of the kids and was able to hold my granddaughter right away. Now I'm almost content. They fill my life with so much happiness. I make it known to them not to have anything to do with drugs. Now they are here for me to spoil, I don't want to waste any time having fun with them while I'm still somewhat alive but still suffer with jail branded into my brain. When I got home, I just couldn't stay still. I had to open my garage, look at all my stuff in my body shop, just couldn't wait to start working on cars again. I couldn't stop looking at my Corvette that my mother helped me buy with the money she left me.

I was at home just for a couple of days, and I watched a car come up the street. A cop got out of a car and started to walk over to me right away. I noticed that it was a CO that I knew years ago. As he walked up, I had that hate in me right off the bat, and I wanted to know what the hell he wanted as I reached for a bat I had by the door. He looked at me and asked me if I recognized him. Of course I said yes. This fuckin' asshole asked me if I could get him some cocaine. I looked at him and said, "Are you joking or what?" He just looked at me dumbfounded. I just couldn't believe what I just heard. I just said no! I looked at him and said, "Get the fuck out of my face, away from my home, never come back." I wonder, just think to this day, was it a setup? This I will never know and don't care. Thinking about it, I just can't believe what he was asking me after me doing five years, To see a CO walk up my driveway to my house, I just wanted to hit him with a bat I had next to the door of my garage.

I had a good amount of cash that my so-called attorney returned to me. My daughter had let a lot of the bills go behind, but she managed to keep the house, so in my mind I had to find work to cover the bills that were left behind. I found a job in a body shop, a mechanic shop, and both jobs didn't last long. I guess they did a query on me, and it showed that I was incarcerated, so they laid me off. Every boss or should I say all the bosses that I worked for reminded me of COs. I hated them all because of the way they would bark orders at me. They all made me feel like I was still in jail, so of course the dirty looks came from that. I would collect my benefits as long as I could and started to look for work all over again. That was a long, hard process every time. Now unemployment was a joke. Before they give you what you worked hard for, they make you take all these useless programs that amounted to nothing at all, just a waste of time. I tried for disability; they denied my over and over again right to this day and with all the shrinks reports and internal problems I had, they said that I can still work. All I can say is that the judge that reviewed my case was as useless as the COs and doctor that I was in jail with or even better, the Judge that gave me five years. They never wanted to hear what you had to say, nor did my lowlife attorney do any good for me. My so-called disability attorney put in for an appeal, but I heard from the disability office before I did from her another piece of shit. I wish they could have been plugged into my head to see what I was going through in everyday life, maybe they would realize what was really going on in my head. So I did what I could to stretch out what money I had. My daughter helped with what little money she had coming in, and I was able to take in a few jobs in my garage to make ends meet and cover the mortgage. It took me four years to find a job. The job I ended up getting was from the neighbor that lived across the street from me named Tony. He happened to be a boss in a garbage company, and he asked me if I needed a job, so I said yes. It took me a couple of months to start to do work at the job that I had no experience in, but I learned real quick. Of course I was treated real bad, but I needed the work so I put up with all the shit they threw at me. It was no different from jail, but I made a lot more money than at all the other places I was at. This job lasted about four and a half years. When I came in on one Friday, the guys told me that the boss that hired me was fired. I was called into the office shortly after and was also let go. That was a day after Christmas. What heartless bastards the bosses were. They said that it was because there was a lack of work. All I can say about that was bullshit. They got rid of me, hired two guys in my place, and another guy to take my old boss's job for less per hour who didn't last long because he was caught doing cocaine on the job and was let go also. How can there be a lack of work when there was so much garbage in the city? All the money they made, this is a good example of greed. All I say about that I hope it comes back on them three times. I really think is that they did a query on me; they found out that I was incarcerated; they let me go along with the boss that hired me. Before they let me go, they kept giving me very large amounts of work to do I guess to try to get me to quit, but after being in jail, I learned what was handed down to you has to get completed no matter what, sick or not. If they couldn't break me in jail, no boss was going to do it either. That part of my brain was already damaged from being in jail.

Prior to me getting laid off, they gave me a couple of trainees and asked me to teach them the job that I was doing. They kept doing things without being told, doing these things without telling me. On this one occasion, they let this large door down just a little, didn't let me, the door was damaged, because the top of a truck hit it. The guy that I was teaching the job to had lowered the door and raised the forks on the truck while I was filling out the work orders on now because of this it hit the door. They asked me if I would pay for the damage, and I said that I would take the days off instead of paying for the damage. This was an option they gave me. Now because of this, they sent me for a drug test to see if I was on drugs, not telling the bosses that every guy they gave me were fuckin' assholes as they were in jail. So after numerous drug tests trying to get me for taking drugs, they couldn't, so they said that there was a lack of work, gave me my walking papers. Most of the guys that worked for this company were all like the guys that I had to deal with in jail, were not the sharpest tools in the shed. I tried so hard to get along with them but had a real hard time doing so because they were all ass kissers. I couldn't believe what the night boss did. He just sat in his office most of the time and watched the cameras to see who he could fuck with, mostly it was me because I stopped him from eating my food I brought in for myself. He called himself Jay I guess because he couldn't remember his name or it was too hard for him to spell, but anyways he was also a fuck nut along with his son and just wonder how fucking assholes like these two get jobs like they do.

It's been quite a few years. Of course I will have all the things that were done to me stuck in my head. I know it will be for the rest of my life. The thing that I still can't get over is when I was ready to leave, I forgot to tell the CO Hinny Wrecker that fucked with me the most, "Fuck you!" It killed me not to be able to do so. This was my regret. All I can say is that the prison life is and always be burned into my head. Remember how bad I was treated, how they tried to take my life on the outside away from me. I see some of the COs from time to time, and they won't say a word to me about anything, usually rush out of every store when I see them in when they make eye contact with them. The best one was the body shop manager. He was in the variety store that was right next to my house. I picked up on his truck because he had a propeller on the back of his truck. I walked in and saw that he was buying lottery tickets. He made eye contact with me and rushed right out of the store. I never saw him again. This guy was always trying to teach me body work the way he did it. Of course, I told him that my way would work better. He said that he wanted it done his way. When he went to lunch, I did it my way, and he said when he came back to see it worked out real good didn't it. I just agreed with him and said, "Oh yeah." He thought he knew body work better than me. If this was true, why he would keep asking me how I would do it, referring to jobs to be done. The shop was full of Spanish guys. I was told to see if I could teach them some body work, and they would all want to work real hard, fast. I got mad and said, "Take your time. It's not going anywhere." You're in jail, you're not expected to kill yourself working in jail for five dollars a week. Yes, five dollars a week. Well, of course, they ratted me out to the CO. I was not picked up anymore to go to the body shop. What I really missed was the food that we got off the loading trucks. I always wanted so much to talk to some of the COs that I met from time to time to tell them what fuckin assholes they were but never got a chance to do so.

When I returned home as I mention I was almost a yes man even though I didn't mean it. Whenever I was asked a question, I just said yes, I know what you mean, did things my way. When I went to the first store with my daughter, it was real bad. Most of the time I had my back to the wall and was always looking over my shoulders, surrounding my food with my arms when I ate. I guess it's just a jail thing that stood with me when I got out. I trusted no one, watched everyone very closely. The only one I really trusted was my daughter, grandson, and my sister-in-law who was really upset when she saw me. As I was shopping with my daughter, I would be asking her if I could get all stupid kinds things like paper, stamps rice, peperoni, all stuff I would get through the canteen when I was in jail. If she didn't let me get it, I was mad at her, and she would look at me and say, "You don't need that stuff anymore. You're home now."

I started to wander off. After a while, my daughter let me use her car. Of course, I would go to the stores, buy what she told me that I didn't need anymore. I would be gone for hours. The reason for this was because it was real hard to face people; I would drift off and have to remember how to get back home. Sometimes I would wait outside the store until most of the store was empty because I didn't want to face people. But it did take me that long to buy the things I needed, and I would stand back until the register had no people at it before I checked out. I really think this was like a form of being brainwashing from all the different prisons that I was at. I started to make some of the food that I made in jail. My grandson loved it, and my daughter did also. She just said all I had to do was to tell her what I wanted to do with what I was buying because I was always yelling at her for no good reason. I kept telling her that I was all right, but I could see it in her eyes that she could see some of what I was going through. I was having a real hard time adjusting to the outside world and was still living the jail life even though I've been out for a while now. I was still stuck in the past. It was like I was still living in the nineties like before I went into jail, and I'm trying so hard to bring myself back to the present time. This to me was real hard to do. I still think that they gave me too much time for what I did but not what I was accused of. I know I messed up but you don't lock someone away like that for drugs, say to the courts that I was a big-time dealer, and know they didn't have the proof of it either. After the first night in jail, that was enough. The five to follow I will never be right in the head ever again. For what I got caught with, this would be possession. I still think one or two years would have been long enough for me, the rest in community service. Then if I messed up, if I had anything to do with drugs, I would have to do the rest of the time incarcerated.

Since then I haven't touched drugs as I did before I went to jail, just take what the doctor gives me. I have a hard time even doing that.

I finally got in touch with my wife. I still looked at her as still being my wife. I was so happy to see her when she pulled up in front of the house. I had to call her to ask her if I could have the stuff that she was holding for me in her attic. She said that she would drop it all off for me as soon as possible. She called me back in a couple of days, and she said that she was coming over with my stuff. I kept looking out the window, waiting for her to pull up the street as I waited for them to call me for her visits. I couldn't wait to see her. You know when you love someone you just can't remember what happened in the past. I have the tendency to block out all the bad stuff that happened when you were together. As she pulled up, I walked over to her real fast. I was just glad to see her. I wanted to kiss her, hug her, real happy to see her face. She pulled back like I was a stranger. I just backed off, then remembered we were divorced. It was just so hard for me to accept. I just stared at her, and she said that she had a boyfriend, and it was serious. I just said to her that she was my best friend. I couldn't help my actions. Her reply was now her new boyfriend was her new best friend. When she told me this, it just tore me apart. It hurt real bad. It was like someone ripped my heart from my chest. We exchanged things. When we went up in my attic, she wanted all our old wedding things because she didn't want to buy it all over again because she was planning to get married again. I thought that was fucked up, but I let her have it all and told her to do what she wanted to do with it. When it was time for her to leave, it killed as it did when she came for a visit when I was in jail. All I could do was watch her drive away. Now she's driving away again but forever, as my daughter's mother did many years before.

When I was incarcerated, all the things that people sent to me in letters about what she was doing to me were the ones she probably was fucking around with. I think this was their way of getting rid of their guilt that they were feeling. This is just a guess. Even to this day it hurts. Some of the guys that I did know were the ones that were telling me these stories. Not one of them ever sent me a penny the whole time I was incarcerated. Some of the letters that I was getting were from guys that I knew, fixed some of their cars, and owed me money before I was sent to jail. I did sent them letters asking for money for the work I did on their cars, but they responded by saying seeing that I was in jail, they didn't have to pay me because the business was no longer open. (What great friends.)

Even after all my wife did to me, I still loved her. I would never tell my daughter this because she would be pissed off at me and wouldn't talk to me. The silence would kill me. But really there was nothing I could do about it. It's just something I felt inside of me. There was no cure for what I had. After I was laid off from the garbage company in New Bedford, I had my record sealed, thinking that it would help me get a fresh start because everyone these days did a query check on you. Even after I had my record sealed, I still couldn't get any jobs that I was applying for no matter what I knew. Even after I had my record sealed, my name still comes up on the computer stating what I did. It will be there I feel till the day I die. I just can't get a break. I've tried so many times to get a decent job but can't. They say that employers will give you a second chance. What a joke. I can't even get in for an interview to talk about what I was in jail for. The only way you're going to get a job is if you open up your own business. When you do that, the government hits you up with taxes that you can't afford to stay open, and you end up closing up because they make more than you do even though it's your business. So the way you look at it, you're dead in the water and don't stand a chance in hell. Now for the job that I have is a night watchman making chump change, just enough to pay the bills plus scrapping metal at a scrap yard. I have a résumé that when shown to an employer will make him look twice at you, give you a look like you can do all this, and end up saying after they do a query that you're overqualified so that would be a plus for them. The way that I look at it, as long as I can pay my mortgage, pay the bills, I'm okay with it. Just know that I will never be wealthy, will never feel what happiness feels like ever again. All I do now is keep up with all the payments on the house. It will all go to my daughter when I die so she doesn't have to work real hard to own a home, as I did. It's a good home for her kids. I will never forget what my daughter had to do to keep my home with no help from anyone. In many ways, she has my spirit and just hope she doesn't lose her soul as I did in jail. One more thing, I don't care who you talk to, doctors, wives, all they do is help with the stress. No one can fix you like you can. It's so hard to do this what I'm doing because of the things that goes on in my head, and no one really knows how much pain you're in. I really feel for the guys that are in longer than what I was in for. It fucked me up. Just imagine what they go through.

Now what I can say is thank you to the court system for putting me in jail for such long time, messing up my ability to get employment, as they say by paying my debt to society for a nonviolent crime (bullshit). But most of all making it a mandatory sentence, it being day for day to keep me from making money in jail to send it home to my daughter to help pay for bills. So while I'm in jail, she had to go to a strip club in which she hated to do to pay the mortgage to keep the house because she could afford to go to work doing a forty-hour job because of her son. I just thank God for giving me a daughter as beautiful as she is. Because of that, I didn't lose my home. Again thank you to the police finest that work as fuckin' narcs for lying to no end just to get a conviction and come out smelling like roses. May the ones who said I was selling drugs up the whole East Cost, I hope they rot in hell or even better catch a bullet in between their teeth. What probably made them real happy was the way they humiliated me and my wife during the bust while we were handcuffed. I wish now that they all had body cameras and people could see how bad we were treated and show my dog getting shot in the head. Another thing I hope you fuckin' cops made a lot of money with the cocaine you doctored up and took from my home that was used to support my druggie wife's habit? What will make you real happy I'm doing the same as I was doing when I got caught for so-called selling cocaine up the East Coast, what a fuckin' joke! I'm living fixing cars as I always did, working as a watchman at a boat yard. You can feel real good about yourselves, you fucked up my life (happy?). I have nothing to do with drugs. I live a long, boring life, live just about the way I did in jail but without bars. When the bosses talk to me, I mumble under my breath when I walk away from them. My back is turned away from them as I did to the COs in jail. It's real crazy all the things I had before I went to jail, I still own because I had all legal receipts for everything I had, that's because I worked real hard to keep it. See you, fuckin' narcs. There was never any drug money, as I told you. All you had to do was open your damn eyes instead of thinking of promotions, believing fuckin' rats.

Now I'm trying to retire, I'm thinking of selling the things that I've accumulated throughout the years to see if it's enough to pay off my home. These are all the things from my old business as a body shop. The weird thing about this is if I do, they will probably say it's me selling drugs again. I say, let them check, like before I'll have all the receipts, its stuff I already paid taxes on already. If they try to pin another rap on me, I'll sue the fuckin' shit out of them. At this time I'm still seeing a shrink to see if it can stop the nightmares that I'm getting from night to night. They are real bad at times. They're just things that happened to me while I was in jail dealing with all the scumbags. What the police has got to stop doing is pining labels on people to get them in trouble just to get gratification, a pat on the back. All the police have to say is that you did whatever they said you did, and off to jail you go. Okay, now the courts they just look at all the facts first, then what they find at the time of the busts. What they have to do at the time is to see if the persons or persons are making tons of money or just supporting some ones drug habit as I was. The money that the cops took from my bank account I was able to get back except for the money the lawyer told me to give to the police department to show good faith to the police department. To this day I really wonder if he kept it, but it makes no difference now. He's dead now and is rotting in hell for what he has done to so many people. Now he's got to face his maker. (David, you slimeball.) The people who read this, remember this before you point the finger at anyone for a crime. Look at all the facts before you say he or she should be in jail. Then read what I went through. Think if you can go through what I went through. This was the first time that I was incarcerated. I was never incarcerated before in my whole life. Also remember this, it's like being in a mental asylum and now my life is not my life anymore.

What is stuck in my head to this day is just a lot of the stupid things that my wife wrote to me in letters, there weren't many letters from her because she signed off on me just as I came into jail. I think I did come across a couple more of the letters she sent me of course just saying that she had to tell me something. Oh, of course, letters from her lawyer sent to me stating that she was divorcing me, just like that. At this time I was really broken like something she had used and just discarded, but it will come to a day and hopefully she will realize what she threw away. She was supposed to stay off drugs, and she was still overdosing on stupid pills because she always had her head up her ass the whole time I was with her and got worse after we broke up. What's still on my mind is what the hell she looks like now after all these years of further drug, smoking cigarettes. All I can say is what comes around goes around. I hope I'm alive to see it. What hurts is that she is living a full life and went on with her life like I never existed while I was living my life in hell.

My aunt is a very religious person. She is the one who said that I should write this so people should know what goes on in jail. Maybe it will open their eyes to the fact. One day after I talked to her on the phone, she asked me if I started to write about my time in jail yet, and I said no. As I hung up the phone, I was thinking about what she had asked me, and I went to lay down and woke up in a sweat, so I picked up a pad, and three weeks later I had somewhat of a drift done. While I was writing, it was more like a nonstop cycle. I just couldn't stop, and when I did and read it, I couldn't believe it. I just wanted to go on, didn't want to put the pen down until I had just about everything down on paper. It took five notepads to put down what was in my head at the time. I realized after a while that I wrote right through the night, and when I looked out the window, the sun was starting to come out. As I was reading my letters that I sent home from jail, it still felt like I was still in jail just by reading and holding them in my hands. I still can't believe the way the COs treated inmates. They acted like they were in the worst prison in United States but with words only or saying that they were going to lug you to another prison. Even better, they fucked with you by making you into a sport by putting you in a room where they knew you will have to defend yourself against other inmates or you just get beat up if you don't, and they wouldn't even get their hands dirty. Being incarcerated, it's like being in a mental institution. It stays with you even after you get out. I'm still not right in the head to this day because of what they did to me. I know it will be there till the day I die. It took a little while, but I finally realize why I was in the fog that I was in and I always felt that something was missing. I finally realized what was missing. It was my soul that I lost while I was in jail, and that's something I will never get back. Don't get me wrong, I'm not scared to go back because I know what to expect. The only way that would happen is if someone were to hurt my family. Let me tell you, it wouldn't bother me if I had to hurt someone because of the loss of my inner self along with my soul. That what jail took from me.

Now this is something my grandson found and brought to my attention, something that I didn't know. When President Clinton was in office, one of his policies resulted in 2.4 million people in prison and the 160,000 Americans serving life, which was an immense economic pressure, moral dilemma, and failure in leadership. Not only did he unequally and punitively criminalize nonviolent offenses and even non-abusers, he flushed away the lives of these people, young and old, who still struggle to this day for it. At least he admitted his mistake. In his apology for his failure, Clinton said, "The problem is the way it was written and implemented is we cast too wide a net and we had too many people in prison." We wound up putting so many people in prison that there wasn't enough money left to educate them for new jobs and increase the chances when they came out so they could live productive lives as I found out. This ultimately affected America's people and economics. (Yes, I will vote for a Clinton—not.) He should have done time for his sex crimes that he was accused of, then he would have known what he put so many nonviolent people through on mandatory sentences. I would love to hear him tell guys in jail that he was not a skinner or a rapist and he didn't think blowjobs was sex. To Clinton, it was as it was pronounced as a job that he gave her, didn't consider it as sex, was never accused, was never convicted. Guess he gave himself a pardon. But as most of us who were incarcerated just wanted to be able to use the good time we earned from their foolish programs while being incarcerated, this would be a plus. We earned it like the president got a pardon. (In this case it's who you are.)

(For those who don't know, a blowjob is considered oral sex.)

Now I know for the rest of my life I will still be incarcerated in my head. It's where my mind always drifts off from minute to minute. I realized when I'm talking with people now, I'm looking through them instead of looking at them. Now I'm alone living in my own world. This is where I'm always going to be for the rest of my life even though I've been out for quite some time. I'm still living the past. It's just so hard to explain. I'm just there and I'm always thinking about what I went through while I was in jail along with my convict number that I'm in the habit of still repeating to myself on a daily basis. Where I work at now, I'm able to look out at the ocean, and I can see the beauty that I really missed along with watching the rain fall on rainy days. These are the two things that I took for granted. Now every day I stop and just look around at everything and really know what I lost while I was in jail along with family members. But even now my mind I will always be in jail, thinking of what I went through, and I know I will never forget any of it. Still to this day, I have a lot of hate in my heart for correctional cops and feel myself heat up when I see any of them in uniform. When I see one, my eyes just follow them. In my mind I'm waiting for any of them to say something to me. I really don't know myself anymore. At this time I can't hang around with any of my friends for long period of time because of all the guys I was confined with while I was in jail. As I think now, I know that I will never have a normal life again or any relationships because of the time I spent in jail. I've been noticing changes in the court officer that I've been hanging around with. He's been acting like a correctional officer to me. He just don't know what type of friend he is losing. I curse the narc cop that shot my dog in the head and may he go through what my dog went through and rot in hell. This cop went really overboard after he handcuffed me. this cop is no good, but I hope he made a lot of money after my bust. I hope he chokes on it. Just look together. Like I've said earlier, the government wants their share of money that people make under the table. When marijuana was illegal, people went to jail. That's why the government is making it legal, so the government can make the big bucks instead of guys who don't have jobs. It's been legalized, and the government is holding off until they find the best way of making as much money as possible. They tell you it's for things that the country needs, but it will come to the point that you will see a lot of government people lining their pockets with money from drug sales. They will never do time because it's legal now. I'm all for the legalization of marijuana. They should have the people choose to do it or not but have an age restriction on it as they do for cigarettes. Boy, the cigarettes companies are going to eat this up. Going to show you who are the drug dealer now? (Thinking just always thinking.)

Just to let people know, I'd rather die than go to a place like that again. It's just the scum that's in a place like that, and that's not just some of the inmates. That's COs as well!

Before this comes to an end, does it make you wonder if I got back with my wife whom I loved so much? Well, that will be in the next book I have started to write. It will be forwarded if this book does well.

About the Author

At forty-three years old, it was Zubin Dio's first time being incarcerated. Prior to being in prison, he was a complete hypocrite, completely blinded before he was actually caged up like an animal. Reality definitely set in, and he saw firsthand the substandard living conditions for criminals in the system. This book is his firsthand experience living in the steel cage and why men would rather die instead of going back to this hellhole.

CPSIA information can be obtained
at www.ICGtesting.com
Printed in the USA
FFHW012200160919
55038277-60731FF